What Is a Crime?

Legal Dimensions Series

This series stems from an annual legal and socio-legal research initiative sponsored by the Canadian Association of Law Teachers, the Canadian Law and Society Association, the Canadian Council of Deans, and the Law Commission of Canada. Volumes in this series examine various issues of law reform from a multidisciplinary perspective. The series seeks to advance our knowledge about law and society through the analysis of fundamental aspects of law.

The essays in this volume were selected by representatives from each partner association: Dorothy Chunn (Canadian Law and Society Association), John EcEvoy (Canadian Association of Law Teachers), Beth Bilson (Canadian Council of Law Deans), and Steven Bittle and Nathalie Des Rosiers (Law Commission of Canada).

1 *Personal Relationships of Dependence and Interdependence in Law*
2 *New Perspectives on the Public-Private Divide*
3 *What Is a Crime? Defining Criminal Conduct in Contemporary Society*

LAW COMMISSION OF CANADA
COMMISSION DU DROIT DU CANADA

Edited by the Law Commission of Canada

What Is a Crime?
Defining Criminal Conduct
in Contemporary Society

UBCPress · Vancouver · Toronto

15 14 13 12 11 10 09 08 07 06 05 04   5 4 3 2 1

Printed in Canada on acid-free paper

National Library of Canada Cataloguing in Publication

What is a crime?: defining criminal conduct in contemporary society / edited by the Law Commission of Canada.

(Legal dimensions series)
Includes bibliographical references and index.
ISBN 0-7748-1086-6 (bound); ISBN 0-7748-1087-4 (pbk.)

1. Criminology – Canada. 2. Criminal law – Canada. 3. Sociological jurisprudence. I. Law Commission of Canada. II. Series.

HV6025.W475 2004   364.971   C2004-901786-1

Canadä

UBC Press gratefully acknowledges the financial support for our publishing program of the Government of Canada through the Book Publishing Industry Development Program (BPIDP), and of the Canada Council for the Arts, and the British Columbia Arts Council.

UBC Press
The University of British Columbia
2029 West Mall
Vancouver, BC V6T 1Z2
604-822-5959 / Fax: 604-822-6083
www.ubcpress.ca

Contents

Introduction

Nathalie Des Rosiers and Steven Bittle

On the surface, to ask "what is a crime?" seems to warrant a straightforward answer in that one can simply suggest that "crime is something that is against the law." For those who adopt such a strict definition, or a legal-consensus approach to crime (see, for example, Tappan 1947), studying the law as it is written is sufficient for understanding what society considers harmful behaviour. However, if we take a step back from this literal interpretation to consider the broader social processes that help give meaning to crime and its control, it quickly becomes apparent that there is much more to the question than simply referring to what is written in the law. As Comack and Brickey (1991, 15) remind us, "[l]aw can be said to have a distinctly *social basis*; it both shapes – and is shaped by – the society in which it operates" (emphasis in the original). Indeed, before a criminal statute is even contemplated, there are a whole host of social forces and events that both shape how we conceive of a particular behaviour and influence our decisions on how to respond. In addition, many of these social forces continue to shape our response strategies well after the social wrong becomes part of our legal lexicon. How society thinks about crime and the individuals deemed to be responsible for criminal behaviour influences law enforcement practices and the penalties administered. Why is it that certain behaviour is deemed sufficiently problematic to warrant being labelled a crime? Why is certain behaviour considered a crime while other behaviour is not?

To ask "what is a crime?" is certainly not a novel endeavour. For decades academics from numerous disciplines (such as law, sociology, and criminology) have struggled to understand various aspects of this question. From studies that examine the factors contributing to the enactment of certain prohibitions or the impact of law and its enforcement, to studies that focus on the events that precede the decriminalization of certain behaviour, there are countless examples of scholarly work dedicated to exploring the nature of crime and its control. In the last half of the twentieth century, various scholars noted that crime is not an objective phenomenon and that the way in which certain behaviour is understood and responded to is more a reflection of how society is structured than an indication of any inherent problems with those individuals regarded as criminals. In the 1940s, for example, Edward Sutherland introduced the concept of "white-collar crime" to draw attention to crimes committed by the upper class and corporate elite, thereby challenging the common perception that crime was committed primarily by those in the lower class.

Other critical scholars built upon Sutherland's work by continuing to explore definitions of crime and its enforcement. The 1960s produced a considerable body of literature within this tradition. Howard Becker's (1963) pioneering work on moral entrepreneurship highlighted the process by which the perceptions and claims of certain groups (often criminal justice officials) were shaped by law and law enforcement, emphasizing that, in many instances, there was an absence of empirical evidence to substantiate the level of concern associated with a given problem. Using the emergence of antimarijuana legislation in the 1930s as an example, Becker illustrated how criminal justice officials effectively manufactured a crisis over the nature and extent of drug use, when in actuality drug consumption was rare. According to Becker (1963, 9), "[f]rom this point of view, deviance is *not* the quality of the act the person commits, but rather a consequence of the application by others of rules and sanctions to an 'offender'" (emphasis in the original). Stanley Cohen's work on the sociology of deviance also brought to light the idea that definitions of crime were not objective, by revealing how crime can be produced through "moral panics." In essence, Cohen revealed that if we deem a group and its behaviour to be a threat, and if this belief is supported through media accounts and professional claims, then we are likely to respond as such even though the nature and extent of the concern may be more perceived than real (see, for example, Cohen 1980).

In more recent decades, a new generation of critical criminological, legal, and socio-legal scholars has discussed and debated the nature of crime and law in society. Various feminists, for example, have brought to light different forms of gender bias within notions of law and its enforcement. As Comack et al. (1999, 44) suggest, over the last twenty years, "feminism has made considerable inroads in challenging us to reconsider the traditional approaches to understanding the law–society relation as well as the claims that law itself makes in its Official Version." Critical race scholars have also drawn our attention to racial biases within criminal justice processes, noting that conceptions of crime and its control are rooted primarily in the experiences of white men (see, for example, Neugebauer 2000). Finally, in Canada, scholars (both Aboriginal and not) have pointed to the importance of understanding the colonization of Aboriginal peoples when examining their overrepresentation in the criminal justice system (see, for example,

Williams 2001). In addition to reminding us that crime and law are not objective phenomena, these critical feminist, race, and Aboriginal literatures reveal the troubling differences between how the law is written and how it is enforced.

The late 1970s and early 1980s witnessed a recognition by government agencies that a reflex application of criminal law had become commonplace and that this might not be the most appropriate approach for dealing with complex social issues. In *Our Criminal Law*, for example, the Law Reform Commission of Canada (LRC) argued that criminal law ought to be "pruned" to better differentiate between what the commission considered "real crimes" and public-welfare, or administrative, wrongs. The label of crime, the LRC argued, should be reserved for "wrongful acts seriously threatening and infringing fundamental social values." Similarly, in 1982, the Department of Justice, in *The Criminal Law in Canadian Society*, suggested that criminal law should be reserved for the most serious harms and that we need to consider whether other, less coercive response strategies would be more appropriate.

Of course these are only a few examples from the range of scholarly works and government reports that have, over the years, taken issue with the notion that crime is objectively defined and controlled and that have cautioned against a reflex application of criminal law to deal with what are often complex social issues. As a body of knowledge, the works of these and other scholars reveal the contextual nature of crime and its control – that is, that crime is the product of power relations within society and that the possibility of experiencing conflict with the law is often inversely related to one's social standing. Referring to the subjective nature of crime and its control, Henry and Lanier (2001, 7) suggest that "what counts as crime at one place and time, culture, or location may not be considered criminal at another time, in another culture, or even across the street!"

Why Is It Important to Ask "What Is a Crime?"
In many respects the ability to reflect upon the role of law in our society is an important task, regardless of the context. The ability to think and rethink, ask questions, pose challenges, and change how we deal with unwanted behaviour is a hallmark of learning in a democratic society. At the same time, however, there are several current issues and trends that underscore the importance and timeliness of examining what constitutes a crime.

Exploring the question "what is a crime?" has become more and more relevant during an era in which responses to various behaviours have become increasingly polarized. While some behaviours are subject to greater regulation and criminalization, others are dealt with increasingly through informal processes or are subject to discussions of deregulation or decriminalization (see, for example, McMahon 1992). There is now a considerable range of options available for dealing with unwanted or criminal behaviour (e.g., restorative justice and various community-based programs). David Garland (2001, 120) reminds us of this by arguing that there is "an emerging distinction between the *punishment of criminals,* which remains the business of the state (and becomes once again a significant symbol of state power), and the *control of crime,* which is increasingly deemed to be 'beyond the state' in significant respects" (see also Hudson 1998; O'Malley 2000). What does this transformation mean for how we perceive and respond to crime? When and how is the use of criminal law and the formal legal justice system deemed appropriate?

Also underscoring the importance of examining what constitutes a crime is the blurring of the lines between the public and private realms. Increasingly, the formal control of crime and unwanted behaviour is no longer solely within the purview of the state. For example, the privatization of various criminal justice system functions is very much part of Canadian criminal justice discourse. "Public sector agencies (prisons, probation, parole, the court system, etc.) are now being remodelled in ways that emulate the values and working practices of private industry" (Garland 2001, 18). What does this trend mean for how we define and control crime? Has the criminal justice system simply become, as Nils Christie (1994) has argued, an industry?

The work of Michel Foucault (1979) and various governmentality scholars is also instructive in this regard. Foucault conceptualizes social control as being produced through a complex of power relations: Power is not exercised upon individuals but through civil society. Referring to the "carceral archipelago," Foucault (1979, 298) argues that the techniques of the penitentiary have been transported from the confines of the prison to the "entire social body." As a result the prison does not act alone but is "linked to a whole series of 'carceral' mechanisms which seem distinct enough – since they are intended to alleviate pain, to cure, to comfort – but which all tend, like the prison, to exercise a power of normalization" (1979, 308). As Hannah-Moffat (2001, 7) reminds us, "the insights of Foucault are useful, because he focuses on the relations of power and technologies of power, which are dispersed through society rather than being located specifically in the state [and hence in any law produced by the state]." This realization poses new and interesting questions for those interested in exploring the nature of crime and its control.

Although notions of a "carceral archipelago" provide an important analytical perspective to examine the diffuse ways in which power is exercised in society, there is also considerable evidence that much of the normalizing and disciplinary approach to social order has been overshadowed in recent decades by calls for more punitive crime-control efforts. In both popular culture and criminal justice frameworks, there has been a noticeable increase in crime-control discourse. As Garland (2001, 3) suggests:

> The re-appearance in official policy of punitive sentiments and expressive gestures that appear oddly archaic and downright anti-modern tend to confound the standard social theories of punishment and its historical development. Not even the most inventive reading of Foucault, Marx, Durkheim, and Elias on punishment could have predicted these recent developments – and certainly no such predictions ever appeared.

In Canada discussions of crime and what to do about it have become commonplace. In recent years newspaper articles, community-level discussions, and policy making have all acted as venues through which to express a desire for harsher criminal sanctions – a "lock 'em up and throw away the key" approach to crime. "Such 'lawandorder' talk ... has become a dominant and daily feature of public culture as we embark on this new millennium. In our latter-day 'risk society,' security is purportedly in short supply and menacing outsiders imperil us from all sides" (Menzies et al. 2001, 11). As Garland (2001, 10-11) argues, "the background affect of policy is now more frequently a collective anger and a righteous demand for retribution rather than a commitment to a just, socially engineered solution. The emotional temperature of policy-making has shifted from cool to hot." The question, however, is whether this law-and-order approach represents the most appropriate way to deal with unwanted behaviour.

For many critical scholars a significant concern with the current crime-control agenda is that it does not necessarily reflect what research tells us about the nature and extent of crime in contemporary society. As Menzies et al. (2001, 12) argue, "[e]very piece of criminological evidence available to us shows that the [law-and-order] rhetoric is, quite simply, wrong." In addition, there is a profound imbalance of justice in terms of who is criminalized through this current crime-control discourse. As Snider (2001, 127) argues, "crime and punishment have become a cultural obsession of modernity. But this obsession is one-sided. The harm that primarily powerless individuals do to themselves, their relatives and acquaintances, and occasionally to strangers is demonized, decried and exaggerated, while the harm that corporations do to their employees, communities, competitors and the environment is minimized, rationalized and denied."

Overall, then, there appear to be several reasons for bringing together a range of perspectives on the question "what is a crime?" Embarking upon such a task does not undermine the diverse body of literature that already addresses various aspects of this question but instead emphasizes the importance of continuing this rich tradition. Indeed, we continue to struggle with whether the notion of crime is simply a value-laden term or a necessary construct that delineates appropriate and inappropriate behaviour. Who is a criminal? What is the appropriate response of the state to crime and deviance? These and other questions have confounded the study of crime and its control, and continue to do so.

Issues and Themes

This collection of essays employs a range of critical perspectives to examine crime and its control in contemporary society. Each essay adopts a slightly different approach to the "what is a crime?" question, all the while challenging us to reflect on the processes of defining crime and to consider the impacts of our decisions to criminalize certain behaviour. The perspectives offered by the authors of these essays are as diverse as their respective disciplines: law, sociology, criminology, and socio-legal studies. At the same time, however, it is important to note that this collection does not include economic, psychological, or biological perspectives on crime.

The contested nature and scope of the "what is a crime?" question make it difficult to find unanimity within the authors' fields of study, let alone across disciplines. But therein lies the strength of the six essays included in this collection. The diversity of voices contained herein allows the reader to think about, and indeed to rethink, what it means to say that something is a crime, and what is expected when employing criminal law to respond to unwanted behaviour.

Even though the essays in this collection represent a diversity of perspectives, they also offer some common issues and themes upon which to reflect. Collectively, they represent a critical dialogue on law and governance in contemporary society. Many of the essays raise important issues for other legal and socio-legal scholars to consider in their work as well as challenges for legislators and policy makers who are faced with the question "what is a crime?" in their day-to-day activities. First, the authors remind us that crime is not an objective phenomenon. Second, many bring to light aspects of the infamous title of a book by Jeffery Reiman (1995), *The Rich Get Richer and the Poor Get Prison*. Third, others situate the question "what is a crime?" within the growing body of governmentality literature, particularly as it relates to the notion of social control beyond government. Finally, together the authors provide a familiar warning that the law is not a panacea for complex social issues.

Crime and Its "Realities"

In many respects the notion of crime expresses social unity in that it signifies what constitutes acceptable and unacceptable behaviour. Criminal law provides the opportunity for society as a whole – through the state – to identify "what is *expected* and what is not *expected* by members of society"

(Einstadter and Henry 1995, 9, emphasis in the original). The work of Gottfredson and Hirschi (1990), for example, suggests that crime is of a consensual nature given that everyone has the potential to break rules and that those who transgress the law make a rational choice to do so (based on the need for excitement, risk taking, or immediate satisfaction). In this instance the law necessarily differentiates appropriate from illegal behaviour.

However, as we have already discussed, for decades numerous legal, sociological, and criminological researchers have challenged the idea that crime and its control are objective phenomena. They have also challenged the belief that society unanimously agrees on the nature and extent of the social harm attributed to certain behaviour and that an official response is warranted. The authors within this collection contribute to this rich tradition, bringing contemporary perspectives to a historically rooted question. In various ways they illustrate how our notions of crime are shaped by how we think about or perceive behaviour, the role of certain individuals and groups in defining and responding to crime, and the broader socio-cultural context within which the definition of crime and its control occurs.

In "What Is Crime? A Secular Answer," Jean-Paul Brodeur, with Geneviève Ouellet, critically examines the panoply of criminal law in Canada, focusing on how we might reduce the overreliance on legal responses while also simplifying criminal law as it currently stands. In this sense Brodeur wants to develop a pragmatic approach to reforming criminal law. He does not deny competing analyses of crime and its control (e.g., more normative analyses that focus on challenging how we think about and respond to crime) but instead chooses to focus on addressing the complexities and contradictions found within criminal law in its current form and practice.

Brodeur argues that, despite repeated calls to avoid a reflex application of criminal law, the rush to codification is alive and well in the Canadian context. His analysis of the *Criminal Code of Canada* leads to the argument that (1) the *Code* is not so much about defining a large number of offences as it is about differentiating between them for the purpose of punishment; (2) criminal law is developed on an ad hoc basis, often in response to problems of the day; (3) criminal law is used as a public relations exercise to appease certain concerns or public outcry; and (4) criminal law has a large communication component, or symbolic function. Overall, Brodeur suggests that the criminalization process does not exclusively relate to the nature of the act but has its own logic and serves functions that are not necessarily related to preventing and suppressing crime.

In "Undocumented Migrants and Bill C-11: The Criminalization of Race," Wendy Chan examines the factors that propelled the introduction of new immigration and refugee legislation in Canada. For Chan the emergence of this legislation did not stem from any real or established threats to Canadian security but from racist beliefs that permeate society. In particular she argues that Bill C-11 emerged in a climate of increased concern about "non-white" immigrants entering the country, which was fuelled by sensational media accounts of illegal immigration cases (e.g., recent cases involving boatloads of Chinese migrants off the shores of British Columbia), growing security concerns following the events of 11 September 2001, and the frequent debates by elected officials about these issues. In turn, these concerns prompted what Chan characterizes as an immigrant backlash, thus feeding into stereotypical beliefs that Canada cannot absorb an increasingly diverse immigrant population and that the Canadian way of life is being damaged by the poor quality of recent immigrants.

Chan argues that the threats associated with immigration and refugee claims in Canada are more perceived than real. What she finds particularly troubling is that, instead of challenging these erroneous claims and stereotypes, the government simply enacted new legislation. In fact, the notion of a crisis – that the new legislation was a matter of safety and security – was used as a basis for quelling opposition to Bill C-11.

The work of Steven Penney points to another aspect of the political nature of criminalization. In "Crime, Copyright, and the Digital Age," Penney considers the possibilities of increased criminalization of copyright infringement in the digital era. The increased use of the Internet and the proliferation of high-technology products have raised concerns about the digitization of copyrighted works, including music, text, and video. Penney suggests that any effort to further criminalize copyright infringement in response to digitization would be "doomed to failure."

The basis of Penney's concerns is his suspicion of both moral and economic justifications for increased criminalization. According to Penney, a moral approach, which implies that the behaviour deserves censure, would be ineffective because the "infringement is not self-evidently or incontrovertibly culpable." On the other hand, the economic approach is equally likely to fail. Detecting copyright infringement on the Internet is difficult and costly and, given the sheer number of people using the Internet, would likely overwhelm law enforcement resources. Deterrence is not a realistic goal given the low detection rates and the fact that many people do not view their activities as being criminal (e.g., downloading music files from the Internet). Penney's analysis illustrates the limits of criminal law with respect to copyright in the digital era as well as how the power of middle-class consumers of copyrighted materials makes the possibility and potential effectiveness of criminalization unlikely. According to the author, policy makers may submit to the reflex of criminalizing new forms of digital theft, but the efficacy of these policies will be dubious at best.

Even if one accepts that legislative support for the enactment of a criminal prohibition appears to have a large measure of consensus, the application and interpretation of the unwanted behaviour is constantly being reframed. The authors in this collection provide three examples of the fluid nature of crime and its control. In "Criminalization in Private: The Case of Insurance Fraud," Richard V. Ericson and Aaron Doyle probe the nonobjective nature of crime by examining what happens when its definition and control fall within the purview of the private sector. In particular the authors look at the private insurance industry to determine how cases of fraud are defined and controlled. Within this context the question "what is a crime?" is examined vis-à-vis "the expanding world of private justice."

An important aspect of Ericson and Doyle's analysis is their identification of the dramatic rise of antifraud units in private insurance companies in Canada and the United States within the last twenty years. The authors illustrate how antifraud measures, driven primarily by economic concerns within the industry (i.e., a desire to minimize the rising costs of premiums), flourished in the name of increased profits. Before the emergence of antifraud units, and the associated crackdowns on fraud cases, claims costs were thought to be something to pass along to the consumer. After the crackdowns, however, fraud detection was thought to be necessary for preventing costly fraudulent claims and to encourage the free flow of business.

On the surface, differentiating between fraudulent and legitimate claims might seem relatively unproblematic. However, Ericson and Doyle reveal that the nature and scope of insurance fraud are "ultimately unknowable" and that fraud in the insurance industry is a direct by-product of how the industry organizes itself. For example, the authors reveal that fraud is a highly fluid concept that changes depending upon the context within which it occurs. They reveal a blurring of the lines between what constitutes "hardcore" fraud and mere exaggeration, with the final decision ultimately resting with the individual investigator.

In "From Practical Joker to Offender: Reflections on the Concept of 'Crime,'" Pierre Rainville raises similar points by illustrating how the power to define crime rests with the enforcer. In particular Rainville takes a philosophical look at the distinctions in law that are used to differentiate between "behaviour that is truly criminal" and behaviour that might be regarded as inappropriate or simply a practical joke. Rainville's main concern is that current legal doctrine fails to differentiate seriously between these forms of behaviour. Is it appropriate to label practical jokers criminals? Are certain transgressions, as Rainville asks, "sufficient to justify criminal sanctions"?

By drawing upon examples of the criminalization of pranks and jokes, the author argues that failing to consider seriously what is and isn't appropriate behaviour risks casting the net of the law too broadly and, in the process, challenges the law's legitimacy. As Rainville argues, "[t]he provisions of the *[Criminal] Code* must be interpreted in such a way that the philosophy of criminal law is respected. The intervention of criminal law is specifically reserved for acts that are sufficiently odious or dangerous." He also suggests that allowing the law to overreach its original intents produces undue restrictions on individual liberties.

Rainville's analysis reminds us not only that law is never enforced and interpreted in a vacuum, but also that frivolous use of criminal law strategies seriously undermines the legitimacy of law in society. As the author argues, *"[s]ystematically thrusting practical jokes into the arena of criminal law amounts to detracting from and trivializing the very concept of crime"* (his emphasis).

Finally, in "Poisoned Water, Environmental Regulation, and Crime: Constituting the Nonculpable Subject in Walkerton, Ontario," Laureen Snider challenges us to think about the nonobjective nature of crime and its control by examining how, in certain social contexts, particular acts are not labelled as crimes, or how some actors avoid the stigma of criminalization. Of particular concern for Snider is how "'we' as a society decide where blame is warranted and where it is not." The object of her analysis is the results of the public inquiry into the tragic and deadly contamination of tap water in Walkerton, Ontario. In May 2000 the introduction of E. coli into the town's drinking water left seven people dead and 2,300 suffering from varying illnesses.

One of Snider's first tasks is to examine the political and economic context within which the events in Walkerton occurred. As with most liberal democratic societies, the latter half of the twentieth century witnessed a rise in neoliberal political reasoning (for an analysis of this process, see, for example, Barry et al. 1996). For issues of crime and its control, this way of thinking means that individuals have become increasingly criminalized, while the practices of organizations and corporations (which are often very harmful to society) are seen as essential for the smooth flow of capital and thus subject mainly to regulatory approaches. These changing political sensibilities were thought to play a role in the Walkerton tragedy, something that did not escape the final inquiry report. As Snider argues, massive cuts by the Ontario government to the Ministry of the Environment, which included disbanding specialized teams responsible for monitoring water treatment plants across the province, and privatizing water quality testing, made it difficult to monitor drinking-water sources effectively in that province.

While Snider acknowledges that the Walkerton inquiry report criticizes the role of government decision making in contributing to the contamination of the tap water, she cautions that this accomplishment might be more perceived than real. Although the report challenges some of the government decisions preceding Walkerton, she argues that it does so only in a limited, liberal sense. The report criticizes government but suggests that only minor adjustments are necessary for avoiding similar incidents in the future. Snider also raises questions about who was criminalized or held accountable for the events in Walkerton. In most instances it is the individual, rather than organizations or organizational structures, that are held accountable.

For example, a considerable amount of blame was aimed at the manager of Walkerton Public Utilities, who was described as an untrustworthy and blameworthy criminal actor. In contrast, however, although the report was critical of government policies, there was little evidence of similar language being employed to describe organizational "bad actors."

The overall thrust of these examples is that crime does not exist independently of the social structures and processes that help to define and control it. Crime is not merely the quality of an act but also a judgment. To say that something is criminal is to say that it is wrong and, by extension, to suggest that the person who commits the act is somehow culpable. It is therefore important to understand the contextual nature of crime. The authors in this collection explain and illustrate the political nature of crime, from the enactment of legislation (immigration crisis and middle-class copyright infringement) to the variable enforcement of its provisions (insurance fraud, bad-humour jokes, and criminal negligence in administering water standards).

Building from examinations of the nonobjective nature of crime, several of the authors also explore how the most vulnerable classes in society are criminalized through the introduction and enforcement of criminal law.

Who Is a Criminal? or "The Rich Get Richer and the Poor Get Prison"
A theme that has been and continues to be a considerable area of concern for critical legal scholars is the differences between the law on the books and the law in action, or the differences between laws as they are written and laws as they are enforced. A law is not only something that is brought to bear through (subjective) social processes, but also, once on the books, something that continues to be subject to many of the same societal and institutional pressures that helped define the nature of the criminalized behaviour and the associated response. In particular these pressures help determine the extent to which a certain law is enforced and in what manner.

Previous studies have revealed the impact of the law in action in various ways. Some examples from this important body of literature include:

- how the law is unequally enforced to the detriment of certain groups, as is the case with the overpolicing of Aboriginal peoples and other racial minorities in Canada (see, for example, Manitoba 1991; Williams 2001)
- how domestic violence has been underpoliced (see, for example, Bonnycastle and Rigakos 1998; Tutty and Goard 2002) as well as the unanticipated consequences of mandatory arrest policies, including more women arrested in domestic-violence cases (McMahon and Pence 2003)
- gender bias in the law's unequal application to women – for example, only women being charged with soliciting although the legislation theoretically includes men (see, for example, Layton 1979; Lowman 1986)

There are several examples within the essays in this collection that once again bring to the fore the important issues associated with the enforcement of law in society.

In her chapter Wendy Chan suggests that a potential consequence of the new Canadian immigration legislation is that the criminal label will be cast upon more immigrants and refugee claimants, essentially characterizing them as potential threats to security. As the author argues, the legislation creates a "culture of criminalization" and a means of scapegoating or finding a suitable enemy to blame for our "failures and insecurities." At the same time, the criminal label contributes to an us/them dichotomy by defining who is considered normal and nonthreatening and who constitutes a challenge to social order. This in turn leaves certain (nonwhite) people on the outside of society, thereby preventing them from enjoying the benefits of full citizenship. According to Chan the law and its related policies employ the language of exclusion and, in the case of Bill C-11, rely upon criminalizing and retributive undertones that feed into and result from stereotypical and racist beliefs.

After reviewing numerous components of this new immigration legislation, Chan argues that it has considerable overreach. For example, there are often cases where a person fleeing persecution does not have the time or luxury to obtain the proper documentation. In this situation the individual risks criminalization once he or she arrives in Canada if the rules regarding refugees are tightened, even though he or she has a legitimate claim. Similarly, individuals who have been victimized by human smugglers will be revictimized by overly broad detention provisions within the legislation. Finally, migrants and refugees who want to enter Canada will be forced to take even more drastic and covert measures to enter the country, thereby putting themselves (perhaps unwittingly) at greater risk of breaking the law.

We also see the impact of deciding who to label a criminal in Ericson and Doyle's chapter on the definition and enforcement of fraud in the private insurance industry. First, fraud is a fluid concept whose definition is more reflective of how the insurance companies organize themselves than of the actual nature and extent of insurance fraud. Second, the authors reveal that what constitutes fraud often depends on who the client is. In this respect their analysis sheds light on the how the impact of crime-control strategies can differ when enforced in the private realm, with companies and their more affluent customers benefiting from the application of fraud rules. Companies benefit because the application of the rules ensures the efficient flow of business, while more affluent clients are less likely to have their claims rejected or, even in worst-case scenarios, are more likely to have their claims simply denied and dealt with privately rather than deemed to be fraudulent. It is the more marginalized clients from populations of a lower socio-economic standing, individuals believed to lack the capacity to mount a legal challenge to the claims of insurance companies, who are deemed to be acting fraudulently. Wealthy or more desirable clients are frequently given the benefit of the doubt by investigators and are seen to be only exaggerating. In the end, as the authors note, "in an increasingly privatized society, the practical definition of insurance fraud becomes whatever is consistent with the smooth flow of business."

Snider criticizes the individualization of blame that emerged from the Walkerton inquiry by shedding light on how the notion of who is or is not a criminal is formed as well as on how knowledge and power are employed in a manner that ensures maintenance of the status quo. In the Walkerton example, although the inquiry report recognized the role of government decision making in precipitating the contamination of the town's tap water, there remained a considerable element of individual blame, most notably a focus on the actions of individual town employees in causing the tragic events. As Snider argues, "[f]or those who wish to hold organizations accountable for the harm they do, this phenomenon is one of the central challenges of the Walkerton case. If neither the law nor the public can 'see' crime except through the body of the individual bad actor, the possibilities of disciplining the most powerful entities in the modern social order – the organizations dominating our economic and political systems – appear slim."

There are also elements of the "who is a criminal?" question in Brodeur's chapter. The author suggests that laws are highly varied and subjective and that there is no "inherent characteristic of a behaviour" that implies absolute disapproval. As an example Brodeur notes that many aspects of professional sports rely upon violence as a main attraction (e.g., violence in ice hockey), yet violent acts that occur during such activities are rarely criminalized. Rather, they are characterized and marketed as a necessary part of the business of the sport. The author also uses the example of legalized gambling to highlight the fluid understanding of harm, raising questions about whether the government is justified in maintaining a monopoly over certain forms of gambling while other forms remain illegal. Why is it acceptable for the state to organize certain forms of harmful gambling when it is illegal for individuals to do so?

Finally, Rainville's chapter offers a slightly different glimpse of the subjective processes that influence the decision to criminalize certain individuals. Through an examination of the criminalization of pranks, the author suggests that the law must reconcile two existing tensions: (1) "between the practical joker and the victim of the joke" and (2) "between undue criminalization and the judge's subjectivism." In essence, Rainville suggests that there is a need for balance between the subjective experiences of the victim ("I was offended") and those of the offender ("I was only joking"). As the author notes, "[t]his reconciles the respectability of the victim with the respectability of criminal law: One cannot be achieved at the expense of the other."

Governance beyond Government, or Crime and the Role of the State

In *Visions of Social Control*, Stanley Cohen (1985, 10) suggests that "to write today about punishment and classification without Foucault, is like talking about the unconscious without Freud." Indeed, the influence of Foucault's work has been profound in terms of how we understand what it means to say that something is a crime and that a formal legal response is necessary to sanction a particular behaviour. The punishment of a crime is no longer conceived as an exercise of power exclusively by the state, but instead as a form of control produced through a complex of power relations (see, for example, Foucault 1979).

In recent years Foucault's work has spawned a range of research that examines notions of governance beyond government. As a result there has been an increasing recognition that the formal legal system is only one way that we deal with crime or unwanted behaviour. For example, writers like Garland (2001, 140) have argued that crime and its control are no longer considered the sole responsibility of the state. On the contrary, the state has retreated from its claim to be the "chief provider of security" and has reconceived its response to crime "on a more dispersed, partnership basis. In this arrangement the state works *through* civil society and not *upon* it, and emphasizes proactive prevention rather than the prosecution and punishment of individuals" (emphasis in the original). The lessons gleaned from this and other related work (see, for example, Barry et al. 1996) is that an analysis of what constitutes a crime requires an understanding of social control strategies that extends beyond a strict legal definition to consider a range of control and coercion strategies.

There are at least two notions of governance beyond government that permeate many of the essays in this collection. First, a number of the authors illustrate how the state is not solely responsible for defining crime and its control and argue that this dynamic poses new and interesting challenges for those interested in answering the question "what is a crime?" Second, some of the authors illustrate how power and control are exercised throughout the entire social body, rather than as a direct result only of state-centred functions.

Ericson and Doyle's essay illustrates well the web of control that is exercised through the private insurance realm. The authors reveal how private insurance companies work in collaboration with police to employ the symbolism of the criminal justice system. In particular they demonstrate how the law is used as a threat to remind individuals of what might happen if they do not report their claims honestly. In one example the authors describe how an insurance-claims centre was constructed within a police station, which allowed the insurance company to invoke the symbolic power of the police to deter hit-and-run fraud cases; the insurance company reminded clients that all hit-and-run cases would involve police investigators. Overall, Ericson and Doyle's analysis illustrates how the policing of fraud becomes the responsibility of the individual customer; each person is reminded of the need to report honestly. By employing the notion of a fraud "crackdown," the antifraud message of insurance companies permeates the entire insurance industry, from the individual claims investigator to police agencies and individual insurance consumers.

Snider's analysis also reminds us of the complexities of contemporary control processes. The author illustrates, for example, how neoliberal notions of regulation were employed throughout the Walkerton inquiry in defence of government policy decisions that remove many responsibilities from the hands of the state (in this case, responsibility for tap-water quality) and place them in the hands of private companies, communities, and individuals. Although the Walkerton inquiry report criticizes many of the Ontario government's decisions to privatize water monitoring, there is little evidence of fundamental challenges to status-quo relations of power. Instead, individuals are criminalized or held responsible for their actions, while organizational structures are conceived of in more technical terms – for example, on the basis of how to improve their effective functioning. In this regard Snider raises questions about the potential of holding organizations and organizational structures accountable for serious social wrongs. As the author notes, "[c]riminality resides at the individual level. It is about the blameworthy legal subject, about character flaws in individuals, about willed and wilful misconduct."

Chan provides us with an indication of the impact of governance beyond government as it relates to immigration and refugee legislation. Chan suggests that a "culture of criminalization" has come to characterize the Canadian immigration and refugee landscape. In a sense, racist undertones within society shaped and were shaped by the government's decision to introduce this new legislation. The resulting "culture of criminalization," or the erroneous and stereotypical belief that all immigrants and refugees pose a threat to the security of Canadians, means that everyone (not only the state) will potentially play a role in constituting the criminal subject. All actors, from individual citizens, government officials, and immigration officers to those individual immigrants labelled threats, will participate in the perception (or self-identification) of the migrant as dangerous and worthy of criminalization.

Challenging the Reflex to Apply Criminal Law
A final theme that runs throughout many of the essays in this collection is

that the law is not a panacea for complex social issues and that we must therefore reconsider the role of criminal law in society. Despite a growing recognition of the notion of governance beyond government, these essays also remind us that the control of crime by state actors continues to be a significant and prominent issue within society – that is, the notion of a socially recognized "carceral archipelago" has some important empirical qualifications, which provides context concerning the role of the contemporary state in defining and controlling crime. For example, Brodeur notes and criticizes the expansion of criminalization, arguing that the *Code* "has grown thicker over more than a century now with a host of provisions that have helped to make Canadian criminal law impenetrable." Penney similarly cautions against giving in to persistent demands for criminal law in the context of the infringement of copyright in the digital world, arguing that such criminalization would be doomed to failure and would be perceived by the public as both morally and economically indefensible. Rainville also warns that overextending the reach of the law will in itself challenge the law's legitimacy.

The sombre depiction of the consequences of criminalization in the immigration context, as depicted by Chan, leads to a similar suggestion of the need to avoid overusing criminal law. As other scholars have frequently pointed out, we ought to refrain from using criminal law as a quick response to complex social issues. As Chan's analysis suggests, the introduction of new immigration and refugee legislation will do little to quell the fears associated with the impact of globalization (however perceived or real that impact is); in fact, such legislation will only exacerbate many of the racist beliefs that permeate our society.

The reliance on criminal law and punishment is indeed a dangerous strategy. The essays in this collection provide a challenge to those interested in developing pathways to reforming our current approach to crime. In this regard the authors offer several insights on law reform. A key overall insight is that we need to better appreciate how our ideas of what constitutes a crime are developed. After all, social control in general and criminal justice in particular constitute how we think about crime and unwanted behaviour. In short, as these authors illustrate in various ways, crime is not an objective phenomenon. Thus we need to consider with humility whatever reforms might be suggested.

The essays in this collection also challenge us to reflect on who has a voice in the criminalization process. In particular we need to work toward democratizing the process of defining crime and its control. This is a familiar message for legal scholars, feminists, and criminologists concerned with answering the question "what is a crime?" Certainly feminists have argued (in some cases successfully) for the inclusion of women's voices in defining crime and its control, and they have also warned against the limits of the law in dealing with complex social issues. In the late 1980s some critical scholars (most notably Left Realists) advocated democratizing crime-control processes, especially for the most marginalized groups, which bear the greatest costs of crime (see, for example, Young and Matthews 1992). Finally, Aboriginal communities have argued for a stronger voice in designing crime-control strategies, advocating greater use of restorative justice programs to deal with the problems associated with the overrepresentation of Aboriginal peoples in the criminal justice system. Overall, then, as a society, we need to better support democratic ideals in the hopes of creating a more equitable and accountable process for defining crime and enforcing criminal law.

Finally, the essays contained herein convey the familiar message that we need to search for unique ways to avoid the reflex application of criminal law. Despite repeated calls by academics and government to be cautious about using the law to deal with complex social problems, we continue to turn to the law to provide a quick fix or to scapegoat certain populations for our social insecurities. We have to pause and seriously ask how we might better avoid this reflex in contemporary society.

Conclusion

The essays in this book critically examine the question "what is a crime?" In addition to challenging us to think about what we mean when we say that something is a crime or that someone is a criminal, the authors provide clear illustrations of the various impacts of the criminalization process. The collective issues and questions raised by the authors pose serious challenges for those interested in crime and its control, including academics, policy makers, and law reformers. Why do we criminalize certain behaviours and not others? What are the legal, social, and cultural factors that influence the decision to criminalize or not criminalize unwanted behaviours? What are the consequences of responding or not responding in certain ways to unwanted behaviour? What strategies can we use to avoid the reflex application of criminal law?

Overall, this collection of essays continues a rich scholarly tradition of examining issues related to crime and its control. They signal the importance of rethinking our approaches to defining and responding to behaviour that is deemed unwanted. At the same time, they highlight the importance of asking and reevaluating the question "what is a crime?" In doing so, they encourage us to imagine how things might be different in the future.

References

Barry, A., T. Osborne, and N. Rose, eds. 1996. *Foucault and Political Reason: Liberalism, Neo-Liberalism and Rationalities of Government.* Chicago: University of Chicago Press.

Becker, H. 1963. *Outsiders: Studies in the Sociology of Deviance.* New York: Free Press.

Bonnycastle, K.D., and G.S. Rigakos, eds. 1998. *Unsettling Truths: Battered Women, Policy, Politics, and Contemporary Research in Canada*. Vancouver: Collective Press.

Canada, Department of Justice. 1982. *The Criminal Law in Canadian Society*. Ottawa: Ministry of Supply and Services Canada.

Christie, N. 1994. *Crime Control as Industry: Towards Gulags, Western Style*. London: Routledge.

Cohen, S. 1980. *Folk Devils and Moral Panics: The Creation of the Mods and Rockers*. New York: St. Martin's Press.

–. 1985. *Visions of Social Control*. Cambridge: Polity Press.

Comack, E., and S. Brickey. 1991. *The Social Basis of Law: Critical Readings in the Sociology of Law*. 2nd ed. Halifax: Garamond Press.

–, with S. Arat-Koc, K. Busby, D.E. Chunn, J. Fudge, S.A.M. Gavigan, L.M. Jakubowski, K. Johnson, P. Monture-Angus, L. Snider, eds. 1999. *Locating Law: Race/Class/Gender Connections*. Halifax: Fernwood Publishing.

Einstadter, W., and S. Henry. 1995. *Criminological Theory: An Analysis of Its Underlying Assumptions*. Toronto: Harcourt Brace College Publishers.

Foucault, M. 1979. *Discipline and Punish: The Birth of the Prison*. New York: Vintage Books.

Garland, D. 2001. *The Culture of Control: Crime and Social Order in Contemporary Society*. Chicago: University of Chicago Press.

Gottfredson, M.R., and T. Hirschi. 1990. *A General Theory of Crime*. Stanford, CA: Stanford University Press.

Hannah-Moffat, K. 2001. *Punishment in Disguise: Penal Governance and Federal Imprisonment of Women in Canada*. Toronto: University of Toronto Press.

Henry, S., and M. Lanier. 2001. *What Is Crime? Controversies over the Nature of Crime and What to Do about It*. New York: Rowman and Littlefield Publishers.

Hudson, B. 1998. "Punishment and Governance." *Social and Legal Studies* 7, 4: 553-59.

Law Reform Commission of Canada. 1976. *Our Criminal Law: Report*. Ottawa: Information Canada.

Layton, M. 1979. "The Ambiguities of the Law of the Street Walker's Dilemma." *Chitty's Law Journal* 27, 4: 109-20.

Lowman, J. 1986. "You Can Do It, but Don't Do It Here: Some Comments on Proposals for the Reform of Canadian Prostitution Law." In *Regulating Sex: An Anthology of Commentaries on the Findings and Recommendations of the Badgley and Fraser Reports*, edited by J. Lowman, M. Jackson, T. Palys, and S. Gavigan, 193-213. Burnaby, BC: School of Criminology, Simon Fraser University.

Manitoba. 1991. *Report of the Aboriginal Justice Inquiry of Manitoba/Public Inquiry into the Administration of Justice and the Aboriginal People*. Vol. 1: The Justice System and Aboriginal People; Vol. 2: The Deaths of Helen Betty Osborne and John Joseph Harper. Winnipeg: The Inquiry.

McMahon, M. 1992. *The Persistent Prison? Rethinking Decarceration and Penal Reform*. Toronto: University of Toronto Press.

–, and E. Pence. 2003. "Making Social Change: Reflections on Individual and Institutional Advocacy with Women Arrested for Domestic Violence." *Violence Against Women* 9, 1: 47-74.

Menzies, R., D.E. Chunn, and S.C. Boyd. 2001. "Introduction." In *[Ab]using Power: The Canadian Experience*, edited by S.C. Boyd, D.E. Chunn, and R. Menzies, 11-24. Halifax: Fernwood Publishing.

Neugebauer, R., ed. 2000. *Criminal Injustice: Racism in the Criminal Justice System*. Toronto: Canadian Scholarly Press.

O'Malley, P. 2000. "Criminologies of Catastrophe? Understanding Criminal Justice on the Edge of the New Millennium." *Australian and New Zealand Journal of Criminology* 33, 2: 153-67.

Reiman, J. 1995. *The Rich Get Richer and the Poor Get Prison: Ideology, Class, and Criminal Justice*. Boston: Allyn & Bacon.

Snider, L. 2001. "Abusing Corporate Power: The Death of a Concept." In *[Ab]using Power: The Canadian Experience*, edited by S.C. Boyd, D.E. Chunn, and R. Menzies, 112-29. Halifax: Fernwood Publishing.

Tappan, P.W. 1947. "Who Is the Criminal?" *American Sociological Review* 12: 96-102.

Tutty, L.M., and C. Goard, eds. 2002. *Reclaiming Self: Issues and Resources for Women Abused by Intimate Partners*. Halifax: Fernwood Publishing.

Williams, T. 2001. "Racism in Justice: The Report of the Commission on Systemic Racism in the Ontario Criminal Justice System." In *[Ab]using Power: The Canadian Experience,* edited by S.C. Boyd, D.E. Chunn, and R. Menzies, 200-213. Halifax: Fernwood Publishing.

Young, J., and R. Matthews, eds. 1992. *Rethinking Criminology: The Realist Debate*. London: Sage Publications.

What Is a Crime?

1
What Is a Crime? A Secular Answer

Jean-Paul Brodeur, with Geneviève Ouellet

Before attempting to answer the question "what is a crime?" we must ask what it means. The very wording of the question is ambiguous. On the one hand, it would be possible to narrow down its meaning and attempt to answer the question in relation to a specific crime. The question then might be, for example, "what is murder, tax fraud, or rape?" On the other hand, it can also be understood in the general sense of "what is *crime*?" – that is, in reference not to a particular crime but to the very nature of crime. This is the sense in which we interpret it in this chapter.

However, this initial clarification does not suffice to focus the meaning of our question adequately, leaving two important aspects unaddressed. First, what are we looking for – a concise definition or a more elaborate theory? Second, do we want to account for the fact of criminalization, as it can be described, or do we want to provide a normative standard for future criminalization?

Definition or Theory

One could approach the question either by attempting to produce a *definition* of crime or by devising a *theory* on the various aspects of the concept. As Williams (1955, 108) has reminded us, a definition is a set of words that can be substituted in a process of discovery for the term to be defined. As a substitute for the term being defined, the definition will rarely be much more than a relatively short sentence. A few decades ago it was still possible to respect this requirement because the concept of crime was not problematic then and because few felt any need to provide it with an epistemological foundation. However, following the lasting upheaval brought about by the various "critical criminologies" (Taylor, Walton, and Young 1973, 1975), it is no longer possible to accept a brief definition of crime, and the efforts to do justice to the concept usually take the form of theories that include a constantly growing number of factors (Henry and Lanier 1998).

Fact or Standard

On a different level, it is probably immediately obvious that asking what a crime is on the basis of an examination of behaviours that are *currently* treated as crimes by the law, as opposed to asking what the criteria *should* be for making a given behaviour a crime in the future, are two very different tasks. The first of these activities is based on the facts as they can be apprehended and is descriptive in nature. This description can, in the best cases, be expanded into an explanation of the reasons why certain behaviours came to be treated as crimes. The second activity is located in an ideal realm, wholly normative and subjective in nature, where arguments tend toward ethical justification rather than empirical demonstration.

Our review of thirty or so studies and manuals on criminology that have attempted to answer the question "what is a crime?" has shown that these distinctions are crucial and that the answers given are profoundly influenced by the type of approach adopted by the expert.

The Factual Definition

Most of those who have looked for such definitions are led to a formalistic perspective. By simply positing that crime is a violation of the law, the definition is suitably succinct and thus complies with the requirement stated above. Tappan (1960, 10) provided a prototype for this kind of definition, which was repeated with little variation in more than half the works we reviewed: "Crime is an intentional act or omission in violation of criminal law (statutory or case law), committed without defence or justification, and sanctioned by the state as a felony or misdemeanour."

The Factual Theory

The theories that focus on behaviours that are treated as crimes in the law as it currently stands take the view (which forms the very basis for formalism) that crime is a product of a social reaction. Durkheim (1981, 35) provided the paradigm for this theory, of which the only specific element is that crime is merely the correlate of a sanction.[1] Many authors have subscribed to this paradigm, albeit with a number of critical reservations (Robert 1985; Killias 1991, 341). The essential difference between this approach and the "common sense" approach is that it focuses on the criminal offence *in its full legal dimension*, whereas common sense inquires only into the nature of *serious crime*.

Focusing as it does on the real harmfulness of criminal conduct, the normative approach is in this regard grafted onto common sense.

The Normative Definition

Normative approaches attempt to go beyond the social reaction as such, and try to find, in the features of the behaviour, reasons that might justify treating it as criminal. When the concept of crime was not yet a problem (Garofalo 1968, 46), this kind of definition, based on the concept of harm or damage caused to others, was common. Though this conception of crime was at the very heart of early criminology, fewer and fewer authors now feel that the question of the nature of crime can be resolved by providing a definition of it that is limited to a single phrase (one exception is Gassin 1994, 17, who, following a straight line from Garofalo, defines crime in terms of the violence and/or duplicity involved).

The Normative Theory
Those who seek criteria for criminalizing behaviours inside the behaviours themselves can only develop adequate arguments in the broader framework of a normative theory. Two variants of the normative approach can be found. The first one is *epistemological*. One of the founding fathers of criminology, Garofalo, felt that this new scientific discipline could be scientifically viable only if it had a stable subject. It is in order to satisfy this scientific standard that he developed his theory of "natural crime," which he recognized as applying only to a hard core of criminality. Garofalo has been unfairly criticized by criminologists who simply brushed aside the legitimate epistemological requirement he wished to satisfy, a requirement that critical criminologies have jettisoned in favour of an increasingly wandering theoretical search. The second variant of the norm-based approach is *pragmatic* and consists of systems of thought directed at reforming the existing practices involved in criminalizing various behaviours (Hagan 1977; Young 1992; Henry and Lanier 1998).

This chapter takes the perspective of factual theory and, accordingly, focuses on criminalization in the law as it currently stands. It consists of four parts, followed by a conclusion: (1) preliminary theoretical observations on the parameters of the debate; (2) a study of the various categorizations of criminal offences; (3) a case study on gun control; (4) a case study on lotteries and other games of chance. In the closing section, we move beyond the framework of a descriptive theory and draw a number of conclusions as to whether, and under what circumstances, it is appropriate to criminalize conduct.

Before beginning our analysis, we shall use an analogy to determine the principle that will guide us. The question of the death penalty has provoked some fierce debates and continues to do so, and there are two basic ways to object to capital punishment. First, one can object on principle – that is, on the basis of a moral argument that denounces all forms of killing without exception. However, this objection is unlikely to be decisive since every moral argument against capital punishment has been answered with credibility at some point in the history of ethics.[2] Second, one may object to it on the basis of a practical consideration: Regardless of the legitimacy of the death penalty from the standpoint of principles, its discriminatory application betrays these principles irremediably. In concrete terms many individuals who are extremely guilty avoid the death penalty because they have the resources to assert their rights, if not their privileges, whereas the most disadvantaged individuals cannot escape it because they lack the resources to do so, even if they are innocent or lack the capacity to stand trial because they suffer from serious psychiatric problems. These arguments highlight the gulf that exists between principles and their application. In a similar way, we shall study the actual text of the law through its many changes to show that there is also a large gap between the letter of the law, as it can actually be found in legal codes, and an abstract and fabricated spirit of the law, which only exists in the imagination of those who invoke "the law" without having ever examined how it is actually codified.

Part 1: The Parameters of the Debate

The debate on the nature of crime cannot be separated from the debate about the nature of punishment because these two concepts are closely connected. This means that the debate has been going on at least since classical antiquity. Plato asked what criminal justice was in *The Republic* and in *The Laws*. As a result of its scope and its duration, this debate is at risk of getting bogged down in its own verbosity and needs to be circumscribed by a set of parameters. We believe that these parameters can be kept to a minimum in order to avoid introducing undue restrictions or biases in our discussion.

Heterogeneous Nature of Criminal Offences

As it currently reads, the *Criminal Code of Canada* (CCC; Cournoyer and Ouimet 2001) consists of thirteen parts defining the substance of criminal offences, to which should be added other laws that create their own offences, such as the *Controlled Drugs and Substances Act* or the *Firearms Act*. To illustrate the highly varied nature of our criminal law, we should point out that Part 4 of the CCC concerns *Offences against the administration of law and justice*, Part 5 concerns *Sexual offences, public morals and disorderly conduct*, Part 6 concerns *Invasion of privacy*, Part 8 concerns *Offences against the person and reputation*, and Part 11 concerns *Wilful and forbidden acts in respect of certain property*. Under the heading "Disorderly Conduct" we find the following offences in Part 5 of the CCC:

> indecent acts, exposure, nudity, causing a disturbance, obstructing or violence to or arrest of an officiating clergyman, disturbing religious worship or certain meetings, trespassing at night, possession of an offensive volatile substance and vagrancy.

Part 11 is a catch-all for a wide range of offences that include both arson (CCC, 433) and a prohibition on keeping cockpits (447(1)).

Brief though this listing is, it will serve to underline the wide variety of behaviours that are criminalized, which seems to make it impossible for a person to find any intrinsic characteristic they might have in common. The only aspect that these behaviours might hypothetically share is that *it is felt to be desirable to avoid them*. As the impersonal structure of the phrase "it is felt" suggests, this classification of conduct that should be avoided comes from outside. As we shall see, there is *no* inherent characteristic of a behaviour that would imply total disapproval.

Those who have devised a concept of crime have undertaken to overcome the obstacle posed by this wide variety of offences in two different ways.

We alluded earlier to the first kind of solution, which was suggested in the nineteenth century by Garofalo in order to give criminology a firm scientific foundation. This solution was to avoid engaging in a search for substantive characteristics that were common to all offences, their wide diversity being accepted, and to instead identify a hard core of offences, whose harmful effects were not open to debate and which could be included in a set of so-called "natural" offences (Garofalo 1968; see also Gassin 1994, 1998, although he does not use the terminology of naturalism). These offences, characterized by violence and duplicity, essentially cover the various kinds of aggression against the person, and the variants of theft. The main stumbling block in this substantivism and its multiple applications is the simple fact that it is always possible to find behaviours that display the features of a natural offence but that have not been criminalized. The whole arena of professional sports is marked by violence and duplicity (for instance, in the use of substances that artificially enhance athletes' performances), yet athletes are generally immune to the criminal law in the course of playing their sport, except in extreme cases of physical aggression, where criminal prosecution is intended only to placate public hysteria. Violence on the ice is the main attraction of hockey for North American audiences. Imposing criminal measures to suppress this violence would be tantamount to forcing many teams into bankruptcy, which so far has been avoided for obvious economic reasons.

There is one major implication of the heterogeneous nature of criminal offences for the task of developing a comprehensive theory of crime that we will not address. Fully addressing it is beyond the scope of this text since our concerns here are not epistemological. We shall only mention that a theory of crime must avoid two equally fatal traps. The first one is essentialism, which holds that all crimes must share certain common characteristics. The search for such common features results in the kind of naturalism or substantivism that we have found in Garofalo's thought. The second trap is casuistry, which, as its name indicates, is so immersed in a case-by-case approach, no two cases being viewed as really alike, that it misses seeing the forest by focusing too exclusively on individual trees. Rather, the investigative logic of a comprehensive theory of crime should be based upon the concept of "family resemblance," as developed by Wittgenstein (1953). Family resemblances are broad similarities between individual cases that are neither identical nor share a common core.

Legal Formalism

The second solution designed to dispel any doubts caused by the heterogeneous nature of offences is to define crime formally, as a breach of criminal law. The only characteristic shared by behaviours that otherwise would differ too widely to constitute a single category is that the law makes them crimes and imposes penalties on those who commit them. The resort to formalism is only to be expected given the nullifying effect of the obstacle of heterogeneity. Notwithstanding the tautological aspects of the definition – criminal *offences* share only a single characteristic in that they all involve breaches *of the law* – another objection can also be made, perhaps even more decisively, against formalism. This objection can be stated in two parts.

First, the criminalization of behaviours is a legal act that is itself not uniform; in fact, it occurs in a widely diversified manner. The criminal codes of Western countries make a distinction between minor offences (which can be prosecuted in Canada on summary conviction) and major offences (which in Canada are indictable offences). This distinction between the more and the less serious may be expressed in different ways (*délit* and *crime*, *misdemeanou*r and *felony*), but it can be found in nearly all criminal codes. To complicate matters, in Canada there are also hybrid offences, which can be treated as indictable offences or minor offences depending on how they are committed. Furthermore, the severity of the penalties for the more serious offences varies substantially since they can range from life imprisonment in those countries that have abolished the death penalty to periods of imprisonment of varying duration. Finally, some offences have minimum sentences – for example, CCC, 85(3) – although in Canada most of them do not.

Second, the criminalization of a form of behaviour coincides with its being subject to legal punishment. Since criminalization is not a uniform legal act, *a sentence is also not a fixed penalty but a quantum that varies according to the seriousness of an offence.* Defining an offence solely by the penalty imposed for it, as Durkheim did, is just as abstract an exercise as defining goods by the fact that they have a price. This simply avoids questions about the amount of that price, who determines it, and in what context, which cannot be addressed without examining the laws of the market and the quality of the traded goods. Where crime is concerned, it seems at least equally important for any definition to account for the *differentiation* in the penalties imposed for various offences.

If we do not believe that the severity of sentences is determined by chance, there are two mutually supporting ways to explain the variations in the harshness of punishment for criminal offences. One can first explain it in reference to the fluctuation of social consensus – a problematic notion in itself – regarding the seriousness of certain offences. For instance, paedophilia, which was completely acceptable to the Ancient Greeks, is now viewed as a heinous crime in Western-type societies. One can also invoke changes in state governance: a religious government will punish (female) adultery with great harshness, whereas a secular one might not even criminalize it. The distinctive feature of both attempts is that they explain changes in the severity of punishment from the outside, without taking into explicit account the nature of the punished behaviour itself. For instance, it may well be that attitudes to paedophilia have changed because paedophilia in itself has changed. What was accepted by the Ancient Greeks and condemned by us is the same behaviour only in name (for instance, Greek paedophilia only implied boys as its object, whereas modern paedophilia involves girls as much as boys). Such intrinsic explanations are disqualified in the preceding approach(es). The economic equivalent of these external accounts of the variation of punishment would be the development of a theory of pricing in which assigned monetary values were relatively independent of the nature of the property for sale and deemed to vary solely with the level of demand. This view is not unreasonable in economics, but it faces a substantial problem in the field of criminal justice. There is in fact a certain stability in penalties (prices) over time and across locations and cultures for a whole body of offences (Newman 1976). This stability is not immune to upheavals, as has been evidenced in a number of countries by the restoration of *sharia* (Islamic law), in which the punishment for adultery is stoning to death. The fact remains that a penal value is ascribed to certain behaviours – murder, theft with violence, sexual assault – that transcends cultures; despite their heterogeneous nature, the behaviours that constitute crimes are still punished on a comparable scale of severity. There are clear differences between the rape of a woman as defined by *sharia* and as conceived in the criminal codes influenced by the Christian tradition; yet the fact remains that the search for shared characteristics in these offences and in the punishments meted out for them would not immediately reveal an insurmountable degree of difference.

In this way, therefore, we arrive at a reversal of formalism, now shown to be unaware of the consequences of its own premises. Defining crime by what is criminalized and saying nothing about the variety of sentences is similar to defining temperature by the thermometer reading and failing to note that it is a measuring instrument that does not vary in itself. Just as a thermometer does not vary on its own, the level of difference in sentences is not explained by itself. The comparisons that we have used hitherto – the market and the thermometer – have two things in common: (1) these instruments vary, but (2) their variations cannot be explained by the instruments themselves. Similarly, a sociology of the state that attempts to understand changes in penalties by refusing to consider who and what is subject to criminal sanctions is being wilfully blind.

We shall now see why these comments do not mean that we need to rediscover the natural view of crime of Garofalo and his followers.

Crime from the Viewpoints of Those Involved

Our analysis concerns the nature of crime: Why is it that a particular form of behaviour is classified as a crime? In this regard we need to examine (1) the criminalized behaviour and the actors involved in a crime, namely (2) the victim, (3) the officer of the law, and (4) the offender.

The Criminalized Behaviour

We have already argued that as a category of behaviour, crime has been characterized according to the heterogeneous nature of its elements. We need to add two more general characteristics to this first formal feature. First, as can be seen from the history of the criminalization of behaviours, which was studied in masterly fashion by Durkheim (1900), the initial instances of criminalization applied to behaviours that derogated from the respect owed to a deity (impiety, blasphemy). The criminal codes in the West, having moved in the direction of constantly greater secularism, can easily make us forget that the harmfulness of the crime, which is its primary constituent from a "realistic" perspective, was initially an indirect feature. It was the fear of indiscriminate divine wrath that made religious offences harmful to human beings. Second, we shall distinguish between two types of behaviour: (1) individual acts[3] perpetrated by one or a few offenders, which occur in the form of separate events at various points in time, although the offenders may display compulsive as much as sporadic behaviour; (2) actions complementing each other, which form practices continuous in time and involve the participation of several offenders acting in a concerted fashion. What is referred to as "street crime" consists primarily of individual acts of aggression, whereas organized crime or crimes against humanity take the form of practices that often require elaborate planning. Although recent legislation has focused, at the national level, on organized crime and, at the international level, on crimes against humanity, this trend is relatively new, and the application of these laws by the courts is already facing procedural problems that may be difficult to overcome. Traditionally, it is the individual offence, still much easier to prosecute, that has been criminalized. With the exception of extremely serious crimes against persons, this type of offence has usually been regarded as belonging to the realm of petty or mid-level criminality.

The Victim

A behaviour that causes harm or material damage to others is a crime under two conditions: (1) if the person being harmed was not in the process of criminally aggressing another person – who would then have been acting in self-defence; or (2) if the person is not being harmed by a punishment imposed after a public conviction for a crime in accordance with the canons of due process. We stress that harmful conduct is considered a crime only if its victim is innocent and thus able to make the point that, objectively, a sentence coincides with the perpetration of a crime. In such cases, the death sentence is a homicide, imprisonment is an extended form of kidnapping, probation is a form of harassment, and a fine is a form of government extortion. The consequences of this observation are neutralized by appealing to a (variable) consensus on the legitimacy of socially reacting to criminal behaviour by imposing legal sanctions on the offender (Hagan 1977; Young 1992; Henry and Lanier 1998). The difference between a murder and the death penalty is that the former is a homicide that is *culpable* in the eyes of society, whereas the latter is alleged to be a *justified* homicide because it takes the life of a guilty victim who has already been convicted of murder. Similarly, it will be asserted that kidnapping is a culpable impoundment, whereas imprisonment is justified internment. Although it is sound, this reply does not really exhaust the issue. As the first of our examples shows, a consensus concerning the legitimacy of a sentence can change to its diametrical opposite very quickly since the death penalty is considered to be murder in the eyes of a growing majority of people (the death penalty has actually been abolished in most Western countries, and it is now opposed in the United States by an increasing number of people). Furthermore, the answer to a lack of consensus concerning the criminal nature of a particular kind of behaviour is usually moderate or lenient punishment – the concepts of moderation and leniency being wholly relative in this situation. This solution, which can be considered viable if we limit our considerations to the abstract level of the individual offence, may become catastrophic in the practical context of a behaviour that occurs with a high degree of frequency. Despite its apparent moderation, the systematic application of short periods of imprisonment for very frequent offences can lead to mass incarceration, as has happened in the United States in the case of offences involving the possession of narcotics. Systematically imposing imprisonment for offences that are frequent in great part because they are only mildly disapproved of by large segments of society forfeits the punishment's legitimacy. In such a case, it is pure confinement that peeks out from beneath the illusion of justified incapacitation.

The Officer of the Law

The prime enforcer of the law is the police officer. In many cases behaviours are criminalized simply because the government wants their prohibition to be rigorously enforced. This is easily accomplished by making enforcement a priority task for the police – in other words, by criminalizing the behaviours instead of merely regulating their occurrence through civil or administrative law. For instance, the government may wish to take action following a tragedy on the highway that will have a strong impact on public opinion. Let us assume that the cause of the accident is found to be the use of a cell phone by one of the implicated drivers. Now this problem could be addressed by various regulatory mechanisms, especially through insurance rules. However, if the government wishes to target this conduct with the same rigour as impaired driving, it will label the behaviour a crime. In such cases, it is not so much the harmful nature of the conduct that justifies its designation as a crime as it is the government's desire to be perceived as taking decisive action and its belief that the best way of achieving this result is to package a problem in a way that will allow the police to make it one of their priorities. It hardly needs to be pointed out that the legitimacy of this expeditious mode of criminalization is dubious.

One of the most general assumptions of criminal law and of law enforcement is that the offender and his or her crime are tied in space, crime being rarely perpetrated at a great distance. This common *locus* of the crime event and of its perpetrator greatly facilitates prosecution, the offender being put on trial in the country where the crime was committed and where the offender was generally arrested (extradition is not a frequent practice in criminal law). In the context of globalization, this territorial proximity disappears, as the possibility of committing crimes at a considerable distance, particularly through computers and the Internet, has phenomenally increased. Globalization raises two relatively opposed issues with respect to the question "what is a crime?" First, it shows how much crime is, in practice, defined in relation to local legal traditions and political culture, which thus undermines the notion of universal standards for the assessment of harm. The notion of intellectual property, for instance, seems markedly different in China than in Canada and the United States. Second, it also underlines the urgent need for international norms in the future. Contrary to naturalistic thought, the universality of penal norms is not a given. It must be constructed through negotiations that will take place in a political context.

The Offender

The question of discrimination in its various forms (ethno-racial, economic, religious, etc.) rouses passions in any discussion of criminalization. Yet, regardless of the area of penology that is considered, from the drafting of criminal legislation to release on parole, it is astoundingly difficult to demonstrate that a penal practice is discriminatory (Tonry 1995). To the best of our knowledge, the only express reference made to an ethnic community in the CCC occurs in paragraph 718.2(e) *(Other sentencing principles)*, according to which the judge must consider all the alternatives to imprisonment in a particular case *"with particular attention to the circumstances of aboriginal offenders"* (emphasis in the original). This controversial provision (Stenning and Roberts 2001) was enacted for the benefit of Aboriginal peoples. In the same part of the CCC, the law regards a criminal act's being motivated by prejudice or hatred based on sexual orientation as an aggravating circumstance (718.2(a)(iv)). This subparagraph, which is justifiably viewed as providing increased protection for homosexuals, was the subject of a very lively debate in the House of Commons. As we shall shortly see, there are other examples of positive discrimination.

It could be argued that negative discrimination is not an intentional result of criminalization but stems from the structural characteristics of criminal behaviour as it has been traditionally viewed by law makers. The paradigm for crime is an individual *act,* of which the author can be singled out and stigmatized. Unreported criminal *practices* without personal authorship – such as crimes against the environment perpetrated by companies endowed with an abstract and intangible juridical personality – do not fall within this paradigm. Such delinquent practices are generally the object of civil litigations that carry much less stigma than criminal procedures. Lower-class offenders who perpetrate high-profile crimes – such as robbery – are more likely to be prosecuted than the bosses of organized crime or of private companies causing environmental pollution, who are protected by a phalanx of skilful lawyers. There is an acerbic observation attributed to various French writers (Anatole France, Victor Hugo, etc.) to the effect that the "majestic equality of French law forbids the rich as well as the poor to sleep under the bridges of Paris**.**" The legitimate question raised by this quip is the following: *To what extent can we claim that a completely foreseeable result is not intentional?* This is an embarrassing question for jurists, who often claim that we must legislate "under the veil of ignorance" in order to be fair (Rawls 1971, 136-42).[4]

There is one final observation on the offender that shows the volatility of our conception of crime. Generally, the amount of obloquy directed against an offender is proportional to the amount of harm that he or she has caused, but this link between harm and blame can actually be broken in certain instances. A most interesting case in this respect is that of cyber-criminals ("black hat" hackers of various sorts). The amount of damage that can be done by one successful hacker is quite impressive (millions of dollars). However, computer wizardry carries so much prestige in a competitive context obsessed with intellectual performance that a cyber-criminal may actually be applauded in proportion to the magnitude of the damage inflicted upon a multinational corporation, especially if the offender is not an adult (the offender may indeed by rewarded by lucrative job offers).

A Principle of Criminal Uncertainty

We need to recognize one crucial limitation in our ability to determine what should be considered a crime. In theory, such a determination would map out our future with a claim to universality: It would definitively set standards for all possible future criminalization. In reality, however, our ability to recognize crime is not in any way universal and, above all, operates *retrospectively*. This is the bitter lesson of genocide, which should not be forgotten. Our civilization has conditioned us to respect the powers that be and the letter of the law to a point where it has become difficult to recognize the criminal aspects of an act – even though it may be absolutely monstrous – if it is not *already* classified as criminal by the political and judicial authorities. The idea that genocide is perpetrated by a minority of criminals who usurp the powers of the state is refuted by any serious examination of the mechanisms of annihilation: Murderous enterprises such as the Shoah and the recent genocide in Rwanda could not have been accomplished without a high number of active accomplices and without the tacit assent of the majority. Wanting to catch a criminal *red-handed* without having some legislative precedent as a benchmark for the crime in question is tantamount to wanting to jump further than one's shadow. It is only *after* the mass graves are discovered that the laws are changed and new legislation is enacted.

Part 2: Classification of Crimes

We are all familiar with the difference between the Continental European tradition and the Anglo-Saxon common law tradition in the field of criminal law. The former prefers a systematic codification of the laws and thus freezes the legal conception of delinquency for long periods of time, with one or two centuries passing before new codifications are considered. The latter dislikes codification and works on an ad hoc basis, accumulating layers of jurisprudence as the circumstances require and making the statutes more and more opaque. Canada finds itself somewhere between these two traditions and has inherited the worst features of each. As is well known, Canadian criminal law is the product of a British codification dating back to 1892 (the *Stephen Code*), which was rejected in Britain. Onto this tree and its guilty roots in Continental Europe, Canadians have grafted common law branches, obstinately refusing, despite the substantial efforts of the late Law Reform Commission (Law Reform Commission of Canada 1986) and the recommendations of the Canadian Sentencing Commission (Canadian Sentencing Commission 1987), to revise the codification of 1892 in a systematic fashion. The Canadian *Criminal Code* has grown thicker over more than a century now, with a host of provisions that have helped to make Canadian criminal law impenetrable. On the one hand, this turgidity of the governing statute has benefited legal practitioners, who are brought together as a coven of technicians to exploit the prolix nature of the letter of the law. On the other hand, it baffles theoretical efforts to translate its spirit by attempting to embrace it in its entirety. Still, a disinterested study of the criminal legislation can produce significant results if it pays attention to the detail of what is said. This is what we shall attempt to show by examining a phenomenon easily observable in the first thirteen parts of the CCC, where offences are defined.

One of the most common crimes is that of *robbery (vol qualifié)*, which is theft accompanied by violence. This defining proviso is an instance of *qualification*, an instrument by which the law maker defines the nature of certain offences, distinguishing between different variants of some of the major categories of delinquency and attributing each crime a predetermined level of seriousness. The qualification of offences is systematically used throughout the CCC, and its main governing principles are (1) the degree of their seriousness, (2) the circumstances surrounding their commission, (3) the general context in which they are committed, (4) the characteristics of the offender, (5) those of the victim, (6) in the case of offences against property, the nature of the property stolen, and finally (7) the means used. We have studied the use made of this qualification process in the definition of offences in the CCC as a whole. What follows is a more specific look at the structures used to qualify (and to classify), first, different forms of homicide (as detailed in a segment of Part 8, *Offences against the person*), and second, the offences in Part 9 (*Offences against rights of property*). Note that these structures are far from being the most complex. For instance, Part 10, concerning fraudulent transactions, is far more technical in nature.

Homicide and Other Crimes against Persons

The whole panoply of qualifications is used for homicide, with the exception of the nature of the property stolen, which does not apply in this case. It can be seen that this structure is markedly asymmetrical. First-degree murder is defined very restrictively, whereas second-degree murder is defined merely in a residual manner as not being murder in the first degree.[5] Originally, murder in the first degree was premeditated killing. This qualification has since been joined by others concerning the victim (police officer or correctional officer) and the general context in which the murder is committed: Whether or not it was premeditated, the killing of a police officer or member of the staff of a prison is first-degree murder; the same is true of culpable homicide committed in the context of hijacking an airplane, of sexual assault, or of kidnapping.

Figure 1

Qualifications applying to homicide in the Canadian *Criminal Code*

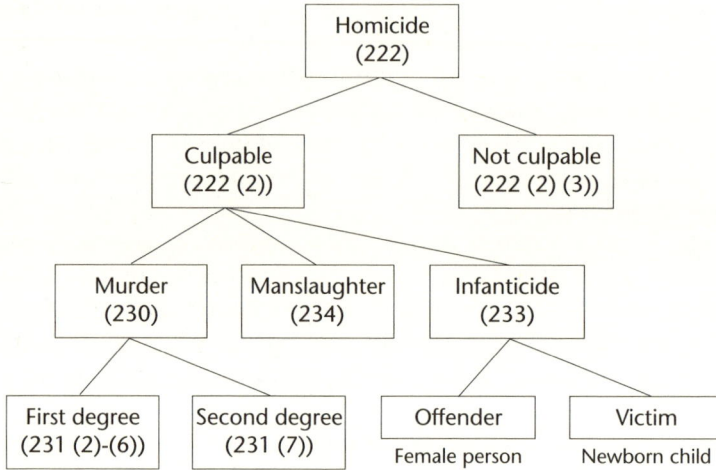

→ Premeditation (231 (2)) → Contracted (232 (3))
→ Victim: Peace officer – police officer or prison guard (231 (4))
→ Context (231 (5)): Hijacking
                     Sexual assault
                     Kidnapping
→ Context: Criminal harassment (231 (6))
→ Context: Terrorist activities (231 (6.01))
→ Context: Using explosives in association with a criminal organization (231 (6.1))
→ Context: Intimidation (231 (6.2))   ↗ Justice system participant (423.1)
                                      ↘ Journalist (423.1)

There remain criminal harassment (CCC, 231(6)) and intimidation (231(6.2)), which further complicate the framework for classifying homicide as first-degree murder. These two crimes are defined by their *repetition*, in the case of criminal harassment (CCC, 264(2)), or by their *repetition/persistence*, in the case of intimidation (CCC, 423.1(2)(c) and (d)). Both of these aspects show a precedence over time that could already serve to prove premeditation, yet the law states that "irrespective of whether a murder is planned and deliberate," a murder committed as part of the offence of harassment or intimidation will be deemed to be first-degree murder. Why saddle the *Code* with such redundancy in the description and such excessive precision? One could imagine a scenario in which an accused could argue that he or she harassed or intimated the victim for a long time but killed him or her without giving it any previous thought.[6] Does this imply that the law maker has a duty to come up with statutory provisions to cover this type of unlikely scenario?[7] If we are to understand these redundant provisions, we will find it more informative to note that the upgrading of a homicide committed in the context of an offence of criminal harassment to first-degree murder coincided with a public campaign against the stalking of women. It is even more enlightening to stress that the criminal aggravation of intimidation was included in the law shortly after two prison guards were murdered and a journalist who was a well-known associate of the police was the victim of an attempted murder.

There is one final element we would like to underline with regard to offences against the person. This does not appear in Figure 1, which refers only to forms of homicide: A provision was recently added to the CCC stating that female circumcision and other forms of genital mutilation of women (268(1) to (4)) constitute aggravated assault and that the person committing them is liable to imprisonment for a maximum period of fourteen years. These provisions apply exclusively to immigrants from the countries of Africa, who alone engage in these practices.

Offences against Rights of Property
The structure of these offences is very different, especially in terms of the nature of the property stolen, which ranges from oysters and cattle to credit cards, gas, electricity, and the unauthorized use of computers. Similarly, a distinction is made on the basis of the offender's status. In the case of some of these qualifications, the law maker's view is relatively clear. Since the physical value of a credit card is minuscule, a person who steals one could be prosecuted only for theft under $5,000, which involves a maximum sentence of two years' imprisonment. A professional thief, however, can steal many cards on the same day and use them fraudulently to acquire property that is worth much more than $5,000. This explains the interest in designating credit card theft an offence the maximum sentence for which is ten years' imprisonment. However, this argument – which is open to challenge – does not apply quite as clearly to the other objects of theft and similar offences (oysters, cattle, gas, electricity, etc.). In the latter cases, one is left wondering why law makers felt they had to specify the nature of the stolen good.

Discussion
Brief though it is, this analysis of the process of qualifying crimes leads us to draw the following conclusions:

The Criminal Code is an exercise in penology. Examining the particulars of a qualification reveals that it does not so much *define* a large number of offences as differentiate them for the purpose of determining the sentences to

Figure 2

Qualifications applying to offences against rights of property in the Canadian *Criminal Code*

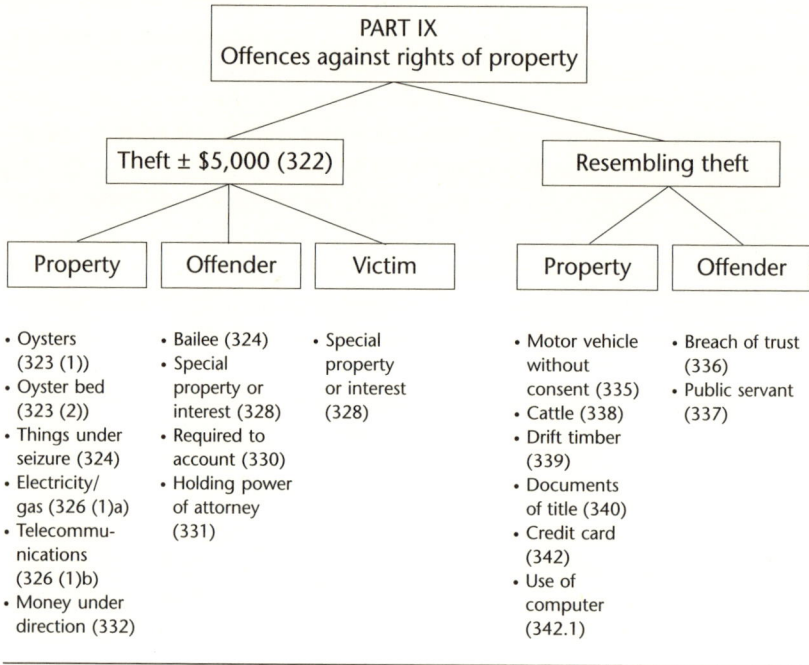

```
                        ┌────────────────────────────────────┐
                        │              PART IX                │
                        │ Offences against rights of property │
                        └────────────────────────────────────┘
                          /                                \
        ┌──────────────────────┐              ┌──────────────────────┐
        │ Theft ± $5,000 (322)  │              │  Resembling theft     │
        └──────────────────────┘              └──────────────────────┘
         /        |        \                      /            \
  ┌──────────┐ ┌──────────┐ ┌──────────┐   ┌──────────┐ ┌──────────┐
  │ Property │ │ Offender │ │  Victim  │   │ Property │ │ Offender │
  └──────────┘ └──────────┘ └──────────┘   └──────────┘ └──────────┘
```

Property	Offender	Victim	Property	Offender
• Oysters (323 (1))	• Bailee (324)	• Special property or interest (328)	• Motor vehicle without consent (335)	• Breach of trust (336)
• Oyster bed (323 (2))	• Special property or interest (328)		• Cattle (338)	• Public servant (337)
• Things under seizure (324)	• Required to account (330)		• Drift timber (339)	
• Electricity/ gas (326 (1)a)	• Holding power of attorney (331)		• Documents of title (340)	
• Telecommu- nications (326 (1)b)			• Credit card (342)	
• Money under direction (332)			• Use of computer (342.1)	

be imposed. The typical example is second-degree murder, defined as that which *is not* murder in the first degree – it would be difficult to say less – and accordingly deserves a lesser sentence. This observation applies, to a large extent, to the qualification process, which is shorthand for *sentencing*. This conclusion supports Durkheim's view that crime is essentially a form of behaviour that is *punished*.

Problem solving. Qualification is also an exercise in resolving legal problems as they arise. In this connection reference will be made to the creation of the offence of credit card theft. The essential nature of this process is that it occurs on an ad hoc basis depending on the needs of the circumstances and solely for technical reasons. The *Code* will be amended in ways that impact on the wording of other provisions with little regard for even the appearance of consistency in the spirit of the law. Furthermore, it is difficult to see any other way to solve criminal law problems than by relentlessly adding to the *Code*.

Public relations. Qualification is also a useful tool for developing legislation that offers a sometimes improvised response to events that scandalize public opinion. For example, the inclusion of murder of prison staff or a journalist in the types of first-degree murder is a prototype for the use of the criminalization process to placate the public. It is revealing, in this regard, that it was a failed attempt to murder a journalist that forced the government to act, while two prison guards had been killed earlier without any provisions being added concerning harassment or intimidation. An indication of the hurried nature of this amendment is that it may well lead to an impasse. The law stipulates, for no particular purpose, that the murder of a journalist is first-degree murder when it occurs as part of a process of intimidation, which is simply a duplication of the concept of premeditation. What would happen if a journalist were killed by a member of a crime organization without it being possible to prove premeditation or an earlier desire to intimidate the journalist? Would this killing then no longer be classified as first-degree murder? Is it less serious to kill a journalist as part of a drug deal than as part of attempted intimidation?

Criminalization as communication. Examples of the use of the criminalization process as a public relations tool could be multiplied. Despite its frequency this phenomenon is merely a manifestation of a more fundamental and widespread function of criminal law, which we shall refer to as a *communication* function.[8] Unlike public relations activities for political purposes, which are generally directed to everyone, criminal communication operates on two levels. Obviously, some of the criminal law messages are addressed to the public as a whole, using the press as the medium. Other messages are geared to a specific public. The criminalization of genital mutilation is a message intended for newly arrived immigrants from countries where these practices are widespread; if an exception is made for male circumcision, the ritual injury of human genitalia is not a common practice in Canada. Criminalization of the theft of specific forms of property, such as oysters or cattle, is a response to a need for local communication (eastern Canada in the case of shellfish farming and the West for cattle raising). However, the informational aspect of legal communication is not its only function. When criminal law is asserted anew with different words and in more specific details, it breathes new life into offences that have become trivialized and have thus lost part of their deterrent power. This function is crucial because the promulgation of the law in itself generates conformity: a substantial number of people complying with the law not out of fear of the penalties but rather out of deference to its symbolic value. Awareness of the importance of this communication function of the criminal law creates obligations for law makers, as we shall see in the concluding section of this chapter.

Part 3: Criminalization and Dissent

When we ask "what is a crime?" we expect the answer to relate more to murder or theft per se than to the theft of oysters or the murder of a journalist. This expectation is reasonable when the question is asked in the abstract or from a normative perspective, which moves from the ideal to something more concrete. But when we think about crime inductively – that is, when we start with the wording of actual criminal provisions – we immediately encounter the phenomenon of qualification. It is neither murder nor theft as such that is considered but rather, to take a very general classification, murder in a certain degree or theft of more or less than a certain amount (currently $5,000 in Canada). We have attempted to show that the process of qualifying offences, which coincides roughly with the process of criminalizing behaviours, is not exclusively determined by the nature of the offences at hand. Rather, it has its own logic, and it performs functions whose connection with the prevention and suppression of crime is problematic and strongly contingent. We shall now move forward with an exploration of the *indirect* relationship of criminalization to concepts such as harm or damage caused to others. To this end, we shall present two studies of criminalization as it applies to specific offences. The first study concerns the development of gun control in Canada, which was (and continues to be) determined by the existence of diametrically opposed currents of opinion in Canadian society.

Origins of the New Gun Controls

The events that we are discussing here began in December 1989 and have not yet ended, as the new legislation came into full force only recently (January 2003). For instance, it was revealed in the course of 2003 that the costs of gun registration were many times what had been initially budgeted. It would be wrong to think that before this period, there was no gun control in Canada and that the situation here was similar to that in the United States. In reality the circulation of guns was already controlled, and in fact many studies contrasting the lack of control in the United States with the controls imposed in Canada were conducted regularly by researchers in the US (for a review of these studies, see Zimring and Hawkins 1997; for an assessment of gun control, see Canada 1983). The new legislation of 1991 (Bill C-17) and 1995 (Bill C-88: see *Firearms Legislation [Législation sur les armes à feu]*, 1999) tightened controls that were already working satisfactorily before.

Two tragedies precipitated the reform. On 6 December 1989 a killer entered the premises of the École polytechnique at the Université de Montréal and embarked on a killing spree that produced twenty-nine victims: Fourteen female students were killed, fourteen other students were injured (eleven women and three men), and the killer turned his gun on himself.[9] The massacre lasted only eighteen minutes. It took place on several floors of the building, the killer using an automatic rifle with a high-capacity magazine (a Ruger Mini-14). One student who escaped the carnage, Heidi Rathjen, circulated a petition that was signed by 500,000 people. She eventually gave up her job and cofounded the Coalition for Gun Control with a professor at the University of Toronto, Wendy Cukier (Rathjen and Montpetit 1999). The Canadian government appeared to give in to the campaign and tabled a bill in the House of Commons (C-80), which proposed only four minor changes to the law as it then existed. However, this was already too much for the opponents of gun control, who succeeded in scuttling it in March 1991. The coalition intensified its campaign and eventually got Parliament to pass a revised version of Bill C-80 (which had by then become Bill C-17) on 5 December 1991 (the eve of the second anniversary of the 1989 killings). This reform was a compromise that fell far below what the coalition would have liked.

On 24 August 1992 Valéry Fabrikant, a lecturer who was upset by the unfair manner in which he felt the authorities at Concordia University in Montreal had treated him, killed four people at the University and injured a fifth using handguns. This second massacre led to a campaign by the students at Concordia to abolish the sale of such guns even though they were already subject to controls. The coalition felt that this demand was unrealistic but took the opportunity to breathe new life into its campaign against assault weapons and to obtain stronger gun registration measures. The gun lobby and the coalition, which succeeded in convincing hundreds of thousands of sympathizers to send postcards to their MPs, confronted one another without an obvious winner emerging. The fault lines between the adversaries are deep and run, on the one hand, between central Canada (Ontario and Quebec) and the West and, on the other hand, between urban Canada and rural Canada, where possession of guns for hunting is widespread. In April 1994 a series of murderous occurrences took place in Canada, and the minister of justice announced that he would table new measures in Parliament. The new Bill (C-68) was tabled in the Commons on 14 February 1995, and the new legislation was proclaimed on 5 December 1995 (once again, the eve of an anniversary of the massacre at the École polytechnique, the memory of which is still very much alive in Canada). Between February and December, supporters and opponents of Bill C-68 held further demonstrations, and the Toronto representative of the coalition was subjected to acts of intimidation. The opponents of the new legislation challenged its constitutionality in the Alberta Court of Appeal, and in 1998, in a split judgment (three judges to two), the Court found that the legislation was constitutional. The case was appealed to the Supreme Court of Canada, which confirmed that the *Act* was constitutional on 15 January 2000. This drawn-out process clearly illustrates the harshness of the debate.

Nature of the Reform

Bill C-68 was a complex reform: It produced the *Firearms Act* (FA, an act related to the CCC that contains 137 sections), a revamped Part 3 of the CCC *(Firearms and other offensive weapons)*, and twenty-two enforcement regulations for the new gun control package. Essentially, the reform consisted of four sets of provisions:

- The introduction of *minimum sentences* for using a firearm in the commission of ten specific offences listed in the *Code* (CCC, s. 85), namely a minimum sentence of imprisonment for one year for a first offence and three years for a repeat offence. These sentences are to be added to the sentence for the main offence and must be served consecutively with any other prison term.
- The creation of an elaborate mechanism for the *registration* of firearms and for obtaining various permits to possess or sell them or to sell ammunition. Possession of a firearm without a certificate and without a permit results in sentences ranging from a fine of $2,000 or six months' imprisonment (FA, s. 115) to a maximum of ten years' imprisonment (CCC, s. 92), in the case of a *deliberate* offence.[10]
- Expansion of the classes of restricted or prohibited firearms and those for equipment (for example, large-capacity magazines) and prohibited ammunition.
- A set of penalties designed to prevent and suppress importing, exporting, and trafficking in weapons.

When Bill C-68 was referred to the parliamentary committee for study in 1995, the minister of justice, the Hon. Allan Rock, stated the objectives of the legislation as follows:

> [T]he bill has three main objectives. First, to create deterrents by establishing new offences and very tough sentences for the criminal use of firearms. Second, to improve the control over firearms belonging to individuals. Third, to reduce the smuggling of firearms into Canada. To achieve that objective, we must strengthen controls at the borders and impose tougher sentences for smuggling and trafficking in illegal firearms. (Transcript of Committee proceedings, 24 April 1995)[11]

Within the debate on gun control, this particular statement happens to invert the objectives of the Bill. In the paragraph quoted above, the minister states that the *first* objective of Bill C-68 was deterrence by creating new offences and, above all, even though this expression did not yet appear in the minister's statement, by making the minimum sentence for the criminal use of firearms more severe (it was to be increased from one year to four years). In fact, this more severe penalty was only included in the gun control reform at a very late stage: It was not mentioned during the debate on the initial reform proposals (Bills C-80 and C-17); it was not one of the coalition's most pressing demands; finally, the discussion of this issue took up very little of the parliamentary committee's time (unlike the question of gun registration, which continues to fuel the controversy). As the authorities at the Department of Justice were forced to acknowledge on several occasions in consultations with "experts," the harsher minimum sentence was in fact designed as a response to the most powerful argument against gun registration:[12] that registration penalized people who had not committed any crime – farmers in the West – by threatening them with penalties if they failed to register their guns, whereas no measures were included in the Bill to punish those who actually committed violent crimes.

The harsher minimum sentence contained in section 85 of the CCC was not only politically expedient, but actually constitutes a step backward in terms of sentencing. Just recently the Canadian Sentencing Commission recommended that the use of minimum sentences be stopped, except for murder and treason (Canadian Sentencing Commission 1987, 206). This recommendation had been quoted with approval by the Supreme Court of Canada in a judgment abolishing the minimum sentence of seven years' imprisonment for importing or exporting drugs as being contrary to the *Canadian Charter of Rights and Freedoms.* When he was questioned about the deterrent value of the new minimum sentence, the minister began by avoiding the question, referred to research that was not conclusive, and finally acknowledged the limits of criminal deterrence (Justice Committee hearings, 24 April 1995, 27-28). In general the authorities were also concerned by a possible substantial increase in the prison population. The government's ambivalence eventually led to a reduction of the proposed minimum sentence from four to three years. This also preserved the judges' discretion, in cases where firearms are used, to impose effective sentences that will not substantially exceed those that were imposed before the new law. One of the consequences of this first compromise was a parallel increase of flexibility in the enforcement of the gun control provisions as such. The law now contained transitional provisions stating that any person who is in possession of a firearm that is not prohibited or restricted would be deemed to hold a registration certificate until 1 January 2003. The time allowed to obtain a permit was extended to 1 January 2001. The length of these delays – eight and six years, respectively – testifies to the extent of the resistance by a number of Canadians to tighter gun controls. Above all, despite the trumpeted harshness of the maximum sentences for failure to obtain a permit and a registration certificate (five and ten years' imprisonment), the law provided an escape route by which an offender did not have to be governed by the CCC but rather by the FA, where the offence is punishable by a simple fine. The provision of various escape routes to offenders offers one of the keys to interpreting the political character of Bill C-68.

Incidental Criminalization

The harshest sentences imposed by Bill C-68 are designed to penalize the unauthorized possession of a firearm where the offender knows that he is not "the holder of (a) a licence under which the person may possess it; and (b) a registration certificate for the firearm," in which case the offence will qualify as having been *deliberate* (CCC, s. 92). The maximum sentence of ten years' imprisonment is combined with a minimum sentence of one year's imprisonment in the case of a repeat offence. How will deliberate defiance of the law be proved? It will be relatively easy to do so where a *prohibited* weapon is used to commit a crime. If an offender uses a prohibited weapon, this person knows by definition that he or she does not have a permit or registration certificate for the firearm in question; this reasoning could be extended to most crimes in which the criminals deliberately use weapons that cannot be traced to them. On the other hand, establishing that a hunter deliberately failed to obtain a permit *and* a registration certificate, both of which are required, could be difficult. Furthermore, it is far from certain that the Crown will be zealous in this regard since the law is so controversial that the prosecution of an individual suspected of an offence other than a deliberate failure to obtain the necessary documentation to possess firearms may well seem to the public like gratuitous vindictiveness.

A process can be described as incidental or indirect when it does not go straight to the heart of the matter and tries to avoid an issue that may reveal itself to be too controversial. The approach taken by the government in creating offences related to gun control can be described as incidental in at least two ways. First, the use of a firearm has not, in itself, been criminalized. It is only when a firearm is used *in the commission of a criminal offence,* as section 85 of the CCC expressly states, that this use is culpable. Such a definition, which provides that the use of a firearm is criminal when it occurs in the commission of a criminal offence, is clearly circular. The use of a firearm is not so much a crime in itself as the means of committing one; the use of this means by an offender is to be treated by the Crown as an aggravating circumstance in any court proceedings. This kind of offence is essentially a *subsidiary* crime or a crime by *implication;* it serves to increase the weight of the basic charge and cannot exist alone. This type of ancillary role would also be played by the deliberate failure to obtain a permit and a registration certificate. As set out in section 92, this failure would be regarded as an additional aggravating factor in the prosecution of a person charged with a crime of violence than as a crime in itself.

If the failure to register a firearm and to obtain a possession certificate is the *only* charge laid against an offender, the law provides that offender with two escape routes to avoid imprisonment. First, as already mentioned, the offender may be prosecuted under the FA, which is far less severe than the CCC. Second, because the offences created are situated somewhere between indictable offences and regulatory offences for this class of offenders, who are not viewed as criminals by the general public, the matter can be dealt with through summary proceedings rather than by means of a full criminal indictment. Again, our law makers have provided a way to ensure that the criminalization of this behaviour will appear to be indirect in respect to gun control.

This intermediate status of the new offences created by Bill C-68 underlines the problem caused by offences classified as "hybrid" by jurists. We have seen how Canadian law allows for the possibility of treating these charges either as indictable offences or as summary-conviction offences (or, to use other terminology, as felonies or misdemeanours). What does it mean when one and the same act can be considered in legal terms to be either an indictable offence or a relatively benign offence in terms of the question "what is a crime?"

Part 4: Guilty Monopolies

The previous part dealt with crimes associated with firearms and their registration. We have seen that the debate is characterized by a complete absence of consensus on the matter of their harmfulness. We shall now examine the case of transactional crime, which involves the exchange of illegal goods or services. The goods being exchanged could be drugs, for example, while the services may be of a sexual nature or fall into the category of games of chance: lotteries, casinos, and so on. We have decided to consider the question of gambling, which is well suited to the kind of demonstration we want to make.

One peculiar feature of the criminalization of illegal transactions is that it targets two behaviours at the same time: that of the client (who is guilty of being in a gambling house or house of debauchery, or of possessing drugs) and that of the supplier. In terms of the underlying concept of harmfulness, the legitimacy of criminalizing the conduct of consumers is problematic. Except in extreme cases, this behaviour does not harm other people or the consumers themselves since they claim, on the contrary, to take pleasure in the activity. When it punishes consumers, the state considers such people to be its ward, for it regards them as incapable of discernment and thus in need of punishment if they are to be taught a lesson. This justification is weak, as can be seen in the history of the shaky attempts to criminalize the behaviour of the clients of prostitutes. Having failed to justify criminalization on the consumer side, attempts were often made to find harmfulness in the conduct of the supplier, who is accused of seducing and then of corrupting and eventually destroying an infinitely renewable clientele. An examination of the history of the criminalization of gambling, which has lately taken a 180-degree turn toward a frenetic legalization of games of chance, should easily show how confusing it can be to attempt to make up for the lack of legitimacy in incriminating the client's behaviour by criminalizing that of the supplier.

Diffident Criminalization

One of the first signs of the federal legislator's ineffectiveness in matters of gambling is the role played by the provinces even though the federal government has exclusive jurisdiction over criminal law. Thus we find in Title 8 *(Police and Good Order)* of the Revised Statutes of Quebec (R.S.Q.) of 1888 the following provision:

> If any journeyman, day labourer, servant or apprentice play at any game of cards, dice, skittles or any other game, for money, liquor or otherwise [...] he shall incur and pay for every such offence, a fine not exceeding four dollars, and not less than one dollar; and in default of payment of such fine within six days, such journeyman, labourer, servant or apprentice shall be committed to the house of correction for a space of time not exceeding eight days. (R.S.Q. 1888, Title 8, Chapter 1, Section 1, ss. 3, *"Labourers, Servants and Apprentices Found Gambling"*)

Here a provincial legislature is enacting a penal statute even though the incriminated conduct is not classified as a criminal offence since a province cannot enact criminal legislation. A second sign of the authorities' ambivalence is that this law is openly discriminatory: Those who do not earn high wages are prohibited from doing what richer people are allowed to do. The status of offenders lies at the basis of this law, which aims to protect the poor from themselves. This paternalistic approach is an ongoing theme of all legislation governing gambling: Even today (2003) in Quebec, consideration is being given to limiting access to a future casino to tourists from abroad in order to protect Quebeckers from the scourge of gambling. Indeed, the experience of support groups shows that compulsive gamblers generally come from the lowest income levels. According to the founder of one of these groups, whom we interviewed, 92 percent of the people who come to his organization for help got hooked on video lottery terminals (VLTs), which are generally installed on premises frequented by a blue-collar clientele (in a profile drawn up in 1992, the typical problem gambler was a young single male with no more than a secondary school education).[13]

Between 1892 and 1956 no fewer than five commissions of inquiry – Rainville (1892), Cannon I (1910), Coderre (1924), Cannon II (1944), and Caron (1956) – evaluated the tolerance shown for illegal gambling by the police and the municipal authorities in Montreal (Brodeur 1984). Throughout Montreal's history, illegal gambling and betting have been constant sources of corruption of police and elected officials, as drug trafficking was later to become. At the present time, behaviours that are criminalized by the CCC comprise keeping a gambling house and being found in such a house (CCC, 201), betting (CCC, 202-3), lotteries and taking part in them (CCC, 206-7, 207.1), and cheating at play (CCC, 209). The penalties provided appear to be gentle since the maximum sentence is not more than three years' imprisonment. However, a second offence will involve a *minimum* sentence of three months' imprisonment (CCC, 202(2)(c) and 203(f)).

The offences related to gambling and betting all share the general characteristic that we suggested is common to transactions deemed illegal: Both the consumer and the supplier may be subject to criminal penalties. A person's presence in an illegal gambling house as well as his or her participation in a prohibited lottery are criminalized in the same way as are operating such a house or organizing such a lottery. As far as service suppliers are concerned, the conduct in question is usually an ongoing activity rather than an occasional behaviour and could thus be labelled "organized crime." Yet, as we noted earlier, it is harder to prove the existence of a criminal enterprise than to prosecute an individual violation of the law. For this reason and, above all, because of the lack of interest shown by the law enforcement authorities, prosecutions for crimes relating to gambling are relatively uncommon, especially if we take into account the high frequency of the activities.

Brazen Legalization

In the field of gambling, the list of exceptions to criminalized conduct is substantially longer than the definition of the offences. There are exceptions to each type of offence: For illegal gambling houses there are the casinos operated by the government or under its authority; for illegal betting there is the *pari mutuel* carried on at race tracks, which are quite legal; for prohibited lotteries there is the vast body of lotteries run by the government. Legalization is encouraged by the complexity of the criminal statutes, which allows for all kinds of interpretations. It takes, for example, ten paragraphs to define lotteries and games of chance (CCC, 206(a) to (j)). It is on the basis of these definitions that the provincial governments, charitable organizations, and the managers of agricultural fairs operate "lotteries" (CCC, 207), the legal term used being "lottery scheme" (207(4)). This extends the meaning of the word "lottery" to activities that are quite remote from the sale of tickets in order to win a prize, namely the operation of casinos (card games or roulette) and slot machines. The latter category includes the notorious video poker machines that have such a frightful attraction for compulsive gamblers.[14] According to a study conducted for the Department of the Solicitor General of Canada, the operation of large numbers of these machines in Quebec falls into a legal "grey area" (Beare et al. 1988, 293).

The movement to legalize lotteries has a long history in Canada. In the 1930s the mayor of Montreal, Camilien Houde, was already demanding that lotteries be legalized (Labrosse 1985, 108). In 1932 a referendum held in Vancouver produced a substantial vote in favour of legalization (more than 25,000 votes for and fewer than 10,000 against). In Quebec bingo games organized in church basements were (and still are) tolerated, and the Catholic Church thus had a monopoly on these games. After 1960 projects to legalize lotteries multiplied in Ottawa, with no fewer than nine bills of legislation tabled in the House of Commons between 1960 and 1965. The first public lottery was created in Montreal by Mayor Drapeau in 1968 to restore the health of the city's finances following the 1967 World Fair. This lottery was described by the mayor as a "voluntary tax" (our translation) and ran from 27 May to 14 September 1968, when it was ruled to be illegal. Following the election of Pierre Trudeau as prime minister, gambling was finally legalized for the benefit of the federal and provincial authorities, charitable organizations, agricultural fairs, and those who held permits issued by the authorities in the various levels of government. The legislation was passed on 14 May 1969 and came into force on 1 January 1970. By 23 December 1969 the government of Quebec had already created the Régie des loteries et des courses and the Société d'exploitation des loteries et des courses. Despite a critical report of the Montreal Urban Community Police in 1985, the Régie des loteries eventually started operating slot machines (Beare et al. 1988, 264). A final clash between the federal government and the Government of Quebec occurred in 1985 and concerned the federal government's refusal to recognize the legality of a new lottery based on hockey results. Quebec was successful in the courts, and the CCC was amended. Since then no limits have been imposed on the growth of lotteries and games of chance in Quebec and the other provinces of Canada (the largest casinos are found in Alberta).

We can easily illustrate this fact with the situation in Quebec. Three lotteries were created in 1970, year one of the legalization of gambling in Canada. From 1970 to 2000, Quebec's Régie des loteries et des courses offered consumers some twenty-two different lotteries,[15] twelve of which are still in operation. Sales of lottery tickets amounted to $51,434,000 in 1971 and reached $1,768,224,000 in 2000, an increase of 3,400 percent. This figure does not include direct revenues from the régie's other activities and the indirect revenues it obtains in the form of royalties and fees for issuing licences to various organizations. Among other products, mention could be made of casinos and the ubiquitous slot machines (VLTs). We should add that the activities of the régie do not cover anything like the whole field of gambling, which also includes *pari mutuel* betting at race tracks and the innumerable draws, bingos, and other games organized by licence holders.

State Monopoly: Between Limitation and Expansion

Given the wide licence that government has granted itself, is there still any reason for a residual criminalization of gambling? If there is, it can no longer be based on a claim that gambling is harmful since the harm is quite clearly not great enough for provincial governments to refrain from having become the main operators of this service. It is generally argued that the criminalization of a phenomenon is designed to control its magnitude by giving government a monopoly over its practice. In Canada this monopoly is particularly evident in the case of lotteries.

Our examination of the legalization of gambling leads us to distinguish between two kinds of monopolies. There is, on the one hand, the limiting monopoly, the express purpose of which is to reduce (ambiguously) the frequency of a particular form of behaviour by restricting it to officers of the state. Its prototype is the monopoly on (lawful) violence held by the state, which has apparently limited the use of violence in democratic states (Elias 1996). This function of state monopoly does not apply in the case of gambling. In fact, the creation of a state monopoly has led to such an overwhelming expansion of gambling that it is possible to speak of an *expansionist* monopoly. Driven by its unrestrained adoption of a private logic of maximum profit, public government has applied the substantial resources at its disposal to promote gambling. Even if we take into account the exponential growth of organized crime, it is hard to imagine that keeping the ban on gambling would have resulted in a 3,400 percent growth in the revenues of illegal lotteries. No criminal organization would have succeeded as much as elected governments in the unfettered development of gambling.

Even when the prohibition of gambling is not rigorously enforced, the state runs the risk of ending up in the following impasse if it keeps gambling in the *Criminal Code:* Either the definition of a crime involves the description of a harmful form of behaviour, in which case government itself is hugely delinquent, or the monopoly held by government is legitimate, in which case the definition of the crime is based essentially on the identity of the perpetrator and not on the harmful nature of the behaviour.

Conclusions

Our analysis has been conducted on the basis of an examination of the facts. This endeavour took both the criminalization process and specific criminalized behaviour into account in the historical and present contexts. Such an approach, rather than opposing the more normative perspective favoured by Henry and Lanier (1998), serves to complement it. To illustrate this, we have presented some of the practical implications of our analyses by taking an approach that is pragmatic – in the sense that it is concerned with actual practice – rather than theoretically normative (see the basic distinctions provided in the introduction to this chapter).

Our analysis of the phenomenon of the classification of offences has led us to observe that the criminal law performs a *communication function*. The existence of such a function has two consequences in practice.

If the law is communication, we should first answer the question of whom this communication is intended for. In effect, given the massive growth in the complexity of the law, the traditional presupposition that the law is a message addressed to the community whose behaviours it legislates must be questioned for the simple reason that this message is now, as presented to that community, largely impenetrable. Thus the question of audience is still pending, since the true target of the law's message must be something else. The best way to answer this question is to distinguish between (1) a number of mediators – the press, the police, legal practitioners – that form the new clergy responsible for interpreting and enforcing criminal law, and (2) the ultimate recipient of the law, which is still, at least in theory, the community at large. In practice the living community is vanishing from the scene and being replaced by public opinion polls and focus groups that can be manipulated at will. If these distinctions appear to be anti-democratic, it will then be necessary to reinvent the methods of legislative communication and make them more effective.

Since the law is also penal communication, and we would like to stress this important point, then it issues an institutional message that may result in actual *penalties* (harm). This simple observation leads very directly to a moral requirement. Even though the law includes an element of language, a process that results in the imposition of penalties should not be the tool for solving problems *that result from communication alone*. For example, by the very admission of the minister responsible,[16] the reform of the criminal legislation governing young offenders was not undertaken to meet any increase in the frequency and/or seriousness of juvenile delinquency but essentially to remedy a problem of public *opinion*; the legal message was, wrongly, no longer seen by part of the public as sufficiently intimidating. When problems result from communication alone, they should be resolved by means that depend solely on communication rather than by criminal communication, which is a mixture of language and penalties. Similarly, the new antiterrorism legislation was the product of a communication problem with the United States, but it is no less a penal message for which Canadians will pay even though there is no significant problem of terrorist violence in this country.

Further, let us note an important side effect of offence qualification, which has so far not been properly analyzed. To put it simply, the more narrowly defined an offence is, the more it focuses on a specific type of criminal. For instance, what is referred to as "insider trading" applies specifically to the holders of stocks and shares. Clearly, there is a discriminating effect here that is not *discriminatory*, and the difference is fundamental. In our opinion criteria need to be developed to help separate those measures that are legitimately discriminating from those that are illegitimately discriminatory.

Throughout this chapter we have emphasized a wide range of criminalized behaviours, their substantial differences, the considerable variations in the level of consensus as to their harmfulness, and finally, the greedy appropriation by the state of practices such as gambling, which had previously been outlawed. At the same time, the gaudy spectrum of criminalized behaviours contrasts sharply with the bland array of their corresponding penalties. While the criminal system strives to introduce a limited variety of penalties into its sentencing practices in an effort to individualize punishment, the basic penology still rests on its two traditional pillars, namely fines and various forms of the deprivation of freedom (probation, suspended sentences, house arrest under electronic surveillance, and imprisonment). Intermediate punishment and restorative justice are still used only on an exploratory basis and, regrettably, sometimes result in regressive experiments (e.g., boot camps for juveniles and public shaming). Still, the monotonousness of criminal sanctions is at its most complete in the legal text itself. With the exception of offences that are punishable only on summary conviction, which offer the judge a choice between *two* forms of maximum sentence (fine and imprisonment), *all the maximum sentences prescribed by the CCC are stated as periods of imprisonment of various length.* The one-dimensional character of these definitions does not imply that the judge is forced to impose a sentence of imprisonment for all crimes. Nevertheless, it provides judges with the *possibility of doing so in all cases.* Consequently, an inextricable link between crime and imprisonment is established and re-inforced, which finds expression in the popular notion of a crime as a behaviour that is deserving of incarceration. In light of the inflationary growth in the number and variety of offences, it would seem logical to contemplate breaking away from the undifferentiated structure of the legal maxima in order to redefine sanctions in more flexible and less punitive terms.

Arguably, the effects of such a redefinition might be negligible. In fact, the offences for which the maximum sentence could be defined as an alternative to imprisonment are of the least serious kind and already involve only relatively minor maximum prison terms (six months to two years), which are in any event only rarely imposed. This objection misses an important point, however. As the report of the Canadian Sentencing Commission stated, the overpunishment of repeat petty offenders is one of the most serious problems of sentencing (Ashworth 1983). This misguided idea that we need the ultimate threat of imprisonment in order to finally deter the petty recidivist is a repressive illusion. The move to imprisonment, as can be seen in the fate of large numbers of Aboriginal repeat offenders in western Canada, favours a punitive escalation that has no effect on criminal behaviour, which persists and even grows worse after eventual release from prison. Another example is provided by the petty shoplifter who ends up in prison, eventually spending increasingly lengthy periods of time there if his or her kleptomania is not treated.

This issue of short sentences also raises a substantive problem when we take into account that justice operates within a penal *system*, where individual glitches become major problems through their systematic reoccurrence, thus generating substantial social costs, namely prison overcrowding. Studies of the causes of overcrowding in our prisons typically offer two explanations for the phenomenon: (1) an accumulation of those serving life sentences, in a model with few prisoners but very long sentences; (2) an increase of the number of offenders serving short terms in prison, in a model with short sentences but very large numbers of prisoners (Canadian Sentencing Commission 1987, Chapter 10; Quebec 1986, 35, 54). Today's mass imprisonment problem is the result of sentences imposed for a small number of offences, among which drug cases play a major role. The principle of proportionality can ensure, on an individual basis, that there will be no abuse in the duration of imprisonment for less serious offences, which gives it a limited anti-overpopulation effect. However, when the frequency of these offences rises significantly, with the same offenders constantly back before the courts, the principle of proportionality is of no help in countering overcrowding because it is merely the result of a multiplication of short sentences. The solution to this problem is not to set a time threshold beneath which a prison term could not be imposed, since this would compel judges who feel that imprisonment is deserved to increase the minimum duration of the custodial sentences they impose. One approach that should be explored is to entirely remove the option of imprisonment for certain offences – no matter how frequently an offender commits them – by no longer indicating the maximum sentence for these offences in terms of imprisonment.

The decision not to define some maximum sentences in terms of imprisonment should be based on studies that bring actual content to the vacuous world of criminal legislation, which otherwise remains paralyzed by the obsessive concept of the harmfulness of crime and by inconsistencies caused, among other things, by the participation of the government in a condemned form of activity such as gambling. Within our "secular," pragmatic, nonjurist approach, factors such as the frequency and distribution of offences and the differential impact of criminalization should be taken into account in law making. Considering the frequency of the offences would ensure that legislation would not be enacted on the basis of an individual case, such as a murder attempt on the life of a high-profile police journalist, and that well-meaning laws whose total social costs are out of all proportion to their benefits would never be enacted.

We should note in this regard that recent sentencing provisions allow great latitude when particular communities, such as First Nations (CCC, 718.2) and other communities, are victimized by criminals motivated by hate. While it may be legitimate for sentencing law to exercise positive discrimination, it is also definitely worthwhile to purge from the *Code* elements that result in negative discrimination and selective law enforcement.

Finally, we have seen that the criminalization process is not a one-way street and that it could also function in the direction of decriminalization and even wholesale legalization, this trend being problematic when it begets inconsistent legislation. The conclusion drawn from our study of gambling can be expressed in a few words: It is not desirable for the state to legalize, for its own benefit, practices that it has previously criminalized and that it continues to criminalize in a residual manner in order to maintain its monopoly over its profits. The spirit of such laws rests at first in a legitimate desire to avoid the contagion that can result from the legalization of practices that are potentially harmful; yet it is quickly subverted by greed, to which government is just as prone as private enterprise and which makes government the principal agent of the contamination it wished to eliminate.

Notes

This chapter is a translation from the original French version.

1 *"We call a crime any act for which punishment is meted out and we make crime that is defined in this way the subject of a special science, namely criminology"* (Durkheim 1981, 35, our translation, emphasis in the original).

2 For example, one of the leading lights of moral thought in the Western world, the philosopher Immanuel Kant, was an uncompromising advocate of the death penalty (Brodeur 1992).

3 Reference should be made here to discrete (discontinuous) behaviours in the *mathematical* sense of the term (as in the reference, for example, to discrete units) although this runs the risk of an annoying confusion with the common adjective "discreet," meaning restrained or subdued.

4 In all fairness, it should be acknowledged that John Rawls expects the principle of fairness to be violated solely in those cases where this discrepancy would benefit the most disadvantaged members of society. Such concern for the underprivileged tends to be an exception among lawyers.

5 "All murder that is not first degree murder is second degree murder" (CCC, 231(7)).

6 Let us imagine that a minor member of an organized crime organization is ordered to intimidate someone. He follows the person openly in the street and leaves threatening

messages on the telephone answering machine. One day the target of the intimidation gets fed up and challenges the persecutor in the street, complaining loudly about the treatment to which he or she is being subjected. The persecutor draws his gun and kills the victim. At trial his lawyer argues that he was provoked. Must we assume that the criminal law has become so labyrinthine in its casuistry that such an argument will convince an unbiased judge and that the Legislature must accordingly indicate that what is involved in these circumstances is first-degree murder?

7 In fact, the problem that the provision concerning intimidation is designed to resolve has never come before the courts.

8 The British philosopher R.E. Duff has developed a theory of criminal penalties in which the penalty is viewed as communication (1986). This function of the penalty is grafted onto the foundations of the criminalization process itself.

9 In his suicide note, part of which was made public, the killer, Marc Lépine, expressed murderous hatred for women, such as civil engineering students, who dared to aspire to jobs that he felt should be reserved for men. In the same note, he listed a number of such jobs – sports commentator, business manager, and so on – and asserted that he would also have liked to have killed the women who held those jobs.

10 One indication of the controversial nature of this legislation is that it makes a distinction between possession of a firearm without a permit or a registration certificate, which is punishable by a maximum sentence of five years' imprisonment (CCC, 91), and possession of a firearm by a person who knows that he or she "*is not the holder of* (a) *a licence under which the person may possess it; and* (b) *a registration certificate for the firearm*" (CCC, 92), emphasis in the original), which is punishable by a maximum term of ten years' imprisonment. To spare individuals who fail to register their guns, a graduated scheme is provided for that distinguishes between inadvertence, which does not constitute a criminal offence; an offence by omission (FA, 112), punishable by a fine; an offence as such (CCC, 91); and a deliberate offence (CCC, 92).

11 These transcripts can be found at <http://collection.nlc-bnc.ca/100/201/301/hoc_comm-e/jula/35-1/evidence/35-1-4/105_95-04-24/jula105_blk201.htm> (accessed summer 2002).

12 We have participated in these consultations with our colleagues on a number of occasions and can confirm the extent to which the increase in the minimum sentence for criminal use of firearms was designed solely for strategic purposes — that is, to make gun registration more acceptable to those who were opposed to it.

13 See <http://www.gnb.ca/0162/reports/vlt/index.htm> (accessed summer 2002).

14 According to the annual report of the government of Quebec on public health, "the risk that gambling will become compulsive is high in the case of slot machines and video lottery terminals" (our translation, <http://www.santepub-mtl.qc.ca/Publication/pdf/chapitre1_2001.pdf> [accessed summer 2002]).

15 See the régie's website: <http://www.loto-quebec.com> (accessed summer 2002).

16 The minister of justice, the Hon. Anne McLellan, has on several occasions acknowledged that she wanted to reform the *Young Offenders Act* not because youth crime had increased but because the public had lost confidence in the *Act* for various reasons. See the *Globe and Mail*, 25 August 1997, A1, and 16 March 1998, A1.

References

Ashworth, Andrew. 1983. *Sentencing and Penal Policy*. London: Weidenfeld and Nicolson.
Beare, Margaret, Wanda Jamieson, and Anne Gilmore. 1988. *Legalization of Gambling in Canada*. Ottawa: Department of the Solicitor General, Report No. 1988-12.
Brodeur, Jean-Paul. 1984. *La délinquance de l'ordre*. Montreal: Hurtubise HMH.
–. 1992. "Cartesian Penology," *The Canadian Journal of Law and Jurisprudence* 5, 1: 15-41.
Canada. 1983. *Gun Control in Canada: An Assessment*. Ottawa: Solicitor General of Canada.
Canadian Sentencing Commission. 1987. *Sentencing Reform: A Canadian Approach – Report of the Canadian Sentencing Commission*. Ottawa: Canadian Government Publications Centre.
Cournoyer, Guy, and Gilles Ouimet. 2001. *Code criminel annoté*. Montreal: Éditions Yvon Blais.

Duff, R.A. 1986. *Trials and Punishments*. Cambridge: Cambridge University Press.

Durkheim, Émile. 1901. "Deux lois de l'évolution pénale." *L'année sociologique 1899-1900:* 65-95.

–. 1981. *Les règles de la méthode en sociologie*. 1895. Reprint, Paris: Presses Universitaires de France.

Elias, Norbert. 1996. "Civilization and Violence: On the State Monopoly of Physical Violence and its Transgression." In *The Germans*, 171-299. Translated from the original German, New York: University of Columbia Press.

Garofalo, Barone Raffaele. 1968. *Criminology*. 1885. Translated 1914. Reprint, Montclair, New Jersey: Patterson Smith Reprints.

Gassin, Raymond. 1994. *Criminologie*. 3rd ed. Paris: Dalloz.

–. 1998. "De la peau de chagrin au noyau dur: Réponse à Jean-Paul Brodeur." *Revue internationale de criminologie et de police technique et scientifique* 51, 1: 46-83.

Hagan, John. 1977. *The Disreputable Pleasure*. Toronto: McGraw-Hill Ryerson.

Henry, Stuart, and Mark M. Lanier. 1998. "The Prism of Crime: The Arguments for an Integrated Definition of Crime." *Justice Quarterly* 15, 4: 609-27.

Killias, Martin. 1991. *Précis de criminologie*. Berne: Éditions Staempfli.

Labrosse, Michel. 1985. *Les loteries ... De Jacques Cartier à nos jours: La petite histoire des loteries au Québec*. Montreal: Stanké.

Law Reform Commission of Canada. 1986. *Toward a New Codification of Criminal Law*. Report 30. 2 volumes. Ottawa: Law Reform Commission of Canada.

Law Society of Saskatchewan. 2002. Colloquy on "Empty Promises: Parliament, the Supreme Court, and the Sentencing of Aboriginal Offenders." *Saskatchewan Law Review* 65, 1: 1-280.

Marvell, Thomas, and Carlisle Moody. 1995. "The Impact of Enhanced Prison Terms for Felonies Committed with Guns." *Criminology* 33, 2: 247-81.

Newman, Graeme. 1976. *Comparative Deviance: Perception and Law in Six Cultures*. New York: Elsevier.

Quebec. 1986. *Rapport du Comité d'étude sur les solutions de rechange à l'incarcération*. Quebec: Gouvernement du Québec, Ministère du Solliciteur général.

Rathjen, Heidi, and Charles Montpetit. 1999. *6 décembre: De la tragédie à l'espoir: les coulisses du combat pour le contrôle des armes*. Montreal: Libre Expression.

Rawls, John. 1971. *A Theory of Justice*. Cambridge, MA: Harvard University Press.

Robert, Philippe. 1985. "Au théâtre pénal: Quelques hypothèses pour une lecture sociologique du 'crime.'" *Déviance et société* 9, 2: 89-105.

Stenning, Philip, and Julian V. Roberts. 2001. "Empty Promises: Parliament, the Supreme Court, and the Sentencing of Aboriginal Offenders." *Saskatchewan Law Review* 64, 4: 138-68.

Tappan, Paul W. 1960. *Crime, Justice and Correction*. New York: McGraw-Hill Series in Sociology.

Taylor, Ian, Paul Walton, and Jock Young. 1973. *The New Criminology*. London: Routledge and Kegan Paul.

–, eds. *Critical Criminology*. 1975. London: Routledge and Kegan Paul.

Tonry, Michael. 1995. *Malign Neglect*. New York: Oxford University Press.

Williams, Glanville. 1955. "The Definition of Crime." In *Current Legal Problems, by George W. Keeton and George Schwarzenberger, on behalf of the Faculty of Law, University College, London*, vol. 8, 107-30. London: Stevens and Sons.

Wittgenstein, Ludwig. 1953. *Philosophical Investigations*. New York: Macmillan.

Young, Jock. 1992. "Realist Research as a Basis for Local Criminal Justice." In *Realist Criminology: Crime Control and Policing in the 1990s*, edited by John Lowman and Brian MacLean, 33-72. Toronto: University of Toronto Press.

Zimring, Franklin E., and Gordon Hawkins. 1997. *Crime Is Not the Problem: Lethal Violence in America*. New York: Oxford University Press.

2
Undocumented Migrants and Bill C-11: The Criminalization of Race
Wendy Chan

> Immigration controls have their origins in racism. They legitimate racism, feed racism, and are explicable only by racism.
>
> –Teresa Hayter (2001, 149)

In the summer of 1999 when four successive boatloads of Chinese migrants arrived on the shores of western Canada, the issue of "illegal" immigration once again made headlines across the country and dominated public discussions over concerns about the effectiveness of Canadian immigration policy. In recent decades similar incidents have sparked similarly heated discussions and debates. In the 1980s, 155 Tamils came to Canada in lifeboats along the Newfoundland Coast, and another 174 Sikhs arrived off Nova Scotian waters a year later, also travelling by lifeboats. Less dramatic and more recent were the concerns about Honduran children who were brought into Canada illegally in the late 1990s and coerced into drug dealing on the streets of Vancouver. In each situation, politicians scrambled to change the *Immigration Act* in reaction to the public outcry and the belief that a "crisis" was taking place. Wanting to quell public criticism by appearing to take a tough stance, the government of the day enacted draconian measures to address the situation. The most recent response to the situation with the Chinese migrants was no different from previous reactions despite the change in governments during these periods.

Successive amendments to immigration policies, particularly to the enforcement provisions of the *Immigration Act,* have resulted in increasingly harsh and punitive measures. Both the language used and the substantive changes contained in various amendments construct negative images of immigrants as "abusers" of Canada's "generous" immigration system, as "bogus" refugee claimants, and as "criminals" who are "cheating" their way into Canada. The introduction of Bill C-11 is the most recent example of the criminalizing and retributive tone that is now commonplace in immigration policy making. Also noteworthy is the bill's specific focus on criminality and its adoption of criminal justice processes, such as the greater use of detention, in an attempt to create more effective enforcement mechanisms. The convergence of criminal justice strategies with concerns regarding immigration control found in Bill C-11, the most comprehensive set of amendments since the introduction of the *Immigration Act* in 1975, marks an important orientation in Canadian immigration policy making.

This chapter argues that the changes to enforcement contained in Bill C-11, the proposed new *Immigration Act,* criminalizes and demonizes racialized immigrants, particularly "illegal" immigrants, in a manner that is far-reaching and deeply punitive. Part 1 of this chapter considers, first, the shifts in immigration legislation toward more repressive and restrictive immigration policies in the 1980s and 1990s and, second, the interplay between racial difference and notions of citizenship and belonging. Race and racism have played a key role in organizing racial identities and enforcing a specific racial reality within Canada. Part 2 discusses four important changes contained in the new bill, the rationale for them, and the responses and criticisms of various nonprofit groups providing immigrant and refugee services and advocacy. Finally, Part 3 addresses how the enforcement provisions in Bill C-11 mark racialized immigrants as criminals and thus as outsiders. I argue that these policy changes are a result of punitive sentiments driven by a range of insecurities and are legitimized by racist ideologies and practices. The stigmatization of immigrants in Bill C-11 will perpetuate their social inequality and social exclusion by fracturing Canadian society into those who are considered part of the nation and those who are condemned to its margins.

Part 1: Racism, Immigration, and Crime

Fortifying Canada's Borders

The perceived need to control the flow of immigrants, particularly false refugee claimants, made a marked resurgence in Canadian immigration policy in the 1980s and peaked in the 1990s. The more liberal policies found in the original provisions of the *Immigration Act* of 1975 underwent numerous transformations, culminating in requirements that were stricter and more exclusionary.[1] Immigration scholars cite various explanations for these shifts. First, there was a breakdown in Canada's refugee process, resulting in a backlog of applications. At the same time, there was a rise in requests for asylum from refugees in developing countries due to conflict and upheaval (Garcia y Griego 1994; Creese 1992). By the 1980s the process for refugee status determination had become overly cumbersome, and charges were made that Canada's refugee system was being abused on the grounds that many of the claims were "manifestly unfounded" (Garcia y Griego 1994, 127-28). Second, the issue of immigration had become deeply politicized within Canada (Arat-Koc 1999; Abu-Laban 1998; Avery 1995). Immigration scholars noted a breakdown of interparty consensus over the appropriate levels of immigration to Canada (Abu-Laban 1998; Malarek 1987) and the use of neoliberal ideas[2] to stave off criticisms (Arat-Koc 1999). The notion of self-reliance, which is rooted in the values of the marketplace, where neo-liberalism emerged, took on a greater role in shaping the criteria for immigration policy making, thus creating the view that independent (business-class, typically male) immigrants were desirable but that dependent (family-class, usually women and children) immigrants were not. Throughout this period, the heated debates and contestations drew upon the racist belief that the different ethnic and racial backgrounds of immigrants entering Canada were eroding Canadian values and traditions (Frideres 1996).

Most scholars acknowledge that the increasing and largely unanticipated numbers of refugee claims in the 1980s placed a major strain on Canada's immigration system (Kelley and Trebilcock 1998; Garcia y Griego 1994; Creese 1992). Moreover, with the decision in *Singh,*[3] which recognized that refugees under the *Charter* had a right to an oral hearing, any hope of streamlining the system to eliminate the backlog of claims was dashed. In response, two major pieces of policy reform were introduced in 1987: Bills C-55 and C-84. Bill C-55, the *Refugee Reform Act,* created the Immigration and Refugee Board of Canada (previously the Immigration Appeal Board) and restructured the refugee determination process to respond to the problem of "unfounded" refugee claims. Under this bill one of the procedures refugees were required to undergo was a screening hearing to determine whether or not there was a credible basis for their claims. The other piece of reform, Bill C-84, the *Refugee Deterrents and Detention Act,* conferred broader powers for the detention and removal of refugee arrivals, particularly those considered criminals or a security threat (Kelley and Trebilcock 1998, 386). Both of these reforms were hotly debated, especially Bill C-84, because many of its critics believed that the changes proposed were reactionary and a knee-jerk response to the alleged refugee "crisis" portrayed in the media, rather than well-thought-out pieces of legislation (Creese 1992, 140-41). Critics challenged the portrayal of Sikh refugees as "illegal" immigrants and "bogus" claimants, arguing that these assumptions were fuelled by racism. As a result of intense debate, both bills did not come into effect until January 1989. Interestingly, the procedure of screening refugees at the beginning of the refugee determination process was eventually eliminated when it was discovered that 95 percent of refugee claims were legitimate (Garcia y Griego 1994, 128).

The next two major pieces of immigration reform, Bills C-86 and C-44, addressed security concerns and spotlighted the growing belief that Canada's borders were being infiltrated and threatened by criminals, most of whom were regarded as "illegal" immigrants rather than legitimate refugees. Bill C-86, introduced in June 1992, proposed primarily restrictive revisions to the refugee determination system. Some of the proposed changes included fingerprinting refugee claimants, harsher detention provisions, making refugee hearings open to the public (these were amended as the bill passed through Parliament), and requiring Convention refugees applying for landing in Canada to have a passport, valid travel document, or "other satisfactory identity document" (Canadian Council for Refugees 2000). In addition, new grounds of inadmissibility were added to exclude individuals with criminal or terrorist links. Then in July 1995 Bill C-44, dubbed the "Just Desserts" bill by the media, was enacted in response to two Toronto killings within weeks of each other by landed immigrants with long criminal records.[4] Sergio Marchi, the minister of immigration at the time, reminded Canadians that immigration is a privilege rather than a right and proposed changes that would "go a long way to stopping the tyranny of a minority criminal element" (Marchi 1995). Bill C-44 made it easier to remove from Canada permanent residents deemed by the minister to be a "danger to the public" by restricting their ability to appeal their deportation orders or submit refugee claims. Additional measures were also enacted to address fraud and multiple refugee claims.

These latter two bills were equally controversial and resulted, like the earlier reforms, in intense public and political debate. Most noteworthy was the focus on the discretionary power given to the immigration minister to deport a permanent resident. Widespread academic and public discussions ensued: Legal scholars argued that returning discretionary power to the minister was "a throwback to a less enlightened era" (Haigh and Smith 1998, 291), and immigration advocates claimed that such provisions were racist and would increase the criminalization of non-European individuals in Canada (Hassan-Gordon 1996; Noorani and Wright 1995). However, not all participants in the debate shared this position. Some still thought that Bill C-44 had not gone far enough in tightening the system against false claimants and criminals. The Reform Party argued that defining "serious criminality" only in respect to offences carrying a ten-year sentence or longer was insufficient since, in their eyes, a "criminal is a criminal" (Kelley and Trebilcock 1998, 434).

These divergent positions highlight how immigration had become deeply politicized and how, contrary to Victor Malarek's (1987) lament that immigration as a public policy issue was not debated at all, it was now one of the most hotly contested policy issues. Teitelbaum and Winter (1998, 188) attribute this change to the presence of the Reform Party and their calls in the 1993 election for abandoning the policy of multiculturalism and significantly reducing Canada's annual immigration levels. The populist political movement in Canada,[5] as elsewhere, recognized that immigration and immigrants were easy targets to blame for the economic decline taking place at the time. Furthermore, such views coincided neatly with the shift to neoliberal approaches in public policy development, which fostered a belief that the more vulnerable sectors of society, such as single mothers and immigrants, were to blame for the lack of jobs or the high crime rate (Abu-Laban 1998, 194). Good immigrants, it was understood, were those who could look after themselves and their families. With this came the "common sense" view that strong immigration controls were a necessary component of any effective immigration system. Arat-Koc (1999) points out how neoliberalism validated the attacks against the rights and entitlements of Canadians, making any political or ideological challenge very difficult. Thus the harsh reforms of the 1980s and 1990s were eventually passed by Parliament, sending the message that security and enforcement were now key priorities in immigration policy making.

Race and Nation

The hostilities expressed toward immigrants in the reforms of the 1980s and 1990s were recognizably disturbing for many antiracist scholars and activists. During this period the anti-immigrant view that immigrants were causing an array of social, cultural, and economic problems and disrupting the core values and traditions of Canada was prevalent. Yet immigration scholars observe that the problem of "illegal" immigration in Canada has never been considered serious (Cox and Glenn 1994; Robinson 1983, 1984). As Canada is an immigrant-receiving country with high levels of immigration, Robinson (1983) claims that a certain amount of "illegal" immigration is inevitable. Buchignani and Indra (1999, 438) convincingly counter claims that the population of "illegal" immigrants in Canada is high by pointing out that there is in fact no adequate or rational means of determining how many people in Canada have not had their immigration status regularized; nor is there any evidence of a significant presence of "illegal" immigrants in any of Canada's major cities.

Indeed, Canada's immigration program has been widely acknowledged to be a necessary factor in maintaining steady population growth. Successive governments have recognized that a declining birth rate, an aging population, and the need for skilled labour demand high levels of immigration to ensure economic prosperity and moderate growth. Yet difficulties in maintaining a reasonable level of immigration and in managing cycles of unemployment, while also upholding international obligations to accept refugees and asylum seekers, led to broad fluctuations in levels of immigration during the 1980s and 1990s (Avery 1995, 219). This sparked a series of debates and public opinion polls about whether or not immigration levels were too high (Laquian et al. 1998, 4-5). During this period Asia and the Pacific region increasingly accounted for a large proportion of all immigrants to Canada. By 2000 the top four source countries were China, India, Pakistan, and the Philippines.[6] The increasing numbers of nonwhite immigrants have not gone unnoticed and have contributed to an immigrant backlash, promoting views that Canada cannot absorb all this "diversity"

(Li 2000) and that the "quality" of immigrants is threatening the destruction of the nation (Thobani 2000b). Within this context, questions about the extent of Canada's "illegal" immigration problem were raised.

It would seem that public concerns and anxiety about "illegal" immigration appear to be linked to "perceived immigrant desirability and legitimacy," as Buchignani and Indra (1999, 416) remark, rather than to any real threat to Canada's borders or sovereignty. Garcia y Griego (1994, 120) concurs, stating that "Canada has never lost control over its borders, but it has, on more than one occasion, lost control over its own admission process." As a social issue of concern, "illegal" immigration has waxed and waned over time, and "each time illegal immigration has become an issue, the appearance of control has been quickly reestablished by change in law, regulations, or practice. While this appearance of control is, in part, illusory, it has functioned to defuse the issue" (Buchignani and Indra 1999, 439). Furthermore, some scholars note that the very concept of "illegal" migrants is only possible when nation-states enact legislation on immigrants to control international migration and thereby create their own undocumented, or illegal, migrants (Castles and Miller 1994). Indeed, the flurry of immigration reforms in the 1980s and 1990s was perhaps more a reflection of the government of the time demonstrating that it had matters under control than a response to a bona fide problem. This position is reinforced by the fact that amnesty programs designed to enable "illegal" immigrants to regularize their status have been ongoing in Canadian immigration control (Cox and Glenn 1994).

That the issue of "illegal" immigration has attained symbolic importance despite the absence of any "real" problem can be understood as a desire for Canada to retain sovereignty over her borders, particularly in the face of global economic disparities between rich and poor countries. Global migration, explains Doty (1996, 173), has the effect of disrupting the relationship between territory, national identity, and political community because "illegal" immigration is beyond the complete control of any nation-state, governed as it is by the reality of globalization. Illegal immigration destabilizes notions of national identity and national autonomy, making it more difficult to distinguish between those on the inside and those on the outside of the nation. This is evident in a speech by Elinor Caplan (2001), who was minister of immigration and citizenship at the time, in which she admits that "Yes, the face of immigration has changed ... The newcomer of 1957 and the newcomer of today may not look alike – but they are far more alike than they are different." As Caplan reassures us, there is nonetheless a shared understanding, an essential sameness, uniting these differences. Doty (1996, 180) believes that this fear that we are losing control of our way of life permeates immigration discourse and allows for the use of war and military metaphors in attempting to reclaim national autonomy because "regaining control of our borders conjures up a mythic past, an age of purity, when the inside was clearly and unambiguously differentiated from the outside." Other scholars share Doty's conclusion, stating that such fears create the necessary "crisis" for nations to participate willingly in the state's politics of exclusion and to view "the nation's racism against nonwhite immigrants as common sense" (Behdad 1998, 110-11).

As the boundaries between insider and outsider become more ambivalent and converge with nostalgia for a bygone period of immigration, immigrants of colour are the ones classified and defined most vocally by right-wing individuals and groups as inauthentic, "illegal," or outsiders. Antiracist scholars allege that racial identity remains a key marker of those who are perceived as not belonging, as not being "legitimate" immigrants of the nation. Even though Canada moved away from blatant forms of discrimination in its immigration policies in the 1960s and 1970s, racism and patriarchy continue to define spatial and/or social margins in portrayals of the dominant vision of the nation (Simmons 1998; Kobayashi 1995). The racialization of immigration, which focuses on the process of constructing racial identities and meanings, enables ideas about "race" to proliferate. Now cultural difference, rather than racial inferiority, have become the distinguishing markers between us and them. Avtar Brah (1996, 165) writes that this form of racism is "a racism that combined a disavowal of biological superiority or inferiority with a focus on 'a way of life,' of cultural difference as the 'natural' basis for feelings of antagonism towards outsiders." This has made it possible, for example, for immigration debates to continue to be characterized by recurring allegations that too much racial diversity will lead to conflict, that immigrants have large families who expect to be supported by the welfare state, that immigrants are criminals and have no respect for the law, or that immigrant workers take jobs away from those already resident because they are willing to work for low wages (Hintjens 1992). Furthermore, the demand that immigrants to Canada must now be able to speak either English or French[7] is an example of how racialization is embedded in immigration policies, and as Thobani (2000a, 293) observes, such demands elevate Europeanness/whiteness over other cultures and ethnicities and clearly realign the national Canadian identity with being "white" while seemingly appearing to be race-neutral.

Part 2: Bill C-11 and Immigrant Criminality

The burden placed on immigrants to challenge and counter negative stereotypes of their communities will become even heavier as a result of Bill C-11, which took effect in January 2003.[8] Many scholars and community advocates believe that the new measures were made possible only by creating the impression that Canada is a nation whose borders are constantly under threat. This impression has been exacerbated by the events of 11

September 2001 and by the introduction of Bill C-36, the new *Terrorism Act.* Both Bills C-11 and C-36 describe a country that can no longer turn a blind eye to its security problems at the borders; nor can she ignore the fact that there are people "clamouring" to come to Canada by whatever means possible and that there are people currently in Canada who should not be. As the Standing Committee on Citizenship and Immigration (2001) affirms, "The *Immigration and Refugee Protection Act* represents a significant step in addressing current security concerns. Even though drafted before September 11, the legislation was clearly created with the threat of terrorism in mind." The Canadian government's response has been an attempt to deter these individuals and their activities by imposing harsher sanctions and increasing levels of scrutiny and authority for immigration officers.

According to Citizenship and Immigration Canada (CIC) documents on Bill C-11, the *Immigration and Refugee Protection Act* is intended to serve a number of different immigration goals, such as attracting skilled workers, protecting refugees, and deterring traffickers. The aim, according to the Liberal government, is to accomplish these goals by simplifying the legislation and striking the necessary balance between efficiency, fairness, and security. In their overview of Bill C-11, CIC claims that there is a need to "simplify," "strengthen," "modernize," and "streamline" the immigration system. A key priority in this set of policy reforms is to "clos[e] the back door to criminals and others who would abuse Canada's openness and generosity." This will be achieved by including in the *Act* the provisions needed to "better ensure serious criminals and individuals who are threats to public safety are kept out of Canada, and, if they have entered the country, that they are removed as quickly as possible."[9] Elinor Caplan stated that Canada would only attract the necessary skilled immigrants once a process for ensuring the integrity of the system was established.[10] CIC claims that the new bill is different from its predecessor, Bill C-31, in that it clarifies a number of different provisions and entrenches important core principles in the *Act* itself rather than placing them in the regulations.[11] Moreover, it is regarded as a progressive bill in that it preserves core Canadian values while also recognizing Canada's evolving values.[12]

There are many aspects of Bill C-11 that will have a significant impact on controlling and preventing "illegal" immigration to Canada. Many different organizations and individuals involved with immigrants and refugees submitted written responses to the proposed *Immigration and Refugee Protection Act* and participated in public consultations. Many of the criticisms levelled at CIC noted that the consultation process was inadequate given the fundamental changes made and the effect they would have on immigrants and refugees (Canadian Council for Refugees 2001; Thobani 2000a). As to the substance of the *Act*, while some immigrant and refugee groups applaud changes to family-reunification and sponsorship requirements, the general tenor of the submissions point to growing concerns and trepidation about a bill that is overly reactive and too "obsessed" with security issues. As the Maytree Foundation (2001, 3) states, "the bill is much more about who cannot come to Canada and how they will be removed, than it is about who we will welcome, who we will protect, and how we will do that." Many organizations expressed uneasiness that racialized immigrants will suffer the consequences of immigration officers' concerns with the need to maintain border security. Moreover, women refugees and immigrants are likely to shoulder the burden of the many changes, which encompass racist and sexist practices, because they are more vulnerable to the negative effects of migration. It is not possible here to touch on all the ways in which "illegal" immigrants will be affected by Bill C-11. Therefore, the following sections highlight some of the key policy areas relevant to this issue.

The Crime of Human Smuggling and Trafficking

Under the enforcement provisions, a new category of criminal activity has been created and added to the new *Immigration Act* in response to the arrival of Chinese migrants in 1999. The crime of human smuggling and trafficking involves several types of activities. It is an offence to organize, aid, or abet immigrants wishing to come to Canada who do not have the necessary travel documents (s. 117). The trafficking of persons through abduction, fraud, or deception, the use or threat of force or coercion (s. 118), and leaving a person or persons at sea for the purpose of helping them come to Canada (s. 119) are also offences subject to criminal penalties.

The penalties for organizing the smuggling of fewer than ten people are a maximum of ten years' imprisonment or a $500,000 fine, or both, for the first offence and a maximum of fourteen years' imprisonment or a $1 million fine, or both, for subsequent offences. Where ten persons or more are involved, the penalty is a maximum of life imprisonment or a $1 million fine, or both. Trafficking persons or leaving them at sea carries a maximum penalty of life imprisonment or a $1 million fine, or both (s. 120). Aggravating factors (s. 121), such as the occurrence of harm or death during the offence or the association of the offence with a criminal organization, will be considered in determining the penalty to be imposed.

The Canadian Council for Refugees (CCR) argues that attempting to deter activities of human smuggling and trafficking can have the unintended consequence of criminalizing family members who help refugees escape. While claimants can escape prosecution if they are found to be refugees (s. 133), their family members are not equally protected. Nor are individuals who apply for asylum in good faith but are rejected. Since these provisions do not differentiate between those who engage in human smuggling for profit and those who are motivated by humanitarian concerns, both categories of individuals will suffer the same penalties. Moreover, while these provisions are intended to bring Canadian immigration policy in line with international protocols and thus have included strong enforcement measures to curtail and deter human smuggling and trafficking in persons, there are no provisions in the bill for protection of those being smuggled or trafficked. As the CCR (2001) points out, "the migrant protocol states that the criminalization measures are not to apply to people who are smuggled into a country, whereas Bill C-11 gives an exemption only to those recognized as refugees." As a result, protection from prosecution is limited only to those who can make a successful refugee claim. Yet obtaining refugee status is a political process, and as the Vancouver Association of Chinese Canadians noted in the government's treatment of the Chinese boat refugees, over 100 people were prevented from making a refugee claim. These provisions will clearly catch many individuals in the attempt to prevent smuggling and trafficking of persons. What is less clear is who will in fact receive protection from being criminalized.

Other organizations echoed similar concerns, arguing that any attempt by the government to combat human smuggling and trafficking should not occur at the expense of further victimization of migrants who have been smuggled or trafficked. The National Association of Women and the Law (NAWL) and the United Nations High Commission for Refugees (UNHCR) claim that by failing to include adequate protection for trafficked or smuggled migrants, the Canadian government is reneging on its responsibility to international protocols. The UNHCR notes that migrants resort to smugglers and traffickers for numerous reasons. While many migrants are searching for better economic opportunities, there are also many migrants who are refugees and whose only option for escape lies with the smugglers or traffickers. NAWL believes that this new category of immigration enforcement will result in smugglers and traffickers charging migrants higher prices to escape. For women and children who are less likely to have the financial resources to pay, the possibility of fleeing persecution, conflict, and human rights abuses will become even more remote unless they are willing to pay the costs in the form of enforced prostitution and sexual violations (NAWL 2001). It has been strongly recommended that the Canadian government provide protection to migrants by granting them immigration relief, access to permanent residency, or the opportunity to submit applications to stay on humanitarian and compassionate grounds.[13] Affording migrants the necessary protection would help to alleviate their vulnerability to the smugglers or traffickers.

Document Offences
In addition to designating human smuggling and trafficking of persons a crime, Bill C-11 significantly reinforces measures to combat offences related to the use of false documents. Under sections 122 and 123, it is an

offence to possess, use, or sell false documents for the purpose of enabling either oneself or another person to enter or remain in Canada. Possessing a false document carries a maximum penalty of five years' imprisonment, while using or dealing with false documents carries a maximum penalty of fourteen years' imprisonment. Only refugees whose documents are found to be false once they have arrived in Canada are exempt from punishment for these offences (s. 133). The government plans to enforce these provisions by increasing the number of immigration officials working overseas – for example, at major international airports – and by imposing penalties on transportation companies that fail to check for appropriate documents adequately.

These provisions not only criminalize a broad range of migrants who use false documents by imposing a sentence of imprisonment, but also fail to make the distinction between refugees and nonrefugees. The CCR contends that it is not at all unlikely that travellers with false documents are legitimate refugees trying to find any means of leaving. Many organizations agree that migrants should not be penalized because their government will not issue adequate identification documents. Even the Vatican has waded into the debate, arguing that "persecution and violence do not allow their victims the luxury of getting passports and visas before a forced departure."[14] Amnesty International concurs, claiming that "sometimes the only way that genuine refugees can escape persecution in their own countries and seek asylum abroad is through 'irregular channels' and by means of false documentation" (2001, 3). If overseas immigration officials and transportation companies prevent migrants from travelling because they are using false documents, being forced back into their country of origin could contravene the principle of *non-refoulement* (not forcibly returning refugees to persecution). Since exemption from prosecution applies only to migrants who make it to Canada and are found to be refugees, those who are interdicted on their way to Canada and found with false documents will be denied access to the refugee process and thus entry into Canada.

The myth that many migrants are "bogus" refugee claimants and that they are simply trying to "jump the immigration queue" underlies the perceived need for increased enforcement and punishment in this area. The punitive nature of these provisions, whereby migrants are treated like serious criminals, has been widely noted. The African Canadian Legal Clinic (2001) states that to define lack of proper documentation as a safety issue is to mistakenly assume that undocumented refugees are simply seeking to enter Canada illegally. Such a definition fails to consider the other factors associated with why migrants might need to resort to the use of false documents. Many organizations question the necessity of taking such extreme measures to protect Canada's borders. As the CCR states, "Canadian borders are not sacred." In an era of increasing globalization, when the gap between rich, developed countries and poor, developing countries is widening, the legitimacy of these provisions needs to be challenged. Michael Szonyi (2000) highlights how, in the Fuzhou region of China, which was home to the migrants who came to Canada in the summer of 1999, local residents seeking to establish small-scale entrepreneurial projects were driven out of business by rising foreign investment. He argues that if Canada wishes to stem the practice of "illegal" immigration, simply closing the borders is a mistake. Rather, there needs to be a critical assessment and understanding of China's current situation and future prospects (Szonyi 2000). Thus Canada's role in contributing to the economic conditions of developing countries makes the criminalization of "illegally"-arrived, usually racialized migrants less tenable.

Detention

Broader powers of detention have been conferred upon immigration officers in the new *Act*. Sections 55 and 56 of the bill state that a person can be detained if there are reasonable grounds to believe the person would be inadmissible to Canada, a danger to the public, or unlikely to appear for future proceedings. For any immigration procedure under the *Act*, enhanced powers have also been given to immigration officers at ports of entry to detain migrants on the basis of administrative convenience, suspicion of inadmissibility premised on suspected security or human rights violations, and failure to establish identity. Immigration officers also have wider discretion to arrest and detain a "foreign national," but not a protected person, without a warrant even in cases where the person is not being removed (s. 55(2)). The length of incarceration is not specified for any of these grounds for detention. Thus someone who fails to provide adequate identification can be detained for the same length of time as a person who is considered a danger to the public (s. 58(1)). Children can be detained but only as a measure of last resort (s. 60).

Many concerns have been raised about the nature of the detention provisions and the manner in which they will be executed. The fear among most immigrant and refugee organizations is that conferring greater powers upon individual immigration officers will result in racial profiling, with a high proportion of racialized migrants ending up in detention. Other worries include the broad, arbitrary use of power by immigration officers, the possibility of long-term detention of migrants who fail to establish their identities, the likelihood that trafficked or smuggled migrants will be criminalized and subsequently detained for the purpose of deterring human traffickers, and the use of detention on the basis of group status rather than on the particular circumstances of the persons involved.

The UNHCR states that it opposes any detention policy that is fashioned to deter asylum seekers or to discourage them from pursuing their refugee claims. Moreover, it cautions against establishing a policy that detains migrants on the basis of being "unlikely to appear" at an immigration hearing because of their *mode of arrival* to Canada since many refugees are forced to use smugglers in order to reach safety (UNHCR 2001, 29, emphasis in the original). Finally, it argues that in determining whether to detain a person for failing to establish his or her identity, immigration officials need to recognize the difference between a wilful intention to deceive and the inability to provide documentation when reaching conclusions about the person's level of cooperation with authorities (UNHCR 2001, 30). The UNHCR joins the voices of others who also recommend that the government establish clear guidelines and criteria as to what constitutes a refusal to cooperate.

Given the unsatisfactory state of detention centres in Canada[15] and the now-increased potential for long-term detention of migrants, concerns that detainees' civil liberties will be violated are not unwarranted, particularly when the majority of them are racialized migrants. Indeed, many organizations believe that the heightened powers of detention in the new *Act* are a racist and reactionary response to the arrival of Chinese migrants in 1999.[16] That the subsequent arrival of additional Chinese migrants that summer resulted in their immediate detention without much public outcry highlights how racism, as exercised through the practice of racial profiling, had been used to gain legitimacy for the government's practices. The assumption was that since one boatload of migrants were "bogus" refugee claimants, all Chinese migrants must be bogus as well, which in turn justified the government's tough stance on "illegal" immigrants.[17] Not surprisingly, issues of due process and other human rights abuses surfaced in a UN Human Rights Commission report over the treatment of the Chinese migrants.[18] The UN investigator said that Canada "needed to avoid criminalizing the victims" (UNHCR 2001). Her report pointed to the poor psychological state of some of the Chinese women who were detained and how mistreatment by penitentiary guards had led one woman to attempt suicide. In her report the UN investigator reminded Canadian authorities that the migrants had been doubly victimized since they were the victims of the traffickers as well.

The drift toward the use of preventative detention to deal with migrants will perpetuate the mistaken and prejudiced perception that those being detained are a threat to public safety and are behaving illegally rather than people who actually need safety from danger (CCR 2001). Indeed, the culture of criminalization within the present immigration system points to disturbing trends for the treatment of migrants. Unlike convicted offenders, migrants can face indefinite lengths of detention as they wait for the arrival of their identity documents, and they can be detained on the basis of suspicion or convenience. The expansion of immigration detention promotes an anti-immigrant prejudice by constructing immigrants as dangerous and promoting the idea that the public needs to be protected from them.

New Categories of Inadmissibility

Several new and revised categories of inadmissibility found in the new *Act* can be used to bar applicants from permanent residency or to render existing permanent residents inadmissible. People who engage in activities such as human smuggling, trafficking, or money laundering have been made inadmissible through the category of "transnational" crime (s. 37(1)(b)), which falls within the broader section of organized criminality (s. 37). Those who misrepresent themselves on their application forms, whether directly or indirectly, will be barred from entering Canada for two years (s. 40). This category includes anyone whose sponsor submitted an application on the applicant's behalf and gave false information or withheld information. People who make excessive medical demands on the Canadian state are inadmissible (s. 38(c)). Exceptions apply to family-class spouses, minor children, and refugees. Finally, representatives of governments against which Canada has imposed sanctions will also be considered inadmissible (s. 35).

Where a positive finding of inadmissibility has been made on the grounds of security, violations of human or international rights, serious criminality, or organized criminality, a permanent resident or "foreign national" will lose his or her right to an appeal with the Immigration Appeal Division (s. 64). Serious criminality here is defined as a sentence of imprisonment for two years or more. Moreover, Bill C-11 no longer gives permanent residents undergoing a security-certificate process access to the Security Intelligence Review Committee (s. 77). They have only the right of minimal review by a federal-court judge.

The new formulation for determining inadmissibility on the grounds of either misrepresentation or the withholding of facts has provoked numerous responses from refugee organizations: They point out that refugees' reliance on others to help them complete application forms can result in unintentional mistakes being made but that this doesn't detract from their need for protection; nor should they be punished for making errors on their applications (UNHCR 2001). Language barriers, cultural differences, and bad advice are among the many factors that can result in a case of "misrepresentation" (CCR 2001, 52). In a stronger statement, the Coalition for a Just Immigration and Refugee Policy has remarked that "the fact that a person can be sanctioned for indirectly withholding information is simply bizarre" (2001, 14). Such a situation could involve prospective immigrants who are found inadmissible because they did not read the immigration officer's mind and did not volunteer relevant material information even though they were not asked the question.

With security concerns taking a central role in the new *Act*, it is not surprising that Bill C-11 devotes significant attention to the issue of criminality. While there is general agreement that it would not be desirable to allow serious criminals into Canada, some of the provisions around inadmissibility in relation to criminality need to be challenged nonetheless. First, determinations of serious criminality committed outside of Canada are made on the basis of the maximum sentence for a crime and do not consider when the crime was committed and whether or not the sentence was suspended. Consequently, a person who is completely rehabilitated may still have to wait for long periods before being able to make a refugee claim. Second, that someone convicted and given a sentence of two years or more in prison should automatically lose the right to appeal to the Immigration Appeal Division has been described by the Law Union of Ontario as "a mandatory, unthoughtful and potentially oppressive procedure." The Coalition for a Just Immigration and Refugee Policy agrees that in ignoring other factors, such as how long the person has lived in Canada, the presence of immediate family members, and whether he or she has been rehabilitated, the bill not only will result in serious harm to the families, but is "grossly unfair." Third, under the new *Act*, anyone convicted of serious criminality within Canada would be automatically ineligible to apply for asylum, whereas anyone who is convicted outside of Canada is ineligible if the minister finds the person to be a danger to the public. It is argued that a similar safeguard should be in place for those who are convicted within Canada since it is possible that a refugee may be encouraged to make a guilty plea in exchange for a suspended sentence. While an individual committing a crime within Canada may not be considered a danger to the public, according to the new provisions, this person would still be ineligible to seek asylum. Finally, the African Canadian Legal Clinic (2001, 4) points out that while it supports denying members of a dictatorial regime access to Canada, it is important to remember that which governments become the subject of sanctions is a political decision motivated by concerns that are not always related to protecting human rights. Therefore, there is a need to ensure fairness in the enforcement of this category of inadmissibility.

Further clarification is also sought for individuals in Canada who are inadmissible because of serious criminality. For example, membership in an organized-crime group will render the person inadmissible, but it is unclear what constitutes being a member and what safeguards will be in place to avoid determinations made on the basis of "guilt by association" (Maytree Foundation 2001, 13). Past practices have demonstrated how whole communities have been placed under suspicion because there was a failure to differentiate between being an active member of a political group, participating in criminal activities, or simply desiring political change (Maytree Foundation 2001, 13). Aiken (2001, 6) contends that "the inclusion of an undifferentiated notion of membership, and the broad discretion built into Bill C-11 leave unacceptably wide scope for xenophobic prejudices and a patchwork of specific biases to inform both administrative and judicial decision making." Other areas requiring further clarification concern the definition of terrorism and the definition of transnational crime, which includes activities such as human smuggling or trafficking. A person who enters Canada with the help of smugglers is not inadmissible, but it is unclear whether or not people who help family members escape through the use of smugglers will be considered inadmissible (Coalition for a Just Immigration and Refugee Policy 2001).

In comparison to the previous *Act*, Bill C-11 clearly broadens categories of inadmissibility, particularly as it relates to issues of criminality. The lack of clarification in some of the provisions and the focused attention paid to ensuring that "serious" criminals do not enter or stay in Canada means that the security net has been significantly widened to catch many more people, not all of whom will be a threat to Canada. As a consequence of these provisions, the myth that a serious threat exists at the frontiers of Canada, where the most undesirable types of people are entering the country, and that these people are immigrants and refugees from racialized countries, is given official backing by the state. The failure to specify adequately within these provisions the criteria that will be used to make determinations of inadmissibility, and the failure to recognize the need to consider individual circumstances allow racist ideas to flourish and to continue being acted upon unchallenged.

Part 3: Criminalizing Race
With perhaps the exception of a few groups, such as the Canadian Police Association, the overwhelming majority of participating organizations who made submissions on Bill C-11 agree that the *Immigration and Refugee Protection Act* will have a detrimental effect on racialized individuals, groups, and communities. Racialized female migrants in particular will experience the impact of the new *Act* in harsh and uncompromising terms since they are typically more vulnerable to the effects of migration. For example, women will be disproportionately affected by the elimination of the option to make a second refugee claim in cases where they do not have the opportunity to explain their persecution in their first claim because their spouses are the principle applicants (CCR 2001, 63). The strong rhetoric of safety, the need for enhanced national security, and the threat of terrorism have not been countered in the new *Act* by any recognition of the need to protect vulnerable migrants as a priority, to provide safety for those suffering from human rights violations, and to do so in a humane and compassionate manner. Instead, by the government's own admission, the new *Act* focuses primarily on preventing "abuse" of the system, using exclusionary mechanisms such as deportation, criminalization, enhanced screening, and interdiction to achieve this end. As a result, one of the messages being sent to all prospective

immigrants and refugees is that nonwhite, unskilled persons who speak neither English nor French need not apply. For "illegal" migrants, particularly those claiming asylum on economic grounds, as the Chinese migrants did in the summer of 1999, any hope of compassion for their desperation is lost.[19]

Bill C-11, however, goes further than simply creating more barriers for access to Canada. It also criminalizes immigrants within Canada by constructing them as potential security threats who require surveillance. This process of "dangerization" means that "[immigrants] do not need to break rules to be excluded ... what is important is their perceived probability of being dangerous and this can even be associated with completely legal behaviour" (Lianos 2000, 263). Nowhere is this more symbolically evident than in the term "foreign national," created to describe those who do not hold citizenship or permanent residency in Canada, and in the requirement that permanent residents returning to Canada carry an "identification card" to prove their immigration status. As NAWL (2001, 4) argues, such a move "symbolically declares that immigrants will remain 'the Other' in Canada." The Coalition for a Just Immigration and Refugee Policy (2001, 11) asserts that the identification cards are "a patronizing mechanism that serves to stigmatize and control people." Other immigration advocates agree, stating that both proposals are highly alienating, promote racist beliefs, and send the message that noncitizens deserve less than equal treatment (CCR 2001; Vancouver Association of Chinese Canadians 2001).

The discourse of exclusion in Bill C-11 helps to reconstitute the authority of the nation-state by reaffirming the stability of national boundaries at a time when it is being heavily challenged by global economic forces. The belief that "illegal" immigrants are threatening Canada's sovereignty is used to justify punitive treatment as a necessary measure to manage those who are "abusing" Canada's immigration system. This punitive drift within immigration has been given legitimacy and has been made possible through the politicization and racialization of immigration issues, which gives anti-immigrant sentiments a public forum, and through processes of exclusion, which demonize immigrants of colour for creating Canada's social problems. Both sets of racist ideas and strategies result from a view of immigrants as either "good" or "bad" and from a nation that is composed of "us" and "them." These views thus create the necessary conditions to argue for and justify a more restrictive and exclusionary immigration policy that imposes harsher penalties on its violators.

The Rise of Anti-Immigrant Sentiments

Bill C-11 is the culmination of a series of ongoing reforms and amendments that took place in the last two decades. As the successor to the 1975 *Immigration Act*, Bill C-11 represents a different era of immigration policy making.

The 1975 *Act* resulted from a perceived need for "race-neutral" categories of eligibility and nondiscriminatory treatment of immigrants and is considered liberal in its approach.[20] Bill C-11, on the other hand, emerged out of the ongoing racialization of immigration, whereby immigrants of colour have come to be viewed as threats not only to the social, cultural, and linguistic order of the nation, but also to the security of the nation. These anti-immigrant sentiments are not new and have been present in various forms during previous immigration debates. However, in recent times, they have come to occupy a greater role in framing immigration debates as a result of the negative representation of immigrants of colour by the media elites in Canada and the reorientation of immigration policy making toward a conservative agenda, illustrated by the views of the Reform/Canadian Alliance Party (Abu-Laban 1998; Teitelbaum and Winter 1998). Moreover, the nature of immigration reforms in the 1990s suggests that these sentiments now have the official backing of the state.

Ivan Light (1996, 59) describes attitudes as being anti-immigrant when there is a call for "a reduction of immigration, the speedy end of immigration, the rapid and entire cultural assimilation of immigrants, or the expulsion of at least some of the existing immigrant population from the host society." He argues that these sentiments arise when there is a belief that immigration no longer serves the interests of the nation economically and politically and has become "a bad deal for the country" because of the racial and cultural costs of immigration (Light 1996, 62). Cynthia Wright (2000, 2) claims that underlying these sentiments are fears about immigrants that give rise to a particular anti-immigrant discourse:

> "[W]e" are being taken over by uneducated, undocumented, non-English-speaking, non-white people who form criminal gangs, steal jobs and destroy the environment through their explosive fertility.

The racialization of immigration thus results in immigrants being constructed as subjects in need of containment, regulation, and control. Wright's study (2000, 4) of the portrayal of Somali refugee women in Toronto found that numerous myths about Somali women were being perpetuated in order to justify the call to limit immigration and be more selective about who gets in.

An examination of the media and political discourse over the arrival of Chinese migrants in 1999 highlights how many of these themes were repeatedly echoed that summer. Politicians argued that Canada should exclude citizens of certain countries from being able to seek refugee status,[21] and accusations were made that the migrants were creating an excessive burden on Canada's welfare system,[22] that many of them were not "genuine" refugees,[23] and that Canada's immigration controls clearly were not tough enough.[24] Charles Campbell's argument (2000, 4) that Canada's failed immigration programs have resulted in a costly infrastructure that has allowed the least desirable people into the country is consistent with the view that immigrants of colour are "causing the destruction of Canadian lives." Rather than challenge these myths, the Liberal government validated such ideas by introducing a revamped *Immigration Act* to "safeguard Canada's humanitarian tradition toward genuine refugees but deter queue-jumpers and *crooks* (my emphasis)."[25] Similar remarks had been made when Tamils and Sikhs arrived on the shores of Canada a decade earlier, igniting the belief that a "crisis" was present, that Canada's refugee process was under attack, and that immediate reforms was necessary (Creese 1992, 129). Public acceptance of immigration reforms was possible because refugees were constructed as "queue-jumpers" or "illegal immigrants" while discussions regarding Canada's humanitarian obligations were sidelined (Creese 1992, 130). Most recently, an Ontario Tory vying for the party's leadership argued that Ontario should be able to regulate its own immigration plan since the province was receiving "garbage" immigrants.[26]

Through the metaphors of war and disaster, these constructions and articulations of immigrants, when combined with official policies that confer negative labels upon noncitizens and force them to carry identification cards, can have devastating effects. The view of immigrants as the aggressors and Canada as the victim reasserts the relationship between immigrants and "Canadians" in antagonistic terms. Not only are immigrant activities challenged as not being law-abiding, but immigrants' very identities are constantly called into suspicion. The situation of undocumented or "illegal" migrants, particularly women and children, is made more precarious with every attempt by the government to control immigration flows. As a piece of legislation, Bill C-11 highlights the xenophobia that has been powerfully reinforced and amplified by the media and by politicians of all stripes. It has successfully amalgamated immigration, illegality, and criminality to create the ideal scapegoat: the "illegal," criminal immigrant. Under the guise of boosting national security and protecting the safety of Canadians, the legislated exclusion of migrants will only further exacerbate their already unequal status in Canada.

Although many advocates have challenged the anti-immigration rhetoric, it has not been an easy battle. The problem with countering anti-immigrant views is that one must try to formulate an argument for immigrant rights and interests without being accused of favouring an "open border" policy, which would result in one's ejection from the political debate altogether (Bosniak 1996, 571). Bonnie Honig (1998, 16) argues that the problem with framing immigration arguments in terms of issues of national interest is that xenophilic[27] and xenophobic attitudes are two sides of the same coin and hence fundamentally problematic:

[T]he liberal xenophilic deployment of the foreigner as the truest citizen (because the only truly consenting one) actually feeds the xenophobic back-lash against the nonconsenting immigrant – the illegal alien – to whom we supposedly do not consent and who does not consent to us. If this analysis is correct, then the iconic good immigrant who upholds American [or Canadian] liberal democracy is not accidentally or coincidentally partnered with the iconic bad immigrant who threatens to tear it down.

Wright (2000) concurs, claiming that focusing on the contributions of immigrants cannot sufficiently counter the deeply embedded sexist and racist assumptions found in anti-immigrant rhetoric. Like other authors (Takacs 1999), she suggests that until a fundamental rethinking of the immigration debate from an international perspective occurs, Canadian immigration policy makers' preoccupation with policing Canada's people and borders at the expense of the rights of undocumented migrants will continue unabated.

Demonizing Immigrants

The demonization of immigrants as "criminals" in Bill C-11 is a manifestation of anti-immigrant sentiments that lends validity to the offensive measures taken. Only by conflating immigrants of colour with crime is it possible to construct their "master status" as criminals and/or terrorists and therefore to justify the strong initiatives used to counteract their activities. Moreover, if immigrants' activities are regarded as criminal, then their treatment is depoliticized because it is transformed from an issue of race into an issue of law and order. It is much more difficult to be opposed to punitive strategies made in the name of safety than it is to oppose punitive treatment of a racial group. Thus any resistance is silenced.

Berlet and Lyons (2000) characterize demonizing strategies as a process that begins with marginalizing individuals or groups from mainstream society, such as being denied access to well-paying jobs in order to create an us/them, good/bad dynamic. Next, the dehumanization or objectification of people or persons occurs through negative labelling, such as the use of the term "foreign national." The basis for exercising dehumanizing practices is the belief that a particular group of people, here immigrants, is inferior or threatening. When the person or group is framed as evil and malevolent, the final step of demonization occurs (Berlet and Lyons 2000, 7). At this stage, it then becomes easier to rationalize the use of stereotypes, discriminatory acts, and even violence toward these individuals or groups (*ibid.*).

The demonization of specific "problem" populations through the use of the criminal justice system has a well-established track record. Roberts (1998) notes that, historically, crime was not just a legal category, but a socio-economic and political category used by authorities to repress immigrants. Criminologists suggest that creating demonized images to bolster government policies is experiencing renewed popularity among policy makers. For example, David Garland (1996) argues that in late modern society, Western democratic governments have been forced to acknowledge that attempts to control crime have not met with overwhelming success. As high crime rates became a social fact of modern life, the response was a shift in focus from the causes of crime to the effects of crime (Garland 1996). While governments were making relatively modest claims about the effectiveness of their crime control measures, politically there remained a need for governments to be seen as effective in containing the crime problem. One of the many strategies that governments adopted to reassert their power was to reposition themselves as being "tough" by embracing a punitive "law and order" agenda (*ibid.*, 460). Punitive policies allow governments to reclaim their power to govern by exploiting the insecurities of the governed. As Garland (*ibid.*) states,

> But together with their expressive or reductionist objectives, these "law and order" policies frequently involve a knowing and cynical manipulation of the symbols of state power and the emotions of fear and insecurity which give these symbols their potency. Such policies become particularly salient where a more general insecurity – deriving from tenuous employment and fragile social relations – is widely experienced and where the state is deemed to have failed in its efforts to deliver economic security to key social groups.

From this punitive approach, a criminology of the "other," of "essentialized difference," develops whereby criminals are defined as having particular social and racial characteristics that are unlike "ours," which then gives rise to the view of them as particularly dangerous. It is a criminology "which trades in images, archetypes and anxieties, rather than in careful analyses and research findings" (Garland 1996, 461). Hallsworth (2000, 146) adds that while the "criminology of the other" is irrational because its very basis owes little to rational thought or calculation, it has nonetheless been useful in raising the level and degree of punishment directed toward populations defined as deviant.

This analysis offers a powerful explanation not only for the particular shape and trajectory that certain criminal justice policies have taken in the last several decades, but also for the punitive dimensions of immigration provisions in Bill C-11. Examining the enforcement provisions of Bill C-11 in the context of a "criminology of the other" makes it clear that the process of blaming and punishing immigrants, particularly undocumented migrants, creates a "suitable enemy" to blame for the problems of society (Christie 1986). Few strategies are as effective as processes of criminalization for reinforcing an ideology of "us and them," with the immigrant – usually understood as nonwhite, poor, and/or female – occupying the status of the outsider (Bannerji 2000). The racialized, gendered, and class-based nature of this marking ensures that access to the "Canadian" identity as it is constructed and defined is far from equal. Casting immigrants in the role of the "other" has been an effective means of addressing public fears and insecurities about immigrants "terrorizing" Canadians, taking jobs away from Canadians, and overtaxing the welfare system. Increasing the degree of punishment to offenders allows immigration authorities to reclaim their ability to secure Canada's borders and to argue that the integrity of the immigration system has not been compromised by "illegal" migrants. It also allows governments to demonstrate their power through the use of force. Such has been the case in the United States, where the use of detention to address the problem of "illegal" immigrants is increasingly the de facto response (Welch 1999; Simon 1998) and where the Immigration and Naturalization Service (INS) uses delinquency and criminality to legitimate the perpetual surveillance and control of the immigrant population (Su 2000).

The punitive measures adopted in Bill C-11 become intelligible when we locate them in our need to find a "suitable enemy" for whom we can blame all our failures and insecurities. Demonizing immigrants grants legitimacy to punitive immigration policies since these policies are premised on the view of offenders as "criminals," "bogus claimants," and "queue-jumpers." It is within this context that racism finds its most potent articulations. Beisel (1994, 18) notes that immigrants are often "containers for projected lawlessness." Regarded as the "infectious other," they have served an important function for what he calls "group poisons," which historically have included supposed associations between cholera and the Irish, bubonic plague and the Chinese, and polio and the Italians. Today immigrants of colour are the scapegoat containers for a variety of economic and cultural insecurities. As Sherene Razack (1999, 173) argues, the national story that Canada likes to tell is the one where "generous, legitimate Canadians welcome genuine refugees and construct a wonderful, racially and culturally diverse society which is undermined by illegal immigrants as well as by citizens of colour who are disloyal to the nation." Bill C-11 demonstrates how "illegal" immigrants have become our "poison" containers. Racialized, undocumented immigrants' "violation" of Canadian values and ethics demonstrates all that is "wrong" with society and in need of fixing. Thus Canada the "good" is cast in juxtaposition to the "bad," criminal immigrant. This construction of a "suitable enemy" is made possible through a logic of exclusion that is founded on "common sense" criteria such as criminality. Buttressed by anti-immigrant sentiments, which hold that immigrants are "undeserving," inferior, and potentially "dangerous," the process of demonizing immigrants as "enemies" of the state and punishing them for violating the rules of immigration completes the fantasy that "we" are now safe from "them."

Conclusion

With Bill C-11 immigration has been redefined as a matter of security akin to that of organized crime and terrorism at both the level of discourse and in terms of the regulatory measures imposed. While the government claims to be taking a balanced approach, it is unclear how this has been achieved since the increased penalties for "illegal" migration have not been countered by greater protection to guard against the victimization of migrants. Instead, penal and police practices have been applied in a focused and exacting manner against "illegal" migrants, as evidenced by the treatment of the Chinese migrants. The end result of framing immigration debates in terms of the dangers posed by migrants is the criminalization of all immigrants, who are then constructed as potential suspects and become the targets of immigration authorities. Their continued surveillance and control by the state is authorized by immigrants' overwhelming "threat" to the safety of the nation. Through the metaphors of war, disaster, and crisis, repressive state responses to immigration have been normalized.

Bill C-11 is a clear response to the tensions emerging from the globalization of the market economy, which requires that nation-states reprioritize the relationship between the political and the economic (Takacs 1999, 592). As globalization challenges the sovereignty of the nation, Bill C-11 attempts to reassure citizens of their place in the nation by reconstructing and bolstering the image of the "illegal, criminal" immigrant as the outsider. Like previous immigration acts, it demonstrates how "membership" in the national family is not equally available to all. Exclusionary mechanisms have consistently limited and continue to limit who is considered part of the national family. The Liberal government's willingness to enact legislation that promotes a racist and xenophobic agenda confirms the unequal position immigrant communities occupy. As a consequence of such legislation, migrants and refugees seeking to enter Canada will be forced to engage in more clandestine and "illegal" acts in order to escape their desperate situations.

Notes

1 This is not to suggest that previous eras of immigration policy making were more inclusive or less racist. On the contrary, immigration scholars have noted how immigration legislation in the first half of the twentieth century included some of the most exclusionary provisions in Canadian immigration policy making, aimed directly at specific racial and ethnic groups. See Kelley and Trebilcock 1998, Roberts 1998, and Avery 1995.

2 The main ideas of neoliberalism include unfettered access to the marketplace, reducing social services, deregulation, privatization, and an emphasis on individual responsibility. See Brodie 1997.

3 *Singh* v. *Minister of Employment and Immigration*, [1985] 1 S.C.R. 177.

4 These two cases involved the killings of Vivi Leimonis and police officer Todd Baylis. O'Neil "Tiger" Grant was found not guilty in the killing of Leimonis, whereas Clinton Gayle, who had been ordered to be deported twice, was convicted of killing Baylis. See A. Wilson-Smith, "A Few, Too Modest Reforms," *Maclean's,* 18 July 1994.

5 For the purposes of this paper, this phrase refers to right-wing populism, represented most clearly in Canada by the Reform and Canadian Alliance Parties, now part of the Conservative Party of Canada. Harrison and Johnston (1996, 161) note that "populist movements and parties typically exhibit a high degree of political alienation from the traditional power bloc and political elites."

6 In 2000, 16 percent of immigrants were from China, 11 percent from India, 6 percent from Pakistan, and 4 percent from the Philippines, for a total of just over 87,000 immigrants out of an overall total 227,209 immigrant arrivals. See Citizenship and Immigration Canada 2001.

7 Ian Austin, "Immigrants Must Speak in English or en français," *Vancouver Province,* 5 April 2002.

8 "Good First Step," *Toronto Star,* 28 February 2002.

9 Citizenship and Immigration Canada. *Bill C-11 – Immigration and Refugee Protection Act: Overview.* June 2001.

10 Citizenship and Immigration Canada. *Immigration and Refugee Protection Introduced.* 21 February 2001.

11 Bill C-11 includes a statement of key principles for the administration of immigration and refugee programs. Some of these principles include respect for the multicultural character of Canada, support for the development of English and French linguistic minority communities, and the notion that new immigrants and Canadian society have mutual obligations. Citizenship and Immigration Canada. *Backgrounder #1: Changes from Bill C-31.* March 2001.

12 Citizenship and Immigration Canada. *Bill C-11 – Immigration and Refugee Protection Act: Overview.* June 2001.

13 See briefs by the National Association of Women and the Law (NAWL), the Canadian Council for Refugees (CCR), and the United Nations High Commission for Refugees (UNHCR).

14 Vatican. *The Solidarity of the Church with Migrants and Itinerant People.* Rome, 2000.

15 Schlein, Lisa. "UN rights report criticizes Canada for treating migrants like criminals," *Canadian Press,* 12 April 2001.

16 See briefs by the Coalition for a Just Immigration and Refugee Policy, the National Association of Women and the Law (NAWL), the Getting Landed Project, the African Canadian Legal Clinic, and the United Nations High Commission for Refugees (UNHCR).

17 "Officials recommend migrants remain in custody," *CBC Online,* 2 September 1999; "Department seeks more teeth to detain migrants," *CBC Online,* 23 September 1999.

18 Schlein, Lisa. "UN rights report criticizes Canada for treating migrants like criminals," *Canadian Press,* 12 April 2001. See also "Chinese migrants denied due process, critics charge," *CBC Online,* 5 November 1999.

19 Of the almost 600 migrants who arrived in the summer of 1999, 234 have been deported back to China. While 444 refugee hearings were conducted, only 24 refugees were approved. See "Chinese boat migrants removed from Canada aboard commercial airline," *Canadian Press Newswire,* 13 October 2000.

20 This view of the 1975 *Immigration Act* has been challenged by critical immigration scholars who contend that while the *Act* did not directly discriminate against particular racial and ethnic groups, the outcome of the point system nonetheless resulted in differential access to immigration. See Thobani 2000 and Jakubowski 1997.

21 "Chinese stowaways faced deportation in US, now facing refugee process in Canada," *Canadian Press Newswire,* 5 January 2000.

22 "Four ships and counting" *British Columbia Report,* 13 September 1999.

23 Bauer, W. "The new arrivals: migrants, refugees or frauds?" *Behind the Headlines* 57, 1 (Fall 1999): 12-19.

24 Bauer, W. "A time for tough measures: our policy plays into the hands of those who traffic in human lives" *Maclean's,* 23 August 1999.

25 "Liberals introduce tough new immigration act to crack down on people smugglers, serious criminals," *Canadian Press Newswire*, 6 April 2000.
26 "Tory Supporter Targets 'Garbage' Immigrants," *Toronto Star*, 6 February 2002.
27 Refers to the attraction to the strange or foreign as opposed to "xenophobic," which is the fear or hatred of the strange or foreign.

References
Abu-Laban, Yasmeen. 1998. "Welcome/Stay Out: The Contradiction of Canadian Integration and Immigration Policies at the Millennium." *Canadian Ethnic Studies* 30, 3: 190-211.

African Canadian Legal Clinic [ACLC]. 2001. *Brief to the Legislative Review Secretariat.* <http://www.aclc.net/submissions/immigration_refugee_policy.html> (accessed January 2004).

Aikcn, Sharryn. 2001. *Comments on Bill C-11 Related to National Security and Terrorism.* Toronto: Centre for Refugee Studies, March.

Amnesty International. 2001. *Brief on Bill C-11.* March.

Arat-Koc, Sedef. 1999. "Neo-liberalism, State Restructuring and Immigration: Changes in Canadian Policies in the 1990s." *Journal of Canadian Studies* 34, 2: 31-56.

Avery, Donald. 1995. *Reluctant Host: Canada's Response to Immigrant Workers, 1896-1994.* Toronto: McClelland and Stewart.

Bannerji, H. 2000. *The Dark Side of the Nation: Essays on Multiculturalism, Nationalism, and Gender.* Toronto: Scholars' Press.

Behdad, A. 1998. "INS [Immigration and Naturalization Services] and Outs: Producing Delinquency at the Border." *Aztlan* 23, 1: 103-13.

Beisel, David. 1994. "Looking for Enemies, 1990-1994." *Journal of Psychohistory* 22, 1: 1-38.

Berlet, Chip, and Matthew Lyons. 2000. *Right-Wing Populism in America.* New York: Guilford Press.

Bosniak, Linda. 1996. "Opposing Prop. 187: Undocumented Immigrants and the National Imagination." *Connecticut Law Review* 28, 3: 555-619.

Brah, Avtar. 1996. *Cartographies of Diaspora: Contesting Identities.* New York: Routledge.

Brodie, Janine. 1997. "Meso-Discourses, State Forms and the Gendering of Liberal-Democratic Citizenship." *Citizenship Studies* 1, 2: 223-42.

Buchignani, N., and D. Indra. 1999. "Vanishing Acts: Illegal Immigration in Canada as a Sometimes Social Issue." In *Illegal Immigration in America,* edited by D. Haines and K. Rosenblum, 415-50. Westport, CT: Greenwood Press.

Campbell, Charles. 2000. *Betrayal and Deceit: The Politics of Canadian Immigration.* Vancouver: Jasmine Books.

Canadian Bar Association. 2002. "Submission on Immigration and Refugee Protection Regulations." Part 1 to 17. January.

Canadian Council for Refugees. 2000. "A Hundred Years of Immigration to Canada, 1900-1999: A Chronology Focusing on Refugees and Discrimination." <http://www.web.net/~ccr/history.html> (accessed January 2004).

–. 2001. "Bill C-11 Brief." March. <http://www.web.net/~ccr/c11brief.PDF> (accessed January 2004).

Caplan, Elinor. 2001. "Notes for Remarks to the Rotary Club of Toronto-Don Valley." Toronto, 18 January.

Castles, S., and M. Miller. 1994. *The Age of Migration: International Population Movements in the Modern World.* Basingstoke: Macmillan.

Christie, Nils. 1986. "Suitable Enemies." In *Abolitionism: Towards a Non-Repressive Approach to Crime,* edited by H. Bianchi and R. van Swaaningen. Amsterdam: Free University Press.

Citizenship and Immigration Canada. 2001. *Facts and Figures 2000: Immigration Overview.* Ottawa: Minister of Public Works and Government Services.

City of Toronto. 2001. "Submission to the Standing Committee on Citizenship and Immigration on Bill C-11." Toronto.

Coalition for a Just Immigration and Refugee Policy. 2001. "Position Paper on Bill C-11." Toronto.

Community Legal Education Ontario. 2001. "Bill C-11: Some Key Pieces." April. <http://www.cleo.on.ca> (accessed January 2004).

Cox, David, and Patrick Glenn. 1994. "Illegal Immigration and Refugee Claims." In *Immigration and Refugee Policy: Australia and Canada Compared*, edited by H. Adelman et al. Toronto: University of Toronto Press.

Creese, Gillian. 1992. "The Politics of Refugees in Canada." In *Deconstructing A Nation*, edited by V. Satzewich, 123-43. Halifax: Fernwood Publishing.

Doty, Roxanne Lynn. 1996. "The Double-Writing of Statecraft: Exploring State Responses to Illegal Immigration." *Alternatives* 21: 171-89.

Frideres, James. 1996 "Canada's Changing Immigration Policy: Implications for Asian Immigrants." *Asian and Pacific Migration Journal* 5: 449-70.

Garcia y Griego, Manuel. 1994. "Canada: Flexibility and Control in Immigration and Refugee Policy." In *Controlling Immigration: A Global Perspective*, edited by W. Cornelius, P. Martin, and J. Hollifield, 117-40. Stanford: Stanford University Press.

Garland, David. 1996. "The Limits of the Sovereign State." *British Journal of Criminology* 36, 4: 445-71.

Getting Landed Project. 2001. *Too Many Missing Pieces: A Brief in Response to Bill C-11*. March. <http://www.cpj.ca/getting_landed/docs/c11brief.pdf> (accessed January 2004).

Haigh, Richard, and Jim Smith. 1998. "Return of the Chancellor's Foot? Discretion in Permanent Resident Deportation Appeals under the *Immigration Act*." *Osgoode Hall Law Journal* 36, 2: 245-92.

Hallsworth, Simon. 2000. "Rethinking the Punitive Turn: Economies of Excess and the Criminology of the Other." *Punishment and Society* 2, 2: 145-60.

Harrison, Trevor, and Bill Johnston. 1996. "Special Interests and/or New Right Economics?" *Canadian Review of Sociology and Anthropology* 33, 2: 159-80.

Hassan-Gordon, Tariq. 1996. "Canada's Immigration Policy: Detention and Deportation of Non-Europeans." Anti-Colonial Action Alliance, 14 September, <http://www.hartford-hwp.com/archives/44/032.html> (accessed January 2004).

Hayter, Teresa. 2001. "Open Borders: The Case against Immigration Controls." *Capital and Class* 75: 149-56.

Hintjens, H.M. 1992. "Immigration and Citizenship Debates: Reflections on Ten Common Themes." *International Migration* 30, 1: 5-17.

Honig, Bonnie. 1998. "How Foreignness 'Solves' Democracy's Problems." *Social Text* 16, 3: 1-27.

Jakubowski, L.M. 1997. *Immigration and the Legalization of Racism*. Halifax: Fernwood.

Kelley, Nanette, and Michael Trebilcock. 1998. *The Making of the Mosaic: A History of Canadian Immigration Policy*. Toronto: University of Toronto Press.

Kobayashi, Audrey. 1995. "Challenging the National Dream: Gender Persecution and Canadian Immigration Law." In *Nationalism, Racism and the Rule of Law*, edited by P. Fitzpatrick, 61-73. Aldershot: Dartmouth.

Laquian, Aprodicio, et al. 1998. "Asian Immigration and Racism in Canada: A Search for Policy Options." In *The Silent Debate: Asian Immigration and Racism in Canada*, edited by A. Laquian et al., 3-28. Vancouver: Institute of Asian Research.

Law Union of Ontario. 2001. "Submissions Re: Bill C-11." <http://www.lawunion.ca/briefs/BillC-11.shtml>.

Li, Peter. 2000. "The Racial Subtext of Canada's Immigration Discourse." Vancouver: Pan Canadian Lecture Series, November.

Lianos, M. 2000. "Dangerization and the End of Deviance: The Institutional Environment." *British Journal of Criminology* 40, 2: 261-78.

Light, Ivan. 1996. "Nationalism and Anti-Immigrant Movements." *Society* 33, 2: 58-63.

Malarek, Victor. 1987. *Haven's Gate: Canada's Immigration Fiasco*. Toronto: Macmillan.

Marchi, Sergio. 1995. "Speech: Tougher Tools for Deporting Criminals." *Canadian Speeches* 9, 5 (August/September).

Maytree Foundation. 2001. *Brief to the Senate Committee on Social Affairs, Science and Technology regarding Bill C-11, Immigration and Refugee Protection Act.* Toronto, October.

Maytree Foundation. 2002. *Brief to the Standing Committee on Citizenship and Immigration Regarding Proposed Immigration and Refugee Protection Regulations.* January.

Mohamed, Hamdi, and Harry Kits. 2002. *The Getting Landed Project – Protecting the Unprotected: Submission to the House of Commons Standing Committee on Citizenship and Immigration.* February.

National Association of Women and the Law [NAWL]. 2001. *Brief on the Proposed Immigration and Refugee Protection Act* (Bill C-11). April.

Noorani, Arif, and Cynthia Wright. 1995. "They Believed the Hype: The Liberals Were Elected as 'the Friend of the Immigrant': A Year Later, They're Fanning the Flames of Crime Hysteria with Their New Pals, the Tabloids and Preston Manning." *This Magazine* 28, 5 (December/January): 29-32.

Razack, Sherene. 1998. *Looking White People in the Eye.* Toronto: University of Toronto Press.

–. 1999. "Law and the Policing of Bodies of Colour in the 1990s." *Canadian Journal of Law and Society* 14, 1: 159-84.

Roberts, Barbara. 1998. *Whence They Came: Deportation from Canada, 1900-1935.* Ottawa: University of Ottawa Press.

Robinson, W.G. 1983. *Illegal Migrants in Canada: A Report to the Honourable Lloyd Axworthy, Minister of Employment and Immigration.* Ottawa: Employment and Immigration Canada.

–. 1984. "Illegal Immigrants in Canada: Recent Developments." *International Migration Review* 18: 474-85.

Simmons, Alan. 1998. "Globalization and Backlash Racism in the 1990s: The Case of Asian Immigration to Canada." In *The Silent Debate: Asian Immigration and Racism in Canada,* edited by A. Lacquian et al., 29-50. Vancouver: Institute of Asian Research.

Simon, Jonathan. 1998. "Refugees in a Carceral Age: The Rebirth of Immigration Prisons in the United States." *Public Culture* 10, 3: 577-607.

Standing Committee on Citizenship and Immigration. 2001. *Hands Across the Border: Working Together at Our Shared Border and Abroad to Ensure Safety, Security and Efficiency.* December.

Su, Julie. 2000. "The INS [Immigration and Naturalization Services] and the Criminalization of Immigrant Workers." In *States of Confinement: Policing, Detention and Prisons,* edited by J. James, 245-57. New York: St. Martin's Press.

Szonyi, Michael. 2000. "China: The Years Ahead." *International Journal* 55, 3: 475-84.

Takacs, Stacy. 1999. "Alien-Nation: Immigration, National Identity and Transnationalism." *Cultural Studies* 13, 4: 591-620.

Teitelbaum, Michael, and Jay Winter. 1998. *A Question of Numbers: High Migration, Low Fertility and the Politics of National Identity.* New York: Hill and Wang.

Thobani, Sunera. 2000a. "Nationalizing Canadians: Bordering Immigrant Women in the Late Twentieth Century." *Canadian Journal of Women and the Law* 12: 279-312.

–. 2000b. "Closing Ranks: Racism and Sexism in Canada's Immigration Policy." *Race and Class* 42, 1: 35-55.

United Nations High Commissioner for Refugees. 2001. *Comments on Bill C-11.* Ottawa, March.

Vancouver Association of Chinese Canadians. 2001. *Presentation to the Parliamentary Standing Committee on Citizenship and Immigration: Vancouver Hearing on Bill C-11.* 2 April.

Welch, Michael. 1999. *Punishment in America: Social Control and the Ironies of Imprisonment.* Thousand Oaks, CA: Sage Publications.

Wright, Cynthia. 2000. "Nowhere at Home: Gender, Race and the Making of Anti-immigrant Discourse in Canada." *Atlantis* 24, 2: 1-9.

3
Crime, Copyright, and the Digital Age
Steven Penney

States have long imposed criminal penalties for copyright infringement. The significance of these penalties, however, has traditionally paled in comparison to civil remedies. Copyright violation was viewed primarily as a wrong affecting private, commercial interests. Criminal prosecutions were rare and typically resulted in modest, noncustodial punishments.

This may be changing. The computer revolution has altered the practical landscape of copyright protection. The digitization[1] of copyrighted works, including text, music, and video, has dramatically increased the efficiency of unauthorized copying. Infringers can produce thousands of perfect copies of copyrighted works at little cost. The emergence and rapid proliferation of the Internet has compounded the problem immensely. The Internet allows copyrighted material to be distributed instantaneously and globally, again at nominal cost.

Copyright owners have attempted to combat these threats in numerous ways: They have sued the providers and users of online file-sharing networks; they have developed technological barriers to unauthorized copying; and they have lobbied governments to strengthen legal protections. As part of the latter strategy, copyright owners have pressed legislatures to adopt more comprehensive and punitive criminal sanctions for infringement. They have also encouraged police and prosecutors to use criminal copyright law more liberally.

The purpose of this chapter is to describe and evaluate efforts to criminalize copyright law in the digital era. I begin by relating the history of criminal copyright legislation and enforcement in the United States and Canada. This history reveals a longstanding legislative and administrative reluctance to impose criminal punishments on copyright infringers. It also shows, however, that in recent decades legislatures have become more willing, in the face of new technological threats and industry pressure, to expand the scope and severity of criminal copyright offences. This has culminated in two novel responses to the threat of digitization: the criminalization of noncommercial infringement and the prohibition (enforced by civil and criminal sanctions) of circumventing copy-protection technology.

I then explore the impact of digitization on the economics of copyright enforcement, describing the weakening of civil enforcement mechanisms wrought by digitization and canvassing the normative debate surrounding the appropriate scope of copyright protection for digital works. I note that the extent of copyright protection on the ground depends heavily on the availability and efficacy of remedies and argue that criminal law principles should play a prominent role in determining the extent to which these remedies are criminalized.

Next I attempt to articulate limiting principles for the application of criminal penalties to copyright infringement. Here I canvass moral theories of criminalization, including approaches grounded on analogy, consensus, and harm. While these theories generate useful insights, especially on the interaction between law and shared social norms, none provide a compelling argument for or against the criminalization of copyright infringement. In this section, I also turn to economic analysis. The standard economic model of crime predicts that optimal deterrence can be achieved by adjusting enforcement and punishment levels. Econometric and socio-legal research reveals, however, that under certain conditions deterrence may not be achievable. I argue that this is likely to be the case for certain types of copyright crime, including noncommercial, online file sharing and technological circumvention. This failure of deterrence results from strategic interactions often associated with digital copyright infringement, including low visibility, widespread disobedience, risk aversion, substitution effects, and most important, disjunction between criminal punishments and social norms. Under these conditions, criminalization is likely to be ineffective and harmful.

In concluding, I recommend restraint regarding the expansion of criminal copyright law.

A Brief History of Criminal Copyright Legislation and Enforcement

Criminal punishments for copyright infringement[2] have been on the books for many decades.[3] But they have traditionally not played much of a role in copyright regulation. Infringement was generally considered a private, economic wrong – pursued by copyright owners through private lawsuits and remedied by injunctions, damages, and other civil remedies.[4] Legislatures geared criminal sanctions toward transient commercial entities not adequately deterred by civil remedies.[5] Consequently, criminal copyright offences generally required the prosecution to prove that infringement was wilful and motivated by profit.[6] And even when these requirements were met, infringement was not considered a serious offence: Criminal codes provided for only light punishments;[7] police did not make copyright infringers a high priority; and prosecutors were reluctant to proceed with charges.[8] And the few cases that did proceed typically resulted in lenient, noncustodial sentences, even when the conduct involved was egregious.[9]

Legislative attitudes toward infringement began to change in the 1970s. The growth of the record industry in the postwar decades had resulted in substantial increases in the piracy, counterfeiting, and bootlegging of music recordings.[10] Lobbying by the record and motion picture industries[11] prodded Congress to extend copyright protection to sound recordings;[12] loosen the *mens rea* requirement for all criminal copyright offences to capture financially motivated infringement not resulting in actual profit;[13] and increase fines for music and movie piracy.[14] Congress resisted pressure to impose felony penalties, however.[15] Copyright infringement, it reasoned, was "essentially an economic offence."[16]

This policy changed in 1982. Entertainment industry lobbyists argued strenuously that new copying technologies[17] were enabling unprecedented levels of piracy.[18] Congress responded by imposing felony penalties for the mass piracy of sound recordings and audiovisual works.[19] Legislators felt that existing misdemeanour penalties were not severe enough to deter large-scale, commercial infringement.[20]

Canada followed suit in 1988. In response to industry lobbying,[21] Parliament stiffened summary penalties and for the first time gave prosecutors the option of pursuing infringers by way of indictment.[22] Severe punishments, legislators contended, would send a signal to the courts that copyright infringement was a serious crime.[23]

The criminalization of copyright infringement continued with the dramatic expansion of personal computer use in the 1980s and 1990s. Computers permitted the perfect and virtually costless replication of copyrighted works in digital form.[24] Software publishers, whose products are necessarily produced in digital form, were the first to be affected.[25] Following the example of the entertainment industry, they lobbied hard for enhanced criminal penalties.[26] Congress responded in 1992 with legislation imposing felony penalties for mass piracy of all types of copyrighted works, including computer programs.[27] Legislators asserted that harsher penalties would spur law enforcement agencies and prosecutors to take copyright infringement more seriously.[28]

In the 1990s the spectacular growth of the Internet prompted further reforms to criminal copyright law. The first development was the *No Electronic Theft (NET) Act*,[29] which closed the "loophole" highlighted in *United States* v. *LaMacchia*.[30] David LaMacchia was a twenty-one-year-old MIT student who set up an electronic bulletin board on the Internet. The bulletin board enabled others to download popular copyrighted software programs without paying licencing fees to the copyright owners. Prosecutors alleged that the scheme had cost software publishers over $1 million in lost sales. The problem, however, was that LaMacchia neither sought nor derived any financial benefit from the scheme. His behaviour was therefore not captured by the copyright-offence provision, which required a motive of "commercial advantage or private financial gain."[31]

Prosecutors consequently charged him with violating the federal wire-fraud statute.[32] This legislation prohibits the use of interstate electronic communications to facilitate the fraudulent taking of property. Following the Supreme Court's decision in *Dowling* v. *United States*,[33] the court acquitted LaMacchia, finding that the legislation was not intended to protect intellectual property.

Software publishers were outraged by *LaMacchia* and pressed for a legislative response.[34] Congress obliged by enacting the *NET Act*. It expanded the definition of "financial gain" in the *Copyright Act*'s offence provision to include the "receipt, or expectation of receipt, of anything of value, including the receipt of other copyrighted works."[35] It also criminalized the copying of works having a total retail value of more than $1,000, even in the absence of financial motivation or benefit.[36] Responding in part to concerns that these changes would criminalize relatively harmless activity, Congress clarified that, in itself, evidence of copying is insufficient to establish wilful infringement.[37] But the precise meaning of wilfulness in this context is unclear.[38]

Canada never had a loophole to close. As mentioned, the *Copyright Act* has always permitted conviction for distribution "to such an extent as to affect prejudicially the owner of the copyright."[39] But as far as I have been able to determine, authorities have only very recently begun using this provision to prosecute noncommercial infringers.[40] In a case similar to *LaMacchia*, the Nova Scotia Court of Appeal interpreted this provision as covering the unauthorized, noncommercial uploading of copyrighted software to the Internet.[41]

The most recent extension of criminal copyright law was also motivated by the growth of the Internet and the increasing digitization of copyrighted works. In 1998 the US Congress enacted the controversial *Digital Millennium Copyright Act* (DMCA).[42] Passed in part to comply with international treaty obligations,[43] the DMCA prohibits the circumvention of copyright-protection systems. Such systems exist in the analog, real-space world.[44] But they are particularly prevalent in the digital realm. Just as digitization facilitates unauthorized copying and distribution, it also makes it easier to impose technological barriers to such activity.[45] Content providers are increasingly employing "trusted systems" to secure content against unauthorized use, copying, and distribution.[46] Movies encoded on DVDs,[47] for example, are protected by the Content Scrambling System (CSS).[48] The CSS encrypts DVD content so that it can be played only by licensed DVD players. But what can be encrypted can usually be decrypted.[49] Programmers have managed to "crack" the CSS and distribute software[50] allowing people to easily copy DVD movies, play them on unlicensed players, and distribute them over the Internet.[51] By banning this technology, the DMCA bolsters the copyright protection provided by code. Specifically, the DMCA prohibits: circumventing a "technological measure" controlling access to a copyrighted work;[52] trafficking in circumvention technology;[53] and tampering with copyright management information.[54] None of these provisions requires actual copyright infringement. People may violate the DMCA simply by unlocking an "electronic lock" to gain access to a work even if they do not subsequently infringe the copyright in that work – for example, by copying for the purposes of "fair use."[55] These provisions may be enforced by both civil[56] and criminal[57] sanctions. Criminal penalties are limited to persons acting "willfully and for purposes of commercial advantage or private financial gain."[58] Canada does not yet have an anticircumvention law, but the federal government is considering adopting one.[59]

Legislation, of course, tells only part of the story. As I have mentioned, justice-system officials have traditionally been reluctant to treat copyright infringement as a serious crime.[60] In part this has been a result of the relatively lenient penalties associated with copyright offences. Now that sentences have been increased, have officials changed their attitudes? The short answer is that it is too early to tell. There are signs that large-scale, commercial piracy is being taken more seriously.[61] Police raids against unlicensed CD, videocassette, and DVD copying operations have made headlines.[62] And governments are devoting more resources to combatting intellectual property crime.[63]

But efforts to stem noncommercial infringement have been at best sporadic. There have been a few high-profile arrests and convictions in *LaMacchia*-type cases. These cases involve people, often members of so-called "warez" piracy networks, who use web sites and bulletin boards to distribute software, movies, and video games that have been stripped of copy protection.[64] But such prosecutions have been rare and have typically resulted in modest, noncustodial sentences.[65] Despite the enhanced penalties now available, and continued pressure from the copyright lobby, law enforcement officials appear reluctant to view digital copyright pirates as "real" criminals.[66] As one prosecutor reported, "defendants tend to be young and without a profit motive, [and] they are more sympathetic than most criminal defendants."[67]

Copyright and the Digital Revolution

We can see, then, that despite the increasing breadth and severity of criminal copyright penalties, they remain a relatively marginal part of copyright enforcement on the ground. At this early stage of the digital era, copyright infringement is still viewed chiefly as a private, civil wrong. College students are much more likely to be arrested for smoking a joint than for downloading music files. We have, however, travelled some distance down the road of criminalization. The central concern of this chapter is to gauge whether we have travelled too far or not far enough. To begin answering this question, I will outline in greater detail the threat that digitization poses to copyright enforcement.

New technologies have always influenced copyright law.[68] Printing presses, piano rolls, motion pictures, record players, photocopiers, audio and video tape recorders, and other technologies have forced lawmakers to revise pre-existing conceptions of copyright.[69] In one sense, digitization is simply the latest novel technology. But even if it does not end up revolutionizing copyright law, it will clearly have (and already has had) a significant impact.[70] As I have mentioned, digital technology permits the easy, inexpensive, and perfect duplication of copyrighted works.[71] Equally important, it allows for the rapid, global, "one-to-many" distribution of that content through digital networks.[72] In short, digitization increases the technical quality of copyrighted content and reduces the cost of delivering it to consumers. In economic language, digitization dramatically reduces the fixed costs of copying and reduces the marginal costs of copying to (virtually) zero.[73] These efficiencies promise to spur economic growth, benefiting both producers and consumers of digital content.[74]

But digitization increases efficiency for illegal as well as legal markets. Economists would say that digitization renders the subjects of copyright more like perfect public goods. Public goods are both nonexcludable and nonrivalrous.[75] A good is nonexcludable if people can't be prevented from consuming it without paying for it.[76] It is nonrivalrous if one person's consumption does not reduce the amount or quality of the good available to others.[77] Under these conditions there is little incentive for production. One unit of a good will satisfy an infinite number of users at close to zero marginal cost. Thus, if we leave the production of a public good to the private market, "free riding" may result in underproduction.[78]

In their physically embodied forms, copyrighted works are not public goods. Books, CDs, and DVDs are excludable and rivalrous. Publishers can prevent people from using works without paying for them, and consumption diminishes the quantity of works available in the market. Once published, however, such works can be copied and distributed by people who do not have to incur the costs and risks borne by initial publishers.[79] If competition from subsequent copiers reduces the price to the marginal cost of production, then the initial publisher will have no incentive to distribute the work in the first place.[80] To ensure sufficient incentive, the law therefore gives initial publishers the protection of copyright. Copyright, in other words, substitutes legal excludability for physical excludability.[81]

Digitization weakens the material and legal barriers to copyright infringement. In the analog world, copying is expensive. Large-scale, commercial copying usually requires substantial investment. This in itself deters infringement. But it also makes infringement relatively easy to detect.[82] The equipment and personnel required for such operations render them visible and obvious.[83] Commercial infringers are also likely to have assets to pay damages awarded in civil-infringement actions.[84] It is not surprising, therefore, that policy makers traditionally believed that civil remedies were sufficient to deter all but the most judgment-proof infringers.

However, in the digital world civil enforcement may not be sufficient. Mass digital copying does not require significant investments in equipment or personnel.[85] As we saw in *LaMacchia*, one person of limited means can facilitate large-scale infringement. And as the Napster phenomenon reveals, people with personal computers, broadband Internet connections, and peer-to-peer file-sharing software can easily engage in piracy on a massive, global scale.[86] The low cost of copying technology also means that people may engage in large-scale infringement from noncommercial motives, most commonly for the opportunity to obtain free copyrighted works in return. This greatly increases the pool of potential infringers. Few noncommercial infringers, moreover, are likely to possess assets sufficient to satisfy a civil judgment.[87] The ease of Internet-based file sharing, moreover, may incline people to infringe copyright without giving much thought to the consequences.[88] Many of these people may not even believe that they are doing anything wrong.[89] Digitization, in short, is creating a large group of new copyright infringers who may be beyond the reach of conventional civil enforcement mechanisms.

What, if anything, should we do about this? Broadly speaking, there are two camps. Copyright minimalists assert that digitization should not result in the bolstering of copyright protection. There are numerous variations of this argument. For some, strong digital copyright protections threaten free expression and democratic participation.[90] Others contend that fair use rights should be buttressed in the digital environment by "fair access" rights that thwart attempts to "enclose" the public domain.[91] Still others maintain that digitization eliminates the need for copyright as an incentive for distribution and that for at least some types of works, copyright is not required to induce production.[92] In short, minimalists argue that innovation, economic growth, and creativity will flourish only if copyright protection is thin.[93]

Maximalists, in contrast, argue that these same objectives can be achieved only by strengthening and extending copyright protection to "every corner where consumers derive value from literary and artistic works."[94] This position is premised on the assumption that current copyright limitations exist only because it is too costly to enforce property rights against marginal users. Fair use, for example, is tolerated only because of the onerous transaction costs associated with detecting, controlling, and negotiating certain limited, unauthorized uses of copyrighted works.[95] Digitization, maximalists note, promises to decrease these costs dramatically.[96] Rights management systems give producers fine-grained control over the uses of content, enabling more perfect price discrimination and increasing production and overall efficiency.[97]

Evaluating the merits of these arguments is beyond the scope of this chapter. I do not therefore intend to subject substantive copyright law to a normative critique. I assume that copyright protection in the digital age should remain as extensive as it was in the analog era. My only concern is whether we should respond to the challenges of digital copyright with increased criminalization. But substance and procedure are not entirely separable. The scope of copyright protection on the ground turns not only on the substantive reach of copyright, but also on the availability and effectiveness of enforcement mechanisms. For instance, if policy militates against criminalization in a certain context, and there is no other effective means of protecting copyright, then practically speaking copyright will not be protected. If that is the case, so be it. Copyright crime is as much about criminal law as copyright law. Efforts to maintain the copyright status quo in the digital era should not automatically trump settled views regarding the limits of the criminal sanction. This does not mean that increased criminalization is always a bad idea or that the criminal law should remain immutable in the digital era. It does mean, however, that proposals to protect digital copyright through criminal sanctions should be scrutinized through the lens of criminal law as well as copyright law.

This begs the question of how to determine the appropriate scope of criminal liability. To begin, I should define what I mean by "criminal." There are several ways in which the law responds to violations of legal rights. It can treat violations as civil wrongs, regulatory offences, or crimes. There is considerable overlap between these categories.[98] Misconduct may also give rise to more than one form of liability.[99] For the purposes of this chapter, however, we can define crime as a publicly enforced legal wrong punishable by sanctions that include the possibility of imprisonment.[100] As I have discussed, all existing copyright offence provisions in Canada and the United States conform to this definition.

How then do we decide whether conduct warrants criminal punishment? We could take an extreme positivist position, defining crime as anything that the legislatures say is a crime. But if we want to be normative, this gets us nowhere.[101] First, we cannot assume that the outcomes of the legislative process are justifiable.[102] Second, there are aspects of copyright criminalization that have not yet been dealt with by legislatures, particularly in Canada.[103] And third, legislatures are not exclusively responsible for determining the practical scope of criminal copyright law. As I have already discussed, police, prosecutors, and courts have much to say about how criminal copyright offences are enforced "in action."[104]

To answer normative questions, we must canvass normative theories. There are two candidates. One approach is to consider criminalization as a deontological question: Is the behaviour so morally culpable that it is deserving of a criminal sanction? The second approach, which is utilitarian-economic, is to ask whether criminal punishment efficiently deters the behaviour.[105] I discuss each strategy in turn.

Normative Theories

The Moral Approach

As its name suggests, the moral approach conceives of crime as conduct deserving of moral opprobrium. A criminal sanction is characterized by the "judgement of community condemnation which accompanies and justifies its imposition."[106] Criminal acts, on this view, violate the fundamental values of the community. They are not simply punished for some instrumental purpose like deterrence. They are inherently *wrong*.[107] Admittedly, this conception is not without its ambiguities. Civil wrongs may induce moral disapproval, and crime encompasses a broad range of culpability. The moral approach maintains, however, that crime is categorically more condemnable than noncriminal legal wrongs.[108]

This approach works well enough in most cases. We have little difficulty deciding that a person who causes a serious car accident while severely drunk is more morally culpable, and more deserving of criminal punishment, than a person who causes a similar accident by driving slightly faster than is prudent. But how culpable is copyright infringement? The answer isn't self-evident – at least not to me. So we must explore techniques for defining infringement's moral status.

One strategy is to gauge the analogical fit between copyright infringement and behaviour that is uncontroversially criminal. Copyright is a species of intellectual property, so the obvious comparator is ordinary property. With few exceptions, we consider the unauthorized taking of ordinary property to be criminally culpable.[109] Some therefore contend that copyright infringement is morally equivalent to the theft of ordinary property.[110]

But is intellectual property truly analogous to ordinary property? This is a large and difficult question, requiring the resolution of fundamental controversies regarding the normative virtue of both intellectual property[111] and property rights generally.[112] Fortunately, I do not have to engage this debate here. I want only to show that the equation of copyright with ordinary property is contentious and that the moral status of infringement cannot therefore be determined by simple analogy. Copyright, like other forms of intellectual property, is subject to limitations that do not exist for ordinary property. It is granted for a limited term[113] and is circumscribed by the doctrines of "fair use"[114] and "first sale"[115] as well as by constitutional free-speech guarantees.[116] As Richard Posner puts it, copyright is an "incomplete" property right.[117] Courts, moreover, have resisted equating copyright violation with the theft of ordinary property.[118] The United States Supreme Court, for instance, has stated that copyright protects interests that are "carefully defined and carefully delimited" and "distinct from the possessory interest of the owner of simple 'goods, wares, [or] merchandise.'"[119] Copyright infringement, the Court thus concluded, "does not easily equate with theft, conversion, or fraud."[120]

There are also good normative arguments for limiting copyright. Ordinary property, as we have seen, is rivalrous. Since one person's consumption of a good makes it unavailable to others, we use strong property rights and the invisible hand of the market to allocate the good to its highest value use.[121] Being nonrivalrous, intellectual property does not need to be protected in the same fashion. Though physical media carrying copyrighted works may be taken from their owners, depriving them of their use, the underlying work cannot.[122] Copying does not diminish the quantity or quality of the work available to the author or others. We don't need copyright, in other words, to prevent overconsumption or efficiently allocate scarce resources. If we want authors to create, we may still need to provide an incentive, which is why we grant copyright in the first place.[123] But copyright may not have to be as extensive as ordinary property rights to provide that incentive.[124] Copyright can thus be viewed as a balance between the rights of authors and the rights of other members of society to access information.[125] This balance, we hope, achieves an optimal mix of incentive and dissemination.[126]

It turns out, therefore, that the uncontroversial moral intuition that "theft is wrong" cannot be readily translated to copyright infringement. We could, of course, take a view of copyright that plays up similarities between intellectual and ordinary property. We could discount judicial rhetoric, noting that it has been uttered in the context of interpreting legislation designed with tangible property in mind. We could point out limitations on ordinary property that balance owners' and community interests.[127] And we could argue, with considerable theoretical support, that robust property rights are needed to induce the production and dissemination of copyrighted works.[128] But we would still be left with the realization that viewing infringement as theft requires the making of contestable policy assumptions.

Even if we can't uncontroversially assert that copyright infringement is "theft" in the traditional sense, we might conclude nonetheless that it is morally culpable. Intellectual property *is* property after all, and unauthorized copying is in most contexts legally wrong. If the moral approach defines crime as conduct transgressing fundamental values, then we should consider whether people regard the sanctity of copyright as a fundamental value. As the Law Reform Commission of Canada puts it, criminal law should not be used for "things most people reckon not really wrong or, if wrong, merely trivial."[129] On this view, infringement should not be criminalized. Most legal commentators have concluded that, as a rule, copyright infringement is not culpable enough to justify criminal sanctions.[130] Courts have agreed, expressing reluctance to criminalize copyright infringement in the absence of clear legislative direction.[131]

Ordinary people seem to share this view, at least with respect to noncommercial infringement. Polls reveal, for example, that many people don't believe that downloading copyrighted music is stealing.[132] Not surprisingly, this attitude is more common among Internet users and music downloaders than in the general population.[133] But according to several surveys, a majority of Americans think that downloaders aren't doing anything wrong.[134] Downloading music is also an increasingly widespread activity. By the spring of 2001, 37 million Americans had retrieved music files from the Internet.[135] And the number is growing quickly, among virtually all demographic groups and among people with varying levels of online experience.[136] Such views, moreover, are not restricted to the online music phenomenon. People think that many types of copyright infringement are morally acceptable. As Jessica Litman observes, people "find it very hard to believe that there's really a law out there that says the stuff the copyright law says."[137]

It is tempting to conclude therefore that copyright infringement is not intrinsically wrongful. It is, according to the traditional distinction, *malum prohibitum*, not *malum in se*.[138] From this we could deduce that criminal sanctions are either inappropriate or justifiable on purely instrumental grounds. Such a conclusion, however, would ignore the fact that social norms are changeable. Though people may not currently believe that music downloading and other types of copyright infringement are wrong, this attitude could shift. There are many activities that people have only recently come to consider criminally culpable. Think of marital and "date" rape, spousal abuse, certain forms of environmental pollution, insider trading, and anticompetitive activity. Governments were slow to criminalize these behaviours because their benefits accrued to large or powerful segments of the population. Their costs, in contrast, were either highly distributed (and hence less visible) or borne by less powerful groups.

Copyright infringement shares many of these attributes. Its benefits flow to a broad segment of the population. Even noncommercial infringers profit by obtaining for free what they would otherwise have to pay for. The direct costs of infringement, in contrast, are borne only by producers of copyrighted works. Producers may not be a particularly vulnerable group, but they are dwarfed in number by consumers. If infringement leads to underproduction, then consumers may also be harmed. But this harm is indirect, intangible, and accumulative. It is much less visible than the harm caused by the theft of ordinary property. Equally important, almost everyone owns ordinary property. If the law fails to protect it against unauthorized takings (even when it is owned by big, impersonal corporations), then the security of our own property is threatened. Since few people own intellectual property, it is more difficult to comprehend (and easier to ignore) infringement's long-term economic consequences. It may be especially difficult in the digital era. The speed, anonymity, and intangibility of digital copying may encourage people to cast off norms governing their behaviour in real space.[139]

To summarize, there are good reasons to discount people's assessments of the morality of copyright infringement. The intuition that infringement isn't wrong corresponds with most people's immediate self-interest.[140] And the damage that infringement causes to long-term, collective interests is difficult to discern. So it is possible that public attitudes toward copyright infringement could change. Governments have instituted educational campaigns to convince people of the importance of intellectual property rights.[141] Criminalization may also play a role. Criminal law does not simply respond to prevailing values. It also plays a role in shaping social norms.[142] By decreeing minimum standards of behaviour, criminal law has an educative, moralizing, and socializing effect.[143] Whether the increasing criminalization of copyright is likely to cause more people to believe that copyright infringement is wrong is a question that I take up later. For the moment, I want only to establish that the current consensus that copyright infringement isn't morally culpable does not provide a sufficient reason to oppose criminalization.

If the moral status of copyright infringement cannot be determined by analogy or consensus, then where do we turn next? Liberal legal philosophy presents a possibility: the harm principle. Joel Feinberg offers the most elaborate articulation of this approach.[144] For Feinberg, criminalization is justified when it is necessary to prevent the risk of serious harm to others.[145]

Applying the harm principle to copyright crime is no easy matter. The first problem lies in defining legally relevant harm. For Feinberg, it is an unjustifiable invasion of a person's interests.[146] Copyright infringement is unjustifiable because it violates a legal rule. It also violates a cognizable proprietary interest.[147] But how do we decide whether this harm is sufficiently "serious" to warrant criminalization? Feinberg suggests that we consider three factors: the magnitude of the harm, the probability of its occurrence, and the social value of the conduct creating the risk of harm.[148] For copyright infringement, each of these factors is problematic. Infringement may harm the economic interests of copyright owners. Calculating the probability and magnitude of harm, however, is more difficult than is the case for ordinary property. When ordinary property is unlawfully taken, the owner's economic loss is both certain and easily quantifiable. This is not always the case for copyright infringement. Unauthorized copying will only result in economic loss when it deprives the owner of revenue. If the copier would not have been willing to pay the owner's price for the work, then there is no loss.[149] In some circumstances, moreover, infringement may increase sales of legal copies of copyrighted works. This may result from an "exposure effect," where advertising or sampling from unauthorized copies induces sales of legitimate copies.[150] There is some evidence, for example, that peer-to-peer music sharing may increase spending on legitimate works.[151] Legitimate sales may also be encouraged by "network effects," which arise when "the value consumers place on a good is a function of the number of individuals who use the good."[152] It has been suggested, for instance, that widespread illegal copying of certain word-processing programs has increased sales of legitimate copies.[153]

Even if infringement generally constitutes a net harm to copyright owners, we must also consider its benefits to society as a whole. This includes the private interests of copiers. More important, it also includes the public interest served by the dissemination of content. In many cases, dissemination is probably best served by enforcing copyright.[154] After all, copyright gives owners a healthy incentive to create new works and distribute them as widely as possible. By reducing the number and quality of works available for consumption, infringement may thus constitute a net harm to society. In some circumstances, however, enforcement may inhibit dissemination. Some have argued, for instance, that by unbundling production from distribution, digitization diminishes the incentive required to disseminate musical recordings, thereby eliminating the need for copyright protection.[155] Feinberg admits that the harm principle cannot be applied straightforwardly in circumstances calling for this type of interest balancing.[156] But he offers little guidance on how to determine whether infringement is a net harm or whether any such harm is so morally serious that it warrants criminalization.[157]

Lastly, even if we decide that copyright infringement causes serious harm, either in general or in a specific context, it is by no means certain that criminalization is necessary to prevent it. According to Feinberg, criminalization is only justified when there is no other means of preventing the harm "that is equally effective at no greater cost to other values."[158] This approach recognizes that criminalization entails profound social costs, both private and public, and should therefore be used reluctantly and with restraint.[159] The harms posed by copyright infringement may in many cases be limited by noncriminal mechanisms, including technological protection, civil remedies, and compulsory licensing schemes.[160]

The harm principle, then, provides little support for the criminalization of copyright. But neither does it emphatically reject it. The conceptual tools that Feinberg provides are not refined enough to discern whether infringement's harms justify criminal punishment. At best, we can say that like other iterations of the moral approach, the harm principle preaches skepticism toward the criminalization of copyright infringement. The harm principle does improve upon other morality-based approaches, however, in recognizing that assessing the merits of criminalization requires a careful balancing of competing interests. In this it resembles economic theories that attempt a more thoroughgoing calculation of the costs and benefits of criminalization.[161]

To summarize, the moral approach cannot tell us whether the criminalization of copyright infringement is a good idea. It certainly establishes that infringement is not self-evidently or uncontroversially culpable. It also reveals the existence of social norms tolerating some forms of infringement. It does not demonstrate, however, that criminalizing infringement is itself morally unjustifiable.

The Economic Approach

Though it is by no means novel,[162] the economic approach to criminal law has traditionally played a fairly marginal role in mainstream criminal law theory.[163] But there is reason to think that economic theory might be useful in determining the appropriate scope of criminal copyright law. As we have already seen, lawmakers have tended to view copyright crime through the lens of deterrence – the prime mover in economic analyses of crime.[164] The primary argument for copyright offences, after all, is that they are needed to deter potential infringers who are insufficiently threatened by civil remedies.[165]

Economic analysis posits that potential wrongdoers weigh the benefits of crime against the probability and magnitude of punishment.[166] Governments may therefore increase deterrence (and reduce crime) by increasing the quantity and quality of law enforcement and the severity of sanctions.[167] Each of these interventions is costly, however. Reducing crime to the efficient level requires setting the penalty at a value equal to the external, "social costs" of the crime,[168] with an amount added to account for the fact that not all crime will be detected. The *ex ante* expected cost of the crime to the potential wrongdoer should therefore equal the cost that the crime imposes on society.[169]

There are a number of circumstances, however, in which optimal deterrence is difficult to achieve. An important example is low-visibility crime. When it is difficult for police to collect evidence of illegality, people (correctly) perceive that the probability of detection is minimal. Compliance is accordingly low.[170] Of course, economic theory provides a solution: inflating the penalty.[171] If detection is minimal, then severe punishments are required to maintain optimal deterrence.

Unfortunately, empirical research has cast a cloud over this theoretical model. It turns out that in deciding whether to commit a crime, most people give more weight to the certainty of punishment than its severity.[172] Certainty and severity, in other words, are not proportional. This is a consequence of the general social stigma attaching to criminal conviction and, more specifically, its negative impact on access to the labour market.[173] This effect is exacerbated for individuals with large investments in social conventionality.[174] For "ordinary," middle-class individuals – who have so much to lose from accusation, prosecution, and conviction – the quantum of punishment may at best be an afterthought. Tax evasion research confirms, for example, that most taxpayers are highly averse to the risk of criminal exposure.[175]

Sociological and econometric studies also suggest that when the severity of punishment is out of proportion with social norms, sanctions are less likely to be enforced. Police, prosecutors, and courts exercise considerable discretion in applying legislative sanctions.[176] When punishments are viewed as disproportionate to culpability, justice-system officials find ways not to impose them.[177] This "inverse sentencing" phenomenon may result from a variety of practices:[178] Police may devote little energy to detection; prosecutors may drop or reduce charges; judges may narrow the ambit of offence and punishment provisions; and juries may be reluctant to convict.[179] Researchers have observed these effects in the context of a wide variety of offences.[180]

I have argued that norms are unreliable indicators of intrinsic morality. Put simply, they are too changeable. Moreover, criminal law itself plays an important role in shaping them.[181] But norms are not determined by law. They have an independent impact on how people respond to legal prescriptions.[182] Shared social norms influence behaviour in two ways. First, they help to shape our internal moral codes: our sense of obligation to abide by certain behavioural rules.[183] Second, they form the basis for informal community sanctions: the stigma and other social consequences that flow from norm-offending behaviour even when conduct is not labelled criminal or when criminal justice officials do not apprehend, convict, or punish the wrongdoer.[184]

In most cases, criminal conduct also violates social norms. However, if the gap between law and norms is too great, the law is less likely to be obeyed.[185] People will not internalize legal prescriptions as subjective morality, and disobedience will not result in informal social punishment. This is the other side of the deterrence coin. People obey the law not only because the costs of official sanctions outweigh the benefits of crime, but also because they believe that crime is wrong and fear that wrongdoing will incur social ignominy. If there is a widespread belief that a crime isn't wrong, then it will be more difficult to deter people from committing it.[186]

Widespread disobedience may also overwhelm the capacity of law enforcement officials to respond even if they are inclined to do so. As a consequence, the system loses its "capacity to project a credible enforcement threat."[187] Moreover, when people perceive that many of their neighbours and peers are engaging in an illegal activity, they are more likely to infer both that the activity isn't wrong and that the risk of detection is low. This may induce them to take up the activity, further increasing the pool of offenders and rendering enforcement efforts even more difficult.[188]

So when enforcement is minimal and the law conflicts with social norms, the threat of sanctions – no matter how severe – may not deter crime. Perversely, harsh punishments may in these circumstances *increase* criminality. If minor crimes carry stiff penalties, people may be induced to commit more serious offences. This "substitution" effect is a result of the failure of marginal deterrence.[189] As George Stigler puts it, "if the thief has his hand cut off for taking five dollars, he had just as well take $5,000."[190] Substitution is especially likely when apprehension rates are low.[191]

Punishment may occasionally fail to deter even when enforcement is robust. The standard economic model predicts that a substantial risk of detection will deter most offenders, even with low to moderate punishments. But where punishment contradicts norms, the stigma associated with conviction may be eroded.[192] As Katyal notes, when we label "'ordinary' citizens lawbreakers, the ability of the law to shape the behavior of that community is compromised."[193] Stigma depends, after all, on the rarity of conviction. If too many people bear the mark of conviction, that mark will incur less disapproval, paradoxically diminishing deterrence.[194]

All of this suggests that efforts to criminalize certain types of copyright crime in the digital era may not be successful. The criminalization of non-commercial infringement is particularly problematic. As I have discussed, criminal copyright offences were traditionally limited to profit-seeking infringement. In the United States this limitation was imposed by statute. In Canada it emerged from the practice of police and prosecutors. This accords with economic criminalization theory. Commercial infringers are relatively easy to detect. Enforcement is therefore relatively inexpensive, and optimal deterrence can be achieved with relatively light punishments. Applying criminal penalties to profiteers also accords with prevailing social norms. Profit-seeking infringers don't simply obtain copyrighted works for personal consumption. They make a living from the fruits of others' labour. They are the dealers, not the users.

Governments have determined, however, that digitization demands the prosecution of the users too. Criminal legislation in both the United States and Canada captures, for instance, much of the peer-to-peer file sharing conducted through Napster and its progeny. Heavy users of these networks readily surpass the monetary and market thresholds for criminal liability set by these statutes.[195] But economic analysis suggests that the criminalization of this kind of activity is not likely to generate significant deterrence. As I have discussed, digitization decreases the visibility of copyright infringement.[196] Detecting infringing activity on peer-to-peer file-sharing networks would likely prove difficult and costly. File sharing is, or can be made to be, relatively anonymous.[197] Where users can be identified, usage data may reveal suspicious activity. However, as sharing technology may be (and increasingly is) used for noninfringing purposes, police may have difficulty establishing probable cause to justify searches for evidence necessary for conviction.[198] In these circumstances, enforcement is likely to entail significant costs to both the state and individual privacy. The sheer numbers of infringers, moreover, would likely overwhelm law enforcement responses.

Compensating for low detection rates with stiff penalties is not likely to be successful. File sharers and other noncommercial infringers – typically ordinary, convention-valuing citizens – are likely to be exceptionally risk averse. Given low detection rates, such persons are not likely to be scared off by the remote possibility of harsh criminal sanctions. Moreover, despite the severe penalties on the books, file sharers who are prosecuted are not likely to be punished very severely. As I have mentioned, the current practice is to treat most noncommercial infringers leniently.[199]

Neither the certainty nor severity of punishment, then, can be readily heightened to deter widespread, low-visibility, noncommercial digital copyright infringement. But could *some* increase in enforcement, even if accompanied by light penalties, be sufficient to shift norms and increase deterrence? Robinson and Darley suggest that criminal law plays an especially important role in shaping norms "in those borderline cases in which the propriety of certain conduct is unsettled or ambiguous in the mind of the actor."[200] These cases often involve apparently harmless behaviour that has destructive consequences.[201] When such behaviour is criminalized, people may defer to the law's authority, even if they do not immediately intuit why the behaviour is prohibited.[202] Something like this happened in the case of drunk driving, where increases in enforcement, education, and punishment changed public attitudes and brought about significantly greater deterrence.[203] Could we see something similar for digital copyright infringement?

We could, but it is unlikely. With impaired driving, the path to deterrence was clear. Well-publicized roadside screening programs, mobile alcohol screening devices, and persistent educational campaigns put drivers on notice that impaired driving was dangerous, socially unacceptable, and readily detected.[204] Courts also facilitated deterrence by permitting public safety concerns to override the privacy interests implicated by arbitrary vehicle stops.[205]

This strategy may not be as effective in deterring noncommercial digital-copyright infringement. Studies indicate that large-scale, random alcohol-screening programs can detect a significant percentage of impaired drivers and effect impressive declines in alcohol-related vehicle fatalities.[206]

Achieving similar detection levels for digital infringement would likely be more difficult, especially for copying conducted over anonymous peer-to-peer file-sharing networks. As I have discussed, detecting such activity is technically difficult, expensive, vulnerable to technological countermeasures, and invasive of privacy. Furthermore, unlike the case of drunk driving, courts are unlikely to view infringement as harmful enough to justify privacy-violating enforcement measures. File sharing and other forms of noncommercial copying, moreover, are much more prevalent than impaired driving. Projecting a credible enforcement threat in these circumstances would be very difficult indeed.

The problem is compounded by the effect of prevailing social norms. As Robinson and Darley contend, when legislators enact a criminal prohibition that conflicts with the moral intuition of the community, "they must convince the community that the community's intuitions are wrong and that justice would be better served by distributing liabilities according to the new principle."[207] This task is much more difficult for noncommercial copyright infringement than for drunk driving. Previously, it may not have been immediately obvious to the average person why impaired driving (or driving with a certain blood-alcohol level) was prohibited. In most cases people who drive after consuming substantial quantities of alcohol do not cause any harm. To law enforcement officials, however, the social costs of impaired driving have always been visible and dramatic.[208] Police not only have access to statistics revealing the destructive consequences of drunk driving, but also personally witness (often in horrific detail) these consequences on a regular basis. As a result, it has not been difficult to motivate them to enforce the law on the ground. Further, the harms of impaired driving, even if not immediately apparent, are on reflection fairly evident to ordinary people. Those costs threaten the health or property of almost everyone. It is not surprising that public education campaigns, supported by governments and sympathetic grassroots victims' advocacy groups, have been relatively successful in changing public attitudes.[209]

The immediate costs of digital copyright infringement, in contrast, accrue largely to unsympathetic corporate interests.[210] Costs to consumers and society as a whole are indirect, obscure, and contestable.[211] It is in most people's immediate self-interest to tolerate infringement. In these circumstances, norms are unlikely to be influenced by merely labelling an infringing activity criminal. Officials will be reluctant to enforce the law, and people will be unlikely to obey it. People may have to perceive a substantial decrease in the production of digital content before they begin to view noncommercial infringement as morally culpable.

The evidence that we have to date on enforcement patterns confirms this assessment. As mentioned, legislators increased penalties for copyright offences in part because they believed that this would induce officials to take copyright crime more seriously. But at least in the case of file sharing, this message does not appear to be getting through.[212] Though millions of North Americans have been sharing copyrighted music files for several years, prosecutions have been almost nonexistent.

For at least certain types of noncommercial infringement, then, enforcement does not appear to be viable.[213] However, let us assume, for argument's sake, that enforcement becomes much more common. If criminalization continues to conflict with prevailing values, then we could witness a marked erosion in the stigma, and hence the deterrent value, associated with criminal conviction. In such an environment, a college student convicted for downloading music would face the same social consequences as a rock star convicted for drug possession.[214]

The criminalization of noncommercial infringement may also diminish marginal deterrence and induce perverse substitution effects. If people believe, for example, that copyright law punishes the downloading of music files in roughly the same manner as copying expensive software programs, those already inclined to do the former will feel less compunction about doing the latter.

The appropriateness of criminalizing technological circumvention is more difficult to assess. As mentioned, the DMCA limits criminal sanctions to profit-motivated activity.[215] From a normative perspective, this limitation is crucial. The criminalization of noncommercial circumvention would suffer from many of the enforcement problems discussed for noncommercial infringement. But the case against anticircumvention laws is even stronger because circumventing copy protections does not necessarily result in infringement. Enforcing criminal penalties for the private use of technology enabling noninfringing uses would very likely be futile.

However, as is the case for commercial infringers, commercial circumventors are relatively easy to detect. Developing circumvention technology may not always require substantial investments in infrastructure or personnel, but getting people to pay for the technology requires considerable visibility. Unlike digital copying, moreover, the development of circumvention technology generally requires significant technical expertise. The number of people engaging in such activity is therefore likely to be small.

According to the standard economic model, therefore, enforcement should be inexpensive and deterrence efficient. But unlike most commercial infringers, some profit-seeking circumventors may evoke considerable public sympathy. This is precisely what occurred in the Elcomsoft case. As I described, in the face of substantial criticism from the technical and activist communities as well as the press, prosecutors decided to drop their case against the programmer who was initially indicted under the DMCA's anticircumvention provisions.[216] It remains to be seen whether future prosecutions will evoke similar responses. But given the intense controversy surrounding the DMCA and the hostility exhibited toward it by many individuals, it would not be surprising if criminal enforcement proved to be ineffective.

Conclusion

In many respects, the push to criminalize copyright infringement is understandable. The effectiveness of traditional civil-enforcement mechanisms is truly imperilled by digitization. Peer-to-peer file-sharing networks, broadband connections, file compression formats, circumvention applications, and other technologies have dramatically expanded the scope of copyright infringement. Whether this represents a net benefit or loss to the public interest is not clear. But it is easy to see why industry and government are worried, and why they have turned to criminal law for solutions.

Students of criminal law, however, tend to be skeptical of the capacity of criminal sanctions to solve complex social problems, especially those lying outside the traditional core of the criminal category.[217] Criminal law is too blunt an instrument, the argument runs, to mediate adequately between the complicated, conflicting interests facing the modern regulatory state. Yet, as many have noted, the criminalization of social policy continues unabated.[218]

Whether or not this skepticism is generally justified, it does seem to be warranted in the case of copyright regulation. Efforts to increase the criminalization of copyright in response to digitization may be doomed to failure. The criminalization of low-visibility, noncommercial infringement, especially in the context of file sharing, is likely to run aground on the shoals of deterrence. Attempts to deduce the inherent nonculpability of this behaviour are not philosophically convincing. But the gap between official and popular conceptions of criminality, in conjunction with strategic effects generated by the nature of digital infringement, are likely to thwart deterrence. Justice-system officials are likely to resist criminalization. And where increased enforcement is attempted, it is likely to be costly and ineffective. Enforcing criminal circumvention prohibitions may also be problematic, although the argument is less definitive.

This leaves policy makers with two alternatives. They can attempt to live with the effects of digitization, hoping that the copyright minimalists are correct. Or they can attempt to deploy noncriminal mechanisms to deter infringement.[219] Such efforts have their limitations, but they are probably at least as likely to succeed as criminalization.

Acknowledgments
Thanks to Norman Siebrasse, Michael Geist, and two anonymous reviewers for helpful comments on earlier drafts; Erin Breen and Kara Patterson for research assistance; and the Canadian Association of Law Teachers, the Canadian Law and Society Association,

the Canadian Council of Law Deans, and the Law Commission of Canada for financial support.

Notes

1 As used in this chapter, "digitization" refers to the representation of data in digital form. In the predigital era, copyrighted works were represented in analog form. Analog technologies capture and convey content, such as music, writings, and images, as physical manifestations of that content. Digital technology reproduces that same content as a series of numbers, represented as binary digits (zeros and ones, or "bits"). See National Research Council, *The Digital Dilemma: Intellectual Property in the Information Age* (Washington, DC: National Academy Press, 2000), 28-30; S. Handa, *Copyright Law in Canada* (Markham, ON: Butterworths, 2002), 10-14.

2 Copyright is a bundle of statutory rights granted to the authors of specific "works," including literary compositions, musical recordings, movies, and computer software. Subject to certain limited exceptions, copyright owners have the exclusive right, *inter alia*, to reproduce and distribute these works. Copyright infringement therefore includes the unauthorized reproduction or distribution of a copyrighted work. See *Copyright Act*, R.S.C. 1985, c. C-42; *Copyright Act*, 17 U.S.C. § 106.

3 In Canada the *Constitution Act, 1867* (U.K.), 30 & 31 Vict., c. 3, s. 91(23), gives Parliament the power to legislate in relation to copyrights. Parliament did not use this power to create exclusive, comprehensive copyright legislation, however, until 1921. See *Copyright Act*, S.C. 1921, c. 24. Before 1924, when the 1921 *Act* came into force, copyright was governed by a host of Imperial, federal, and provincial statutes. The 1921 *Act* provided for criminal penalties enforced by way of summary conviction proceedings. The United States *Constitution* gives Congress the power to legislate in the area of copyright (U.S. Const. art I, § 8, cl. 8). The first federal copyright statute was passed in 1790. See *Act of May 31, 1790*, 1 Stat. 124. But Congress did not enact any criminal copyright offences until 1897. Liability was limited to unlawful performances of dramatic and musical compositions. See *Act of Jan. 6, 1897*, ch. 4, 29 Stat. 481-82. In 1909 Congress imposed criminal penalties for infringements against all types of copyrighted works, except sound recordings. Sound recordings were not protected by copyright. Protection was granted only to composers, not to performers or producers who made recordings. Under a compulsory licensing system, composers were given the exclusive right to license the first recording of a composition. Thereafter, anyone could make recordings of the composition provided that they paid a two-cent per copy royalty to the composer. See *Copyright Act of 1909*, ch. 320, 33 Stat. 1075-82. See generally M.J. Saunders, "Criminal Copyright Infringement and the *Copyright Felony Act*" (1994) 71 Denv. U. L. Rev. 671 at 673-74; C. Noonan and J. Raskin, "Intellectual Property Crimes" (2001) 38 Am. Crim. L. Rev. 971 at 990.

4 See A. Young, "Catching Copyright Criminals: *R.* v. *Miles of Music Ltd.*" (1990) 5 I.P.J. 257 at 257; A. Keyes and C. Brunet, *Copyright in Canada: Proposals for a Revision of the Law* (Ottawa: Consumer and Corporate Affairs Canada, 1977), 185; C. Becker, "Criminal Enforcement of Intellectual Property Rights" (2003) 19 C.I.P.R. 183 at 183.

5 See Note, "The Criminalization of Copyright Infringement in the Digital Era" (1999) 112 Harv. L. Rev. 1705 at 1707.

6 The American legislation imposed liability only if the infringement was "willful and for profit." See *Act of Jan. 6, 1897*, ch. 4, 29 Stat. 481. The criminal provisions of the Canadian *Act* have always required that the accused "knowingly" deal with a copyrighted work for the purposes of trade or "to such an extent as to affect prejudicially the owner of the copyright." See *Copyright Act*, R.S.C. 1985, c. C-42, s. 42(1).

7 In Canada copyright infringement was until 1988 classified as a summary offence. The maximum penalty for a first-time offender was a fine of $200. Subsequent offenders were subject to a maximum of two months' imprisonment. See *Copyright Act*, R.S.C. 1985, c. C-42, s. 42(1). Prosecutors occasionally attempted to obtain harsher punishments by prosecuting copyright infringers under the theft and fraud provisions of the *Criminal Code*. See B. Green, "The Empire Strikes Back: Criminal Remedies for Video Piracy" (1984), 1 I.P.J. 1. But in *R.* v. *Stewart*, [1988] 1 S.C.R. 963, the Supreme Court held that copyright infringement

was not theft. Fraud prosecutions, however, have occasionally been successful. See for example *R.* v. *Leahy* (1988), 21 C.P.R. (3d) 422 (Ont. Prov. Ct.); *R.* v. *Kirkwood* (1983), 35 C.R. (3d) 97 (Ont. C.A.); *R.* v. *Bonamy*, 2000 BCCA 308. In the United States all copyright offences were until 1974 classified as misdemeanours. The maximum punishment was $1,000 or imprisonment for up to one year, or both. See *Dowling* v. *United States*, 473 U.S. 207 at 221 (1985).

8 See Young, *supra* note 4 at 258; E. Grell, "Civil and Criminal Remedies for Copyright Infringement," in *Copyright Law of Canada*, edited by G. Henderson (Scarborough, Ont: Carswell, 1994) 311 at 319; Becker, *supra* note 4 at 183-84; Note, *supra* note 5 at 1710; S. Rep. No. 97-274 (1982) at 6, reprinted in 1982 U.S.C.C.A.N. 127 at 132; *Dowling* v. *United States*, 473 U.S. 207 at 221-22 (1985); K. Walker, "Federal Remedies for the Theft of Intellectual Property" (1994), 16 Hastings Comm. & Ent. L.J. 681.

9 See Note, *supra* note 5 at 1710; D. Nimmer, "Criminal Copyright and Trademark Law: The Importance of Criminal Sanctions to Civil Practitioners" (1987), 9(1) Ent. L. Rep. 3 at 4.

10 See C. McCaghy and S. Denisoff, "Pirates and Politics: An Analysis of Interest Group Conflict," in *Deviance, Conflict, and Criminality*, edited by S. Denisoff and C. McCaghy (Chicago: Rand McNally, 1973), 297 at 301-3. In the context of sound recordings, "piracy" refers to the copying of previously recorded works distributed as unauthorized, "underground" copies; "counterfeits" are copies of previously recorded works distributed as if they were authorized copies; and "bootlegging" refers to the unauthorized recording and distribution of live performances or studio sessions. The same terms are used with reference to motion pictures: Pirates copy previously released videocassettes or digital versatile disks (DVDs) and release them as unauthorized product; counterfeiters pass them off as authorized product; and bootleggers make copies from pre-release versions or surreptitiously recorded theatrical showings. The terms are also used in connection with software infringement. See generally M. Coblenz, "Intellectual Property Crimes" (1999), 9 Alb. L.J. Sci. & Tech. 235 at 267-68; McCaghy and Denisoff, *ibid.*, 298 n.1. Each practice, of course, constitutes copyright infringement.

11 See M.J. Saunders, "Criminal Copyright Infringement and the Copyright Felony Act" (1994), 71 Denv. U.L. Rev. 671 at 674-75; R. Merges, "One Hundred Years of Solicitude: Intellectual Property Law, 1900-2000" (2000), 88 Calif. L. Rev. 2187 at 2197.

12 *Sound Recording Act of 1971*, Pub. L. No. 92-140, 85 Stat. 391. It may seem curious that copyright was not granted to sound recordings until this time. But it was not until the development of magnetic-tape recording and cassette players in the 1960s that high-quality, low-cost copying became possible. See Merges, *supra* note 11 at 2196-97.

13 17 U.S.C. § 506(a) (1978).

14 In 1974 Congress increased the maximum fine for record piracy to $25,000. *Act of Dec. 31, 1974*, Pub. L. 93-573. In its view, "record piracy is so profitable that ordinary penalties fail to deter prospective offenders." H.R. Rep. No. 93-1581 at 4 (1974), quoted in *Dowling* v. *United States*, 473 U.S. 207 at 222 (1985). In the comprehensive 1976 revision of the *Copyright Act*, Congress boosted the maximum fine for general copyright infringement to $10,000 and extended the enhanced ($25,000) penalties to motion pictures. The maximum period of imprisonment remained one year. Repeat offenders faced fines of up to $50,000 or up to two years in prison, or both. 17 U.S.C. § 506(a) (1978).

15 See *Dowling* v. *United States*, 473 U.S. 207 at 222-24 (1985).

16 H.R. Rep. No. 93-1581 (1974) at 4, reprinted in 1974 U.S.C.C.A.N. 6849 at 6852.

17 The threat was posed by audio-tape players/recorders and videocassette recorders. See S. Rep. No. 97-274 at 4 (1982), reprinted in 1982 U.S.C.C.A.N. 127 at 130; Note, *supra* note 5 at 1710 n.46.

18 The lobbying was conducted by the two chief entertainment-industry trade associations: the Recording Industry Association of America, Inc. (RIAA) and the Motion Picture Association of America, Inc. (MPAA). They argued that, despite vigorous efforts to combat piracy through civil enforcement, film and record piracy was epidemic. See Saunders, *supra* note 11 at 675; *Dowling* v. *United States*, 473 U.S. 207 at 224 (1985); L. Loren, "Digitization, Commodification, Criminalization: The Evolution of Criminal Copyright Infringement

and the Importance of the Willfulness Requirement" (1999), 77 Wash. U. L.Q. 835 at 842. These organizations, along with software industry trade associations such as the Software and Information Industry Association (SIIA) and the Business Software Alliance (BSA), remain the chief proponents of expansive copyright protections to this day.

19 *Piracy and Counterfeiting Amendments Act of 1982*, Pub. L. No. 97-180, 96 Stat. 91. The *Act* created new felonies for the reproduction or distribution of at least 1,000 copies of sound recordings over a 180-day period and for the reproduction or distribution of at least 65 copies of audiovisual works. See 18 U.S.C. § 2319(b)(1)(A)-(B) (1982). The penalty was raised to a maximum fine of $250,000 or up to five years' imprisonment, or both. Offences involving 100 to 999 copies of sound recordings, or 7 to 64 audiovisual works, attracted fines up to $250,000 or up to two years' imprisonment, or both. All other forms of infringement continued to be classified as misdemeanours carrying fines of up to $25,000 or up to one year in prison, or both.

20 See *Dowling* v. *United States*, 473 U.S. 207 at 224-25 (1985); Saunders, *supra* note 11 at 675-76; S. Rep. No. 97-274 (1982) at 6, reprinted in 1982 U.S.C.C.A.N. 127 at 132-33.

21 See D. Vaver, "The Canadian Copyright Amendments of 1988" (1988), 4 I.P.J. 121 at 148-49; Sub-Committee of the Standing Committee on Communications and Culture on the Revision of Copyright, *A Charter of Rights for Creators* (Ottawa: Supply and Services Canada, 1985), 1 [hereinafter "Sub-Committee Report"].

22 The maximum penalty for offenders prosecuted summarily was raised to a fine of $25,000 or imprisonment for six months, or both. On conviction on indictment, Parliament imposed a maximum punishment of a fine of $1 million or imprisonment for five years, or both. See *An Act to amend the Copyright Act and to amend other Acts in consequence thereof*, S.C. 1988, c. 15. These penalties remain in force today. See *Copyright Act*, R.S.C. 1985, c. C-42, s. 42(1)(*f*)-(*g*). The decision to proceed summarily or by indictment is entirely within the discretion of the Crown. Unlike the situation in the United States, there are no numerical or monetary thresholds distinguishing between offence categories. But Parliament likely assumed that indictable punishments would be reserved for "serious commercial infringements." J. Erola and F. Fox, *From Gutenberg to Telidon: A White Paper on Copyright* (Ottawa: Consumer and Corporate Affairs Canada, 1984), 71.

23 See Sub-Committee Report, *supra* note 21 at 98.

24 See discussion *infra*, notes 71-4 and accompanying text.

25 Congress first extended copyright protection to computer programs in 1980. See *Act of Dec. 12, 1980*, Pub. L. No. 96-517, 94 Stat. 3015, 3028. The Canadian Parliament specifically protected computer programs in 1988. See *An Act to amend the Copyright Act and to amend other Acts in consequence thereof*, S.C. 1988, c. 15, ss. 1(2)-(3). But courts had previously held that programs were protected as literary compilations. See *Apple Computer Inc.* v. *Mackintosh Computers Ltd.*, [1987] 1 F.C. 173 (T.D.), aff'd (1987), 18 C.P.R. (3d) 129 (Fed. C.A.), aff'd [1990] 2 S.C.R. 209.

26 See Saunders, *supra* note 11 at 678-79; Loren, *supra* note 18 at 844. In testimony before the Intellectual Property and Judicial Administration Subcommittee of the House Judiciary Committee, the Software Publishers Association reported that software piracy was costing the industry $2.4 billion in annual revenues. See *United States* v. *LaMacchia*, 871 F. Supp. 535 at 540 (D. Mass. 1994).

27 *Copyright Felony Act*, Pub. L. No. 102-561, 106 Stat. 4233 (1992). The legislation also lowered the numerical and monetary thresholds for felony penalties, which are now triggered by the making of at least ten copies valued at more than $2,500 over a 180-day period. See 18 U.S.C. § 2319(b)(1). The maximum fine for individuals is now $250,000. The maximum fine for organizations is $500,000. See 18 U.S.C. § 3571. The maximum prison sentence for first-time offenders is five years; for repeat offenders it is ten years. See 18 U.S.C. 2319(b)(1)-(2). These are the current punishments for financially motivated infringement.

28 See S. Rep. No. 102-268 (1992) at 2; Note, *supra* note 5 at 1711 n.55.

29 Pub. L. No. 105-147, 111 Stat. 2678 (1997).

30 871 F. Supp. 535 (D. Mass. 1994).

31 17 U.S.C. § 506(a) (1988).

32 18 U.S.C. § 1343.

33   473 U.S. 207 (1985). In *Dowling*, the Court held that a copyrighted song impressed on a bootlegged phonograph record is not property that is "stolen, converted, or taken by fraud" within the meaning of the *National Stolen Property Act*. 18 U.S.C. § 2314. Justice Blackmun's opinion emphasized Congress's traditional reluctance to subject copyright infringers to serious criminal penalties. *Ibid.*, 221.

34   See Coblenz, *supra* note 10 at 249.

35   17 U.S.C. § 101. Because his bulletin accepted uploads of copyrighted software, LaMacchia would likely have been caught by this provision.

36   17 U.S.C. § 506(a)(2). This provision certainly would have captured LaMacchia's conduct. For the reproduction or distribution of ten or more copies of works valued at more than $2,500, the maximum penalty is three years in prison or a fine of $250,000, or both. For the reproduction or distribution of one or more copies of works valued at more than $1,000, the maximum penalty is one year in prison or a fine of $100,000, or both. 18 U.S.C. § 2319(c). The legislation also allows copyright owners as well as the producers and sellers of copyrighted works to submit victim impact statements detailing the economic impact of the offence. 18 U.S.C. § 2319(d).

37   17 U.S.C. § 506(a)(2).

38   Nimmer suggests that wilfulness means an intent to infringe rather than merely an intent to copy. See M. Nimmer, *Nimmer on Copyright: A Treatise on the Law of Literary, Musical and Artistic Property, and the Protection of Ideas*, looseleaf (New York: M. Bender, 1978) § 15.01[A][2]. However, at least some legislators intended that "reckless disregard" of copyright and ignorance of the law should not allow an infringer to escape conviction. *Ibid.*, § 15.01[B][2] at 15-19 n.129. Most courts have interpreted "wilfully" as requiring a specific intent to violate copyright. But the Second Circuit has held that it requires only an intent to copy. See Noonan and Raskin, *supra* note 3 at 994; Saunders, *supra* note 11 at 687-88; Loren, *supra* note 18 at 872, 877-79. In Canada, as I have mentioned, the prosecution must prove that the accused acted "knowingly." See *Copyright Act*, R.S.C. 1985, c. C-42, s. 42(1). As in the United States, most courts in Canada have required actual knowledge that the act violated the *Copyright Act*. See *R.* v. *Laurier Office Mart Inc.* (1994), 58 C.P.R. (3d) 403 (Ont. Prov. Div.), aff'd (1995), 63 C.P.R. (3d) 229 (Ont. Gen. Div.); *R.* v. *Biron* (1992), 127 N.B.R. (2d) 142; *R.* v. *Harris* (1990), 34 C.P.R. (3d) 392 (Nfld. Prov. Ct); *R.* v. *Ghnaim* (1988), 28 C.P.R. (3d) 463 (Alta. Prov. Ct.), aff'd in part (1989), 32 C.P.R. (3d) 487 (Alta. C.A.). *Contra R.* v. *Photo Centre Inc.* (1986), 9 C.P.R. (3d) 425 (Que. S.C.). In most situations, the criminal law does not require defendants to have known that their conduct was wrong or unlawful. It is sufficient if they were aware of the factual circumstances and consequences associated with the *actus reus*. This is consistent, of course, with the maxim that ignorance of the law is not an excuse. See *R.* v. *Théroux*, [1993] 2 S.C.R. 5; *R.* v. *Finta*, [1994] 1 S.C.R. 701; D. Stuart, *Canadian Criminal Law: A Treatise*, 4th ed. (Scarborough, Ont: Carswell, 2001), 234. But there are circumstances where a specific intent to breach a legal standard has been required. See, for example, *R.* v. *Docherty*, [1989] 2 S.C.R. 941.

39   *Copyright Act*, R.S.C. 1985, c. C-42, s. 42(1)(*c*). Note, however, that s. 80 of the Canadian *Act* states that the copying of sound recordings onto an "audio recording medium for the private use of the person who makes the copy" does not infringe copyright. It has not been established whether this exception applies to the downloading of music files from a file-sharing network to a user's hard drive, but such an interpretation would not be unreasonable. See generally *Re Tariff of Levies to be Collected by CPCC* (1999), 4 C.P.R. (4th) 15 (Copyright Board). Such an exception would not apply, however, to any copying associated with uploading files to a file-sharing network to be downloaded by others.

40   In a search of the Quicklaw "IPLQ" database, which includes cases dating back to 1876, I found only two decisions reporting convictions for noncommercial infringement. In *R.* v. *Rexcan Circuits Inc.*, [1993] O.J. No. 1896 (Ont. Prov. Div.) (QL), the corporate defendant was fined $50,000 for making unauthorized copies of computer programs for use in its plant. Notably, the court and counsel were unable to find any similar cases in the jurisprudence. *Ibid.*, at paras. 26, 40. In *R.* v. *M.(J.P.)* (1996), 107 C.C.C. (3d) 380 (N.S.C.A.), the juvenile defendant was sentenced to eighteen months' probation and 150 hours of community service for uploading software to a computer bulletin board and permitting selected users to download it.

41 See *M.(J.P.)*, ibid., 383, where the Court upheld the trial judge's finding that the defendant's conduct was "clearly prejudicial to the owners of the copyright in that they were deprived of control over their product which they required to ensure quality and also interfere[d] with a legitimate commercial distribution and sale of the product for profit."

42 17 U.S.C. § 1201.

43 The relevant treaties are the *World Intellectual Property Organization (WIPO) Copyright Treaty*, 20 December 1996, 36 I.L.M. 65, arts. 11-12 (entered into force 6 March 2002), and the *WIPO Performances and Phonograms Treaty*, 20 December 1996, 36 I.L.M. 76, arts. 18-19 (entered into force 20 May 2002). The treaties oblige contracting states to "provide adequate legal protection and effective legal remedies against the circumvention of effective technological measures" that protect copyright. They also require contracting states to "provide adequate and effective legal remedies" against persons who "remove or alter any electronic rights management information without authority" or distribute works knowing that such "information has been removed or altered without authority." The United States has signed and ratified the treaties. Canada signed both treaties in December 1997, but has yet to ratify either.

44 See generally N. Katyal, "Criminal Law in Cyberspace" (2001), 149 U. Pa. L. Rev. 1003 at 1038.

45 See L. Lessig, *Code and Other Laws of Cyberspace* (New York: Basic Books, 1999) at 127-30; M. Stefik, "Shifting the Possible: How Trusted Systems and Digital Property Rights Challenge Us to Rethink Digital Publishing" (1997), 12 Berk. Tech. L.J. 137.

46 Trusted systems, also known as "lockware," use encryption algorithms to limit access to digital content to authorized users and uses. These systems may simply prevent copying. Or in the guise of "rights management" systems, they may determine the rights that a user has with respect to that content. For example, the system may: permit the user to make only a certain number of copies or make copies only on certain media; program content to expire after a certain date; or charge the user for each time the content is accessed. See Stefik, *supra* note 45; J. Cohen, "Some Reflections on Copyright Management Systems and Laws Designed to Protect Them" (1997), 12 Berk. Tech. L.J. 161 at 162-63.

47 DVDs are an optical storage medium similar to compact discs (CDs) but with considerably greater storage capacity.

48 CSS was developed by the Copy Protection Technology Working Group (CPTWG), a standards body comprising leading entertainment and consumer-electronics companies. CSS licences are issued by the DVD Copy Control Association (DVD CCA). Movie studios would simply not have made films available in digital format without this type of protection. See *Universal City Studios, Inc.* v. *Corley*, 273 F.3d 429 (2d Cir. 2001) at 436-37. To combat the threat of online piracy, the music industry is attempting to convince consumer-electronics manufacturers to adopt a more sophisticated rights-management system, the Secure Digital Music Initiative (SDMI), to protect digital music. Digital music encoded in the CD format is not copy protected. See S. Kramarsky, "Copyright Enforcement in the Internet Age: The Law and Technology of Digital Rights Management" (2001), 11 J. Art & Ent. Law 1 at 12-15. In the meantime, record companies have tentatively begun releasing CDs carrying various proprietary copy-protection technologies. See P. Boutin, "Phillips Burning on Protection," *Wired News*, 4 February 2002, <http://www.wired.com/news/politics/0,1283,50101,00.html> (8 January 2004).

49 See Kramarsky, *supra* note 48 at 8-9.

50 The most famous example is the "DeCSS" program created by Norwegian teenager Jon Johansen and two others, who developed the program to allow DVDs to be played on computers using the Linux operating system (at the time that they created the program, there was no Linux-based DVD player). Johansen posted the DeCSS code on his website. Soon versions of DeCSS executable by the Microsoft Windows operating system became available on the Internet. These programs enabled the copying of DVD movies. Eric Corley, a publisher of a hacker magazine, posted the DeCSS code, as well as links to other web sites where DeCSS could be found, on his website. The major movie studios obtained an injunction under the DMCA enjoining the posting and linking of DeCSS. See *Universal City Studios, Inc.* v. *Reimerdes*, 111 F. Supp. 2d 294 (S.D.N.Y. 2000). The injunction was upheld by the Second Circuit Court of Appeals. See *Universal City Studios, Inc.* v. *Corley*, 273 F.3d 429

(2d Cir. 2001). Johansen was charged with violating section 145 of the Norwegian *General Civil Penal Code*, which states that any person commits an offence who "by breaking a protective device or in a similar way unlawfully obtains access to data or software which are stored or transferred by electronic or other technical means." See <http://www.ub.uio.no/uJur/ulovdata/lov-19020522-010-eng.pdf> (unofficial translation, accessed 8 January 2004). This provision does not appear, however, to capture Johansen's conduct. In the absence of anticircumvention laws, it is arguably not unlawful to gain access (by whatever means) to data that one owns. The judge presiding over Johansen's trial agreed and acquitted him. The acquittal was upheld on appeal. See T. O'Brien, "Norwegian Hacker, 19, Is Acquitted in DVD Piracy Case," *New York Times* (8 January 2003), C4; "Technology Briefing Software: Verdict Upheld in DVD Piracy Case," *New York Times* (23 December 2004), C5.

51 DVD movie files are extremely large. Internet movie distribution was until recently highly inefficient, requiring more patience and bandwidth than most users could afford. But the growing availability of broadband connections and efficient compression technologies (such as the popular DivX video format) has significantly increased the prevalence of online movie piracy. See E. McCarthy, "Reston Firm Sees Future in Fighting Movie Piracy," *Washington Post*, 25 September 2003, E1.

52 17 U.S.C. § 1201(a)(1). Circumvention means "to descramble a scrambled work, to decrypt an encrypted work, or otherwise to avoid, bypass, remove, deactivate, or impair a technological measure, without the authority of the copyright owner." *Ibid.,* § 1201(a)(3)(A). The circumvention prohibition is subject to a number of exemptions. The Librarian of Congress is obliged to promulgate regulations exempting persons who would otherwise be "adversely affected" by the prohibition in "their ability to make noninfringing uses" of particular categories of copyrighted works. *Ibid.,* § 1201(a)(1)(B)-(E). Libraries and educational institutions are permitted to circumvent protective measures in order to decide whether to purchase a copyrighted work. *Ibid.,* § 1201(d). And exceptions are provided for law enforcement and intelligence operations, reverse engineering of computer programs for the purposes of achieving the interoperability of computer programs, and encryption research. *Ibid.,* § 1201(e)-(g).

53 17 U.S.C. § 1201(a)(2) and (b)(1). The former provision covers persons who traffic in technology that circumvents measures controlling access to copyrighted works. The latter covers technology that circumvents measures that permit access but prevent copying or some other act that infringes copyright. The injunction against Corley's DeCSS postings was based on § 1201(a)(2).

54 17 U.S.C. § 1202. This provision is designed to work along with the prohibitions in § 1201 to thwart the circumvention of digital rights-management systems. Specifically, § 1202 prohibits the provision of false copyright management information; the unauthorized removal or alternation of such information; and the trafficking of works when one knows that such information has been tampered with. 17 U.S.C. § 1202(a)-(b).

55 As I discuss in more detail *infra,* note 114, the "fair use" (or as it is known in Canada, "fair dealing") doctrine permits certain limited uses of copyrighted works without the authorization of the copyright owner. The DMCA only prohibits the circumvention of technological measures preventing *access* to a work. It does not prohibit the circumvention of measures limiting the *use* of a work. If persons lawfully access a digital work (for example, by purchasing a DVD movie), they may legally circumvent rights-management systems to make a fair use of that work (for example, by copying a scene from the movie for private research or educational purposes). But they may not either traffic in technology that facilitates this fair use (such as DeCSS) or employ such technology to gain access to a technologically protected work even if that access would be considered a fair use. See *United States* v. *Elcom Ltd.*, 203 F. Supp. 2d 1111 at 1123-25 (N.D. Cal. 2002).

56 17 U.S.C. § 1203. Civil remedies include injunctions, actual damages, and statutory damages.

57 17 U.S.C. § 1204. The maximum penalties for a first offence are a fine of $500,000 or imprisonment for five years, or both. For subsequent offences, the maxima are $1,000,000 or ten years' imprisonment, or both. Libraries, archives, educational institutions, and public broadcasters are exempted from criminal liability.

58 *Ibid.* Consequently, persons like Eric Corley who simply post circumventing code or links to such code on their websites are likely not subject to criminal prosecution under the DMCA. See discussion *supra* notes 50 and 53.

59 See Intellectual Property Directorate, Industry Canada and Copyright Policy Branch, Canadian Heritage, *Consultation Paper on Digital Copyright Issues* (Ottawa and Hull: Information Distribution Centre, Industry Canada and Copyright Policy Branch, Department of Canadian Heritage, 2001) §§ 4.2-4.3 [hereinafter "Consultation Paper"].

60 See Nimmer, *supra* note 9 at 3.

61 See L. Harris, *Canadian Copyright Law*, 3rd ed. (Toronto: McGraw-Hill Ryerson, 2001), 187.

62 See J. Borland, "Movie Studios Tout First DVD Bust in U.S.," *CNET News.com*, 22 March 2002, <http://news.com.com/2100-1023-867314.html> (8 January 2004); Becker, *supra* note 4 at 185-86.

63 In 1995 the United States Department of Justice formed a Computer Crime and Intellectual Property Section (CCIPS). CCIPS has since initiated a number of high-profile investigations and garnered a significant number of convictions. Many copyright prosecutions, however, result from industry-led investigations, the findings of which have been handed over to law enforcement agencies. See Coblenz, *supra* note 10 at 244; Becker, *supra* note 4 at 188.

64 See L. Bowman, "Net Piracy Ringleader Gets Four Years," *CNET News.com*, 17 May 2002, <http://news.com.com/2100-1023-916824.html> (8 January 2004); K. Ritter, "Florida Man, 20 Others Charged With Net Piracy," *SiliconValley.com*, 13 June 2002, <http://www.siliconvalley.com/mld/siliconvalley/news/editorial/3462495.htm> (8 January 2004); D. Becker, "Copyright Infringement Bad; Hulk Smash!" *CNET News.com*, 25 June 2003, <http://news.com.com/2102-1026_3-1021005.html> (8 January 2004); K. Bernstein, "Net Zero: The Evisceration of the Sentencing Guidelines Under the *No Electronic Theft Act*" (2001), 27 N.E. J. on Crim. & Civ. Con. 57 at 62-65; *M.(J.P.)*, *supra* note 40.

65 This has resulted, in part, from the application of the federal Sentencing Guidelines. A discussion of how the guidelines apply to copyright crime is beyond the scope of this paper. Briefly, the guidelines make it very unlikely that a first-time, noncommercial offender will receive any significant jail time. See Bernstein, *supra* note 64 at 76, 81; Coblenz, *supra* note 10 at 256-57. There have not yet been any prosecutions for users of Napster or other peer-to-peer file-sharing technologies. And there has been only one prosecution under the anticircumvention provisions of the DMCA. Acting in cooperation with Adobe Systems, Inc., federal prosecutors charged a Russian programmer (Dmitri Sklyarov) and his employer (Elcomsoft) for developing and marketing a program that circumvented the rights-management system built into Adobe's eBook Reader software. Sklyarov developed the program in Russia, but it was marketed and sold on the Internet using computer servers located in the United States. The FBI arrested Sklyarov when he attended a conference in Las Vegas. In the face of heavy public criticism, the Justice Department terminated its prosecution of Sklyarov. See J. Lee, "U.S. Arrests Russian Cryptographer as Copyright Violator," *New York Times*, 18 July 2001, C8; L. Lessig, "Jail Time in the Digital Age," *New York Times*, 30 July 2001, A7. The case against Elcomsoft proceeded. After defence motions to dismiss the case on jurisdictional and constitutional grounds were rejected, Elcomsoft was acquitted by a jury. See *United States* v. *Elcom Ltd.*, 203 F. Supp. 2d 1111 (N.D. Cal. 2002); A. Cha, "U.S. Clears Russian Tech Firm in E-Book Copyright Case," *Washington Post*, 18 December 2002, E1.

66 See F. Andreano, "The Evolution of Federal Computer Crime Policy: The Ad Hoc Approach to an Ever-Changing Problem" (1999), 27 Am. J. Crim. L. 81 at 94, 98. See also "Will Ashcroft Target P2P Sites?" *Wired News*, 9 August 2002, <http://www.wired.com/news/politics/0,1283,54460,00.html> (8 January 2004).

67 See Bernstein, *supra note* 64 at 73. There is some evidence, however, that authorities in Europe are beginning to bring criminal proceedings against file sharers. See "Spanish Firms Target File Traders," *Wired News*, 23 July 2003, <http://www.wired.com/news/digiwood/0,1412,59720,00.html> (8 January 2004).

68 See generally Merges, *supra* note 11; P. Goldstein, *Copyright's Highway: From Gutenberg to the Celestial Jukebox* (New York: Hill and Wang, 1994).

69 See Kramarsky, *supra* note 48 at 3. See also discussion *supra* notes 10-23 and accompanying text.

70 See generally National Research Council, *supra* note 1 at 2.

71 See National Research Council, *supra* note 1 at 31-32; R. Shih Ray Ku, "The Creative Destruction of Copyright: Napster and the New Economics of Digital Technology" (2002), 69 U. Chi. L. Rev. 263 at 271. The "perfection" of digital copying, it should be noted, only applies to the copying of a digital original or master. See Handa, *supra* note 1 at 13.

72 See Ku, *supra* note 71 at 270-71. Like analog information, digital information can be transmitted through copper wires as electrical impulses; as light across fibre-optic cable; or as radio waves of the electromagnetic spectrum. The most important of the networks carrying digital content is the Internet, which is a public network (though it flows through mostly privately owned "wires"). But digital content can also be delivered via private, proprietary networks, such as those maintained by cable and satellite television providers and mobile telephony providers.

73 Fixed costs are the initial costs of producing a single unit. The fixed costs of copying and distribution via the Internet are extremely low, comprising approximately $1,000 for a personal computer and between zero and forty dollars per month for Internet access. Marginal cost is the cost of producing and distributing additional units. Save for minuscule energy costs, the marginal cost of Internet copying and distribution is effectively zero. See Ku, *supra* note 71 at 274-75.

74 Governments have expressed the view that secure, copyright-protected broadband distribution of digital content will foster enhanced productivity and innovation. See, for example, Information Infrastructure Task Force, *Intellectual Property and the National Information Infrastructure: The Report of the Working Group on Intellectual Property Rights* (Washington, DC: Information Infrastructure Task Force, 1995), 10-12, <http://www.uspto.gov/web/offices/com/doc/ipnii/ipnii.pdf> (8 January 2004) [hereinafter "White Paper"]; Consultation Paper, *supra* note 59.

75 See generally R. Cooter and T. Ulen, *Law and Economics*, 3rd ed. (Reading, MA: Addison Wesley Longman, 2000), 42-3.

76 *Ibid.*

77 *Ibid.* Private goods, in contrast, are both excludable and rivalrous. One person's consumption means that the good is not available for consumption by another person.

78 "Free riding" occurs when individuals consume a good without internalizing the costs of its production. See Ku, *supra* note 71 at 278; W. Gordon, "Fair Use as Market Failure: A Structural and Economic Analysis of the Betamax Case and Its Predecessors" (1982), 82 Colum. L. Rev. 1600 at 1611.

79 See Ku, *supra* note 71 at 278-79.

80 See W. Landes and R. Posner, "An Economic Analysis of Copyright Law" (1989), 18 J. Legal Stud. 325 at 326; S. Breyer, "The Uneasy Case for Copyright: A Study of Copyright in Books, Photocopies, and Computer Programs" (1970), 84 Harv. L. Rev. 281 at 282.

81 See Gordon, *supra* note 78 at 1612.

82 See D. Vaver, *Copyright Law* (Toronto: Irwin Law, 2000), 295.

83 See B. King, "Record Biz Has Burning Question," *Wired News*, 14 June 2002, <http://www.wired.com/news/mp3/0,1285,53157,00.html> (8 January 2004). Detecting and punishing small-scale infringers, on the other hand, is generally not worth the effort. See Loren, *supra* note 18 at 853-54.

84 *Ibid.*

85 See National Research Council, *supra* note 1 at 31-2.

86 Napster is a software program that allowed users to share "MP3" audio files over the Internet. MP3 is a compression algorithm and file format developed by the Moving Picture Experts Group (MPEG) standards body (MP3 stands for MPEG 1 Audio Layer 3). MP3 files are generally much smaller than CD files. MP3, like other compression technologies, removes redundant and nonessential information from the original file. MP3 files are therefore much more efficiently stored on personal computers and transferred over the Internet than CD files. The sound quality of MP3s, however, approaches that of CDs. See generally *Recording Indus. Ass'n of Am. v. Diamond Multimedia Sys., Inc.*, 180 F.3d 1072 at 1073-74 (9th

Cir. 1999); Kramarsky, *supra* note 48 at 5-7. Napster, which could be downloaded free of charge from the Internet, set up a "peer-to-peer" (P2P) network whereby each user's computer became a server hosting MP3 files for download by other users. Users seeking to download a particular file searched a database maintained on the company's server indexing all files on the network. The system could be used to distribute noncopyrighted material. But most users employed it to obtain copyrighted music files. Typically, users would "rip" (copy) songs from legitimately purchased CDs to the hard drives of their personal computers and convert them to MP3 files. By downloading music files stored on other users' computers, Napster users could readily amass prodigious music collections without paying a cent to copyright owners. Downloaded MP3 files could be stored and played on users' computers, "burned" (copied) to recordable CDs, or transferred to portable MP3 players. By the end of 2000, it was estimated that the service had 75 million users. See *A&M Records, Inc.* v. *Napster, Inc.*, 114 F. Supp. 2d 896 at 902 (N.D. Cal. 2000), aff'd in part and rev'd in part and remanded 239 F.3d 1004 (9th Cir. 2001), injunction granted 2001 U.S. Dist. LEXIS 2186 (N.D. Cal. Mar. 5, 2001), aff'd 284 F.3d 1091 (9th Cir. 2002). At this time, Napster users averaged 140 songs in their libraries. See A. Lenhart and S. Fox, *Downloading Free Music: Internet Music Lovers Don't Think It's Stealing* (Washington, DC: Pew Internet and American Life Project, 2000), 7, <http://www.pewinternet.org/reports/index.asp> (accessed 8 January 2004). Record companies successfully sued Napster for contributory copyright infringement. Napster has since been shut down. But other software companies have rushed in to fill the void. Programs such as KaZaA and Morpheus are similar to Napster but do not rely on a central database server. They also permit the transfer of other copyrighted works, such as images and video. These programs are extremely popular, and despite the demise of Napster, file sharing continues unabated. See J. Graham, "File Sharing Is a Hit, Despite Legal Setbacks," *USA Today.com*, 13 May 2002, <http://www.usatoday.com/life/cyber/tech/2002/05/14/music-sharing.htm> (8 January 2004). Not surprisingly, the entertainment industry is suing many of these companies. In the most important post-Napster decision so far, software providers obtained summary judgment on the grounds that they exercised no control over the way their networks were used and that there were substantial noninfringing uses for the software. See *MGM Studios, Inc.* v. *Grokster, Ltd.*, 259 F.Supp. 2d 1029 (C.D. Calif. 2003). But even if the entertainment companies eventually succeed in shutting down these successors to Napster, there are a number of nonproprietary, or "open source," P2P file sharing programs available, including Gnutella and Freenet. These programs are not owned or distributed by any one company or individual, so there is no single controlling entity to sue. See A. Bailey, "A Nation of Felons?: Napster, the *NET Act*, and the Criminal Prosecution of File-Sharing" (2000), 50 Am. U.L. Rev. 473 at 475-76, 515-17; Lessig, *supra* note 65 at 137; Bartow, *infra* note 130 at 106-7, ns. 35-6. The entertainment companies have thus begun suing individual users of these networks. See *infra* note 219. File sharing through instant messaging networks is also becoming increasingly popular. See Graham, *ibid.*

87 See Loren, *supra* note 18 at 854-55.
88 *Ibid.*, 854.
89 See discussion *infra*, notes 129-37 and accompanying text.
90 See, for example, Y. Benkler, "Free as the Air to Common Use: First Amendment Constraints on Enclosure of the Public Domain" (1999), 74 N.Y.U. L. Rev. 354; J. Cohen, "A Right to Read Anonymously: A Closer Look at Copyright Management in Cyberspace" (1996), 28 Conn. L. Rev. 981; N. Netanel, "Copyright and Democratic Civil Society" (1996), 106 Yale L.J. 283; J. Boyle, "The First Amendment and Cyberspace: The Clinton Years" (2000), 63 Law & Contemp. Prob. 337 at 349-50. Several courts have concluded, however, that the anticircumvention provisions of the DMCA do not violate the First Amendment. See *Universal City Studios, Inc.* v. *Corley*, 273 F.3d 429 (2d Cir. 2001); *United States* v. *Elcom Ltd.*, 203 F. Supp. 2d 1111 (N.D. Cal. 2002).
91 See Lessig, *supra* note 45 at 135-38.
92 See Ku *supra* note 71.
93 See Lessig, *supra* note 65 at 200-2; J. Litman, "Revising Copyright Law for the Information Age" (1996), 75 Or. L. Rev. 19.
94 See Goldstein, *supra* note 68 at 236.

95 See Gordon, *supra* note 78.

96 See T. Hardy, "Property (and Copyright) in Cyberspace, [1996] U. Chi. Legal F. 217 at 236-39; T. Bell, "Fair Use v. Fared Use: The Impact of Automated Rights Management on Copyright's Fair Use Doctrine" (1998), 76 N.C. L. Rev. 557 at 564-67; Goldstein, *supra* note 68 at 224.

97 See S. Liebowitz, *Policing Pirates in a Networked Age*, CATO Institute Policy Analysis No. 438, 15 May 2002, 17-21, <http://www.cato.org/pubs/pas/pa438.pdf> (8 January 2004). Others view fair use in a very different light. For them, fair use is not simply the product of market failure. Rather, it is public value – an informational "commons" – that should be preserved regardless of technology. See Lessig, *supra* note 45 at 135-38; M. Gimbel, "Some Thoughts on the Implications of Trusted Systems for Intellectual Property Law" (1998), 50 Stan. L. Rev. 1671 at 1686-87.

98 To name just a few, civil liability may result in punitive sanctions; private parties may sometimes bring criminal prosecutions; criminal penalties may include compensation for victims' losses; and both regulatory and criminal transgressions may result in incarceration and other deprivations of liberty.

99 Copyright violation, for example, can constitute both a civil wrong and a crime.

100 This definition therefore includes many legal prohibitions that Canadian law classifies, for purposes of statutory and constitutional interpretation, as "regulatory" offences. See *R. v. Sault Ste. Marie (City)*, [1978] 2 S.C.R. 1299; *R. v. Wholesale Travel*, [1991] 3 S.C.R. 454.

101 See generally M. Rizzo, "Economic Costs, Moral Costs, or Retributive Justice: The Rationale of Criminal Law," in *The Costs of Crime*, edited by C. Gray (Beverly Hills: Sage, 1979), 257 at 273-74.

102 Many scholars have argued, for example, that public input into copyright legislation is dominated by content-industry lobbying. See Merges, *supra* note 11 at 2236; J. Litman, *Digital Copyright* (Amherst, N.Y.: Prometheus, 2001), 22-32; R. Merges and G. Reynolds, "The Proper Scope of the Copyright and Patent Power (2000), 37 Harv. J. on Legis. 45 at 53-54. More generally, public-choice theory teaches skepticism as to whether democratic institutions accurately reflect popular preferences. See generally M. Stearns, ed., *Public Choice and Public Law: Readings and Commentary* (Cincinnati: Anderson, 1997). And even if copyright legislation did represent popular opinion, it is not clear that this would be normatively justifiable. As I discuss below, most people are consumers – not producers – of copyrighted works. Individual consumers' immediate self-interest is to favour weak copyright protection, enabling them to "free ride" off producers. But if weak copyright provides insufficient incentive for production, the long-term collective interests of consumers (and of society as a whole) may be better represented by the content industry, which internalizes the benefits of copyright protection. (I thank Norman Siebrasse for this insight.) The point here is not to determine whether the content industry has either too much or too little influence over criminal copyright legislation. Since both conclusions are plausible, we cannot be confident that such legislation is socially optimal.

103 See Consultation Paper, *supra* note 59.

104 I allude, of course, to Roscoe Pound's famous distinction between the law "on the books" and the law "in action." See R. Pound, "Law in Books and Law in Action" (1910), 44 Am. L. Rev. 12.

105 The two approaches lay claim to a venerable lineage: Kant for the moralists and Bentham for the utilitarians and economists. See J. Bentham, 1789, *An Introduction to the Principles of Morals and Legislation*, edited by J.H. Burns and H.L.A. Hart (Oxford: Clarendon Press, 1996), 143-311; I. Kant, 1797, *The Metaphysics of Morals*, translated by M. Gregor (Cambridge: Cambridge University Press, 1996), 104-10.

106 See H. Hart, Jr. "The Aims of the Criminal Law" (1958), 23 Law & Contemp. Prob. 401 at 404.

107 See Law Reform Commission of Canada, *Our Criminal Law* (Ottawa: Information Canada, 1976), 19.

108 See J. Feinberg, *Doing and Deserving: Essays in the Theory of Responsibility* (Princeton: Princeton University Press, 1970), 98; J. Hall, "Interrelations of Criminal Law and Torts" (pts. 1 and 2) (1943), 43 Colum. L. Rev. 753, 967; R. Epstein, "Crime and Tort: Old Wine in Old Bottles,"

in *Assessing the Criminal: Restitution, Retribution, and the Legal Process,* edited by R. Barnett and J. Hagel (Cambridge, MA.: Ballinger, 1977), 231 at 248.

109 Criminal law excuses the unauthorized taking of property in a few limited circumstances, such as in cases of necessity, duress, and self-defence. See generally Stuart, *supra* note 38 at 451-533; W. LaFave and Austin Scott, Jr., *Criminal Law,* 3d ed. (St. Paul: West, 2000), ch. 5. Of course, the unauthorized taking of property also generally constitutes a civil wrong.

110 This view stems from the Lockean, natural-law-based conception of intellectual property as an extension of the self. See L. Weinrib, "Copyright for Functional Expression" (1998), 111 Harv. L. Rev. 1149 at 1222-29. It is clearly the view of the content industry. It is also a view that is increasingly articulated by legislators and government officials. See, for example, Erola and Fox, *supra* note 22 at 205-6. The notion that copyright infringement is theft is reflected in the legislative history and title of the *No Electronic Theft Act.* See Loren, *supra* note 18 at 858 and n.120.

111 See generally F. Easterbrook, "Intellectual Property Is Still Property" (1990), 13 Harv. J. Law & Pub. Pol'y 108; J. Boyle, "Cruel, Mean, or Lavish? Economic Analysis, Price Discrimination and Digital Intellectual Property" (2000), 53 Vand. L. Rev. 2007.

112 See generally B. Ackerman, ed., *Economic Foundations of Property Law* (Boston: Little, Brown, 1975); D. Kennedy and F. Michelman, "Are Property and Contract Efficient?" (1980), 8 Hofstra L. Rev. 711.

113 In Canada copyright for most types of works is granted for the duration of the author's life plus fifty years. See *Copyright Act,* R.S.C. 1985, c. C-42, s. 6. In 1998 Congress lengthened the period of postdeath protection from fifty to seventy years. See 17 U.S.C. § 302. Constitutional challenges to this extension based on the First Amendment and the copyright clause were recently rejected by the Supreme Court. See *Eldred* v. *Ashcroft,* 537 U.S. 186 (2003).

114 The Canadian *Copyright Act* limits "fair dealing" to the unauthorized use of copyrighted works for the purposes of research, private study, criticism, review, or news reporting. See *Copyright Act,* R.S.C. 1985, c. C-42, ss. 29-29.2. In the United States "fair use" is more expansive. The *Copyright Act* states that any fair use of a copyrighted work does not infringe copyright. It specifies that the fair use may be for purposes of criticism, comment, news reporting, teaching, scholarship, or research; but it does not limit the concept to those purposes. The *Act* also instructs courts to consider the following factors in determining whether any particular use is fair: "(1) the purpose and character of the use, including whether such use is of a commercial nature or is for nonprofit educational purposes; (2) the nature of the copyrighted work; (3) the amount and substantiality of the portion used in relation to the copyrighted work as a whole; and (4) the effect of the use on the potential market for or value of the copyrighted work." See 17 U.S.C. § 107. In neither jurisdiction is there a definitive test for determining fair use. Each use requires a case-by-case balancing of interests. See, for example, *Allen* v. *Toronto Star Newspapers Ltd.* (1997), 78 C.P.R. (3d) 115 at 123 (Ont. Gen. Div.); *Harper & Row Publishers, Inc.* v. *Nation Enters.,* 471 U.S. 539 at 549 (1985).

115 Under the first-sale doctrine, the buyer of a copyrighted work may sell it to someone else free of any constraint imposed by the seller. See 17 U.S.C. § 109. The first-sale doctrine is not strictly speaking a limitation on copyright because the resale of a copyrighted work does not necessarily entail copying. Rather, first sale is a restriction on the distribution right granted by the United States statute. The Canadian *Act* does not grant a distribution right per se, so there is no need for a first-sale exception. Instead of granting a distribution right, the *Act* forbids "secondary infringement," which is defined as the unauthorized distribution of copyrighted works. See *Copyright Act,* R.S.C. 1985, c. C-42, s. 27(2).

116 See, for example, *Harper & Row, Publishers, Inc.* v. *Nation Enterprises,* 471 U.S. 539 at 560 (1985).

117 See R. Posner, *Law and Literature,* rev. and enl. ed. (Cambridge, MA: Harvard University Press, 1998), 392.

118 See *R.* v. *Stewart,* [1988] 1 S.C.R. 963; *Dowling* v. *United States,* 473 U.S. 207 (1985); *United States* v. *LaMacchia,* 871 F. Supp. 535 (D. Mass. 1994). See also J. Lipton, "Protecting Valuable Commercial Information in the Digital Age: Law, Policy and Practice" (2001), 6.1 J. Tech. L. & Pol'y 2 § 2.1, <http://grove.ufl.edu/~techlaw/vol6/Lipton.html> (8 January 2004).

119 *Dowling* v. *United States*, 473 U.S. 207 at 216-17 (1985).
120 *Ibid.*, 217.
121 See generally R. Posner, *Economic Analysis of Law*, 2nd ed. (Boston: Little, Brown, 1977), 27-29.
122 See J. Cohen, "*Lochner* in Cyberspace: The New Economic Orthodoxy of 'Rights Management'" (1998), 97 Mich. L. Rev. 462 at 502.
123 See H. Demsetz, "Toward a Theory of Property Rights" (1967), 57 Am. Econ. Rev. 347 at 359. See also United States Constitution, Art. I, s. 8, cl. 8: "The Congress shall have Power ... To promote the Progress of Science and useful Arts, by securing for limited Times to Authors and Inventors the exclusive Right to their respective Writings and Discoveries."
124 Lessig, *supra* note 45 at 134; Lessig, *supra* note 65 at 97.
125 See Landes and Posner, *supra* note 80. See also *Théberge* v. *Galerie d'Art du Petit Champlain inc.*, [2002] 2 S.C.R. 336 at paras. 30-1 [hereinafter *Théberge*]: "The *Copyright Act* is usually presented as a balance between promoting the public interest in the encouragement and dissemination of works of the arts and intellect and obtaining a just reward for the creator ... In crassly economic terms it would be as inefficient to overcompensate artists and authors for the right of reproduction as it would be self-defeating to undercompensate them." It has been argued, however, that while determining an efficient balance between access and incentive is unobjectionable in principle, it requires information that is not available. On this view, it is more efficient for copyright law simply to ensure that property rights are well defined. See N. Siebrasse, "A Property Rights Theory of the Limits of Copyright" (2001), 51 U.T.L.J. 1.
126 Economists and legal scholars have argued, moreover, that overly strong copyright protection may work against the interests of authors. Authors draw upon preexisting works in creating new works. If copyright prevents works from being widely accessible, then fewer new works will be created. See Posner, *supra* note 117 at 391; R. Watt, *Copyright and Economic Theory: Friends or Foes?* (Cheltenham: E. Elgar, 2000), 58-67, 200-1. See also *Théberge*, *supra* note 125 at para. 32: "Excessive control by holders of copyrights ... may unduly limit the ability of the public domain to incorporate and embellish creative innovation in the long-term interests of society as a whole, or create practical obstacles to proper utilization." This problem occurs only because of the transaction costs associated with licensing. If transaction costs were zero, authors whose works are protected by copyright would engage in perfect price discrimination, ensuring both maximum incentive *and* maximum dissemination. See Siebrasse, *supra* note 125 at 9; W. Fisher III, "Reconstructing the Fair Use Doctrine" (1988), 101 Harv. L. Rev. 1661 at 1701-4; Liebowitz, *supra* note 97 at 17.
127 Think, for example, of the law pertaining to easements, perpetuities, zoning, and nuisance. I am grateful to Norman Siebrasse for this point.
128 See generally Goldstein, *supra* note 68; Easterbrook, *supra* note 111.
129 Law Reform Commission of Canada, *supra* note 107 at 28.
130 See Young, *supra* note 4 at 273; D. Vaver, *Intellectual Property Law: Copyright, Patents, Trademarks* (Concord, Ont.: Irwin Law, 1997), 275; Vaver, *supra* note 21 at 295-96; Note, *supra* note 5; Loren, *supra* note 18; A. Bartow, "Arresting Technology: An Essay" (2001), 1 Buff. Intell. Prop. L.J. 95. *Contra* Bailey, *supra* note 86; Bernstein, *supra* note 64.
131 See *United States* v. *LaMacchia*, 871 F. Supp. 535 at 544 (D. Mass. 1994), where the court observed that the government's interpretation of the wire-fraud statute would "criminalize the conduct of not only persons like LaMacchia, but also the myriad of home computer users who succumb to the temptation to copy even a single software program for private use." See also *Dowling* v. *United States*, 473 U.S. 207 at 225-26 (1985); *R.* v. *Stewart*, [1988] 1 S.C.R. 963 at 977-78.
132 A. Lenhart and S. Fox, *Downloading Free Music: Internet Music Lovers Don't Think It's Stealing* (Washington, DC: Pew Internet and American Life Project, 2000), <http://www.pewinternet.org/reports/index.asp> (accessed 8 January 2004); M. Madden and A. Lenhart, Music Downloading, *File-sharing and Copyright: A Pew Internet Project Data Memo* (Washington, DC: Pew Internet and American Life Project, 2003), <http://www.pewinternet.org/reports/index.asp> (accessed 8 January 2004).
133 Lenhart and Fox, *ibid.*, 5-6.

134 Madden and Lenhart, *supra* note 132. Interestingly, this belief is more common among affluent and well-educated persons. Predictably, it is also more common among the young. Lenhart and Fox, *ibid.*, 6.

135 M. Graziano and L. Rainie, *The Music Downloading Deluge: 37 Million Adults and Youths Have Retrieved Music Files on the Internet* (Washington, DC: Pew Internet and American Life Project, 2001), 2, <http://www.pewinternet.org/reports/index.asp> (accessed 8 January 2004).

136 *Ibid.*

137 J. Litman, "Copyright Noncompliance" (1997), 29 N.Y.U. J. Int'l L. & Pol. 237 at 238-39.

138 See *R.* v. *Wholesale Travel Group Inc.*, [1991] 3 S.C.R. 154 at 216, Cory J.

139 See A. Kovacs, "Quieting the Virtual Prison Riot: Why the Internet's Spirit of 'Sharing' Must Be Broken" (2001), 51 Duke L.J. 753; I. Ballon, "Pinning the Blame in Cyberspace: Towards a Coherent Theory for Imposing Vicarious Copyright, Trademark and Tort Liability for Conduct Occurring Over the Internet" (1996), 18 Hastings Comm. & Ent. L.J. 729 at 733-34.

140 This is parallelled on the international plane. Nations that are net producers of intellectual property (IP) tend to favour strong IP protection. Nations that are net consumers do not. See F. Cate, "Sovereignty and the Globalization of Intellectual Property" (1998), 6 Ind. J. Global Legal Stud. 1 at 7.

141 See Lessig, *supra* note 45 at 126; Erola and Fox, *supra* note 22 at 203-10.

142 See Lessig, *supra* note 65 at 181-82.

143 See J. Andenaes, *Punishment and Deterrence* (Ann Arbor: University of Michigan Press, 1974), 112-26; R. Hollinger and L. Lanza-Kaduce, "The Process of Criminalization: The Case of Computer Crime Laws" (1988), 26 Criminology 101 at 114; K. Dau-Schmidt, "An Economic Analysis of the Criminal Law as a Preference-Shaping Policy," [1990] Duke L.J. 1; P. Robinson and J. Darley, "The Utility of Desert" (1997), 91 Nw. U. L. Rev. 453 at 471-78; L. Seidman, "Soldiers, Martyrs, and Criminals: Utilitarian Theory and the Problem of Crime Control" (1984), 94 Yale L.J. 315 at 336-38.

144 See J. Feinberg, *Harm to Others: The Moral Limits of the Criminal Law* (New York: Oxford University Press, 1984).

145 *Ibid.*

146 *Ibid.*, 34-36, 52, 105-6.

147 *Ibid.*, 35.

148 *Ibid.*, 191. Note the similarity of this formulation to Hand's famous negligence formula. See *United States* v. *Carroll Towing Co.*, 159 F.2d 169 at 173 (2d Cir. 1947).

149 See Bartow, *supra* note 130 at 117; Liebowitz, *supra* note 97 at 6.

150 See Liebowitz, *supra* note 97 at 7.

151 See M. Richel, "Access to Free Online Music Is Seen As a Boost to Sales," *New York Times*, 6 May 2002; Bailey, *supra* note 86 at 508 and n.220; B. King, "Record Biz Has Burning Question," *Wired News*, 14 June 2002, <http://www.wired.com/news/mp3/0,1285,53157,00.html> (8 January 2004); Bartow, *supra* note 130 at 114; J. Leeds, "Album Sales Test the Napster Effect," *Los Angeles Times*, 20 June 2001, C1. Not surprisingly, music industry representatives dispute these findings. There is evidence, moreover, that music downloaders do not often purchase music after they have obtained it for free from the Internet. This is supported by theoretical work predicting that unauthorized MP3 copying will increasingly be substituted for purchases of authorized CDs. See Liebowitz, *supra* note 97 at 9-10. It is also often suggested that file sharing is a boon to new, less established artists. There is some evidence to support this. But most downloaders seek out "music that they have heard before, by artists they were already familiar with." See Lenhart and Fox, *supra* note 132 at 6. In *A&M Records* v. *Napster*, 239 F.3d 1004 (9th Cir. 2001), the court noted that there was conflicting evidence as to whether file sharing diminishes the market for CD purchases. But it found that Napster negatively impacted the plaintiffs' potential to exploit the online music market. On the whole, the empirical evidence we have to date on the effect of Napster and other file-sharing technologies on the music market is limited and problematic. For a good discussion of the weaknesses of the empirical record, see Liebowitz, *supra* note 97 at 11-14.

152 The classic example of this is the fax machine. See Liebowitz, *supra* note 97 at 7.

153   *Ibid.*
154   See Breyer, *supra* note 80 at 281.
155   See Ku, *supra* note 71 at 299-300.
156   See Feinberg, *supra* note 108 at 203-4, 214.
157   The best that Feinberg can do is to suggest that the relative importance of competing interests be judged by: "a. how 'vital' they are in the interest networks of their possessors; b. the degree to which they are reinforced by other interests, private and public; [and] c. their inherent moral quality." Feinberg, *supra* note 108 at 217. Other scholars have proffered more detailed analyses of criminal harm, but these approaches also provide little insight into the harmfulness of copyright infringement or other "interest balancing" activities. See A. von Hirsch and N. Jareborg, "Gauging Criminal Harm: A Living-Standard Analysis" (1991), 11 Oxford J. Legal Stud. 1 at 32-35.
158   See Feinberg, *supra* note 108 at 26.
159   *Ibid.,* 4; Law Reform Commission of Canada, *supra* note 107 at 17-19, 27; N. Jareborg, "What Kind of Criminal Law Do We Want?" (1995), 14 Scand. Stud. in Criminology 17; P. Alldridge, "The Moral Limits of the Crime of Money Laundering" (2001), 5 Buffalo Crim. L. Rev. 279 at 316.
160   On the possibility of instituting compulsory licensing schemes for music downloading, see Ku, *supra* note 71; A. Reese, "Copyright and Internet Music Transmissions: Existing Law, Major Controversies, Possible Solutions" (2001), 55 U. Miami L. Rev. 237; J. Graham, "Kazaa, Verizon Propose To Pay Artists Directly," *USA Today.com*, 13 May 2002, <http://www.usatoday.com/life/cyber/tech/2002/05/14/music-kazaa.htm> (8 January 2004).
161   Some commentators therefore view Feinberg's project as combining moral and utilitarian approaches. See, for example, H. Bedau, "Feinberg's Liberal Theory of Punishment" (2001), 5 Buffalo Crim. L. Rev. 103 at 119-22.
162   See Bentham, *supra* note 105; C. Beccaria, 1872, *On Crimes and Punishments* (Indianapolis: Bobbs-Merrill, 1963); C. Montesquieu, 1748, "The Spirit of Laws," in *Great Books of the Western World*, vol. 38, edited by R. Hutching (Chicago: Encyclopedia Britannica, 1952), xi.
163   See R. Posner, "An Economic Theory of the Criminal Law" (1985), 85 Colum. L. Rev. 1193 at 1230; A. Klevorick, "On the Economic Theory of Crime," in *Nomos XXVII: Criminal Justice*, edited by J.R. Pennock and J. Chapman (New York: New York University Press, 1985), 289 at 290.
164   There is skepticism among criminal-law scholars regarding the deterrent effect of criminal sanctions. See, for example, D. Paciocco, *Getting Away with Murder: The Canadian Criminal Justice System* (Toronto: Irwin Law, 1999), 28-35. But among empirical researchers there is a strong consensus that, on the whole, criminal punishments exert a substantial deterrent effect. The real question is whether any particular policy innovation (typically increased enforcement or penalties) will add measurably to the existing preventive effect. See D. Pyle, *The Economics of Crime and Law Enforcement* (New York: St. Martin's Press, 1983), 55, 57-58; D. Nagin, "Criminal Deterrence Research at the Outset of the Twenty-First Century" (1998), 23 Crime & Just. 1 at 1-3; Cooter and Ulen, *supra* note 75 at 440, 461-63.
165   This, in fact, is the dominant economic explanation for the existence of the criminal category; that is, criminal penalties are required when conventional damages are insufficient to limit the social costs of an activity to the efficient level. See Posner, *supra* note 163. More generally, law and economics scholars argue that because voluntary exchange is typically more efficient than involuntary exchange, criminal sanctions will be used in preference (or in addition) to tort remedies to prevent individuals from unilaterally converting property rules (permitting only voluntary exchanges of entitlements) into liability rules (permitting involuntary exchanges with compensation). See G. Calabresi and A.D. Melamed, "Property Rules, Liability Rules, and Inalienability: One View of the Cathedral" (1972), 85 Harv. L. Rev. 1089 at 1124-27; Posner, *supra* note 117 at 1195-1205. This model is not particularly helpful in the case of copyright, which is protected by both liability rules (damages and in some cases compulsory licences) and property rules (injunctions and criminal punishments). Copyright property rules, moreover, provide for both civil and criminal remedies. On the limitations of the economic explanation of the criminal category, see S. Schulhofer, "Is There An Economic Theory of Crime?" in *Nomos XXVII: Criminal Justice,*

edited by J.R. Pennock and J. Chapman (New York: New York University Press, 1985) 329 at 331-35.

166 See Bentham, *supra* note 105 at 178-88.

167 See G. Becker, "Crime and Punishment: An Economic Approach" (1968), 76 J. Pol. Econ. 169. See also Cooter and Ulen, *supra* note 75 at 440. The standard economic model ignores the possibility that redistributive initiatives (such as welfare, housing, education, health, or recreation) may also affect crime rates. See Pyle, *supra* note 164 at 90. This omission is not particularly relevant to the analysis in this paper.

168 These costs include the harm done to the victim as well as the costs borne by society in deterring crime. See G. Skogh, "A Note on Gary Becker's 'Crime and Punishment: An Economic Approach'" (1973), 75 Swed. J. Econ 305 at 306-8; Cooter and Ulen, *supra* note 75 at 443. Generally speaking, "social costs" refer to "resource-using activity which reduces aggregate well-being or welfare in a society." C. Gray, "The Costs of Crime: Review and Overview" in *The Costs of Crime*, edited by C. Gray (Beverly Hills: Sage, 1979) 13 at 21.

169 As Dau-Schmidt explains, "the *ex ante* expected value of the criminal sanction is equal to the probability the criminal will be caught and convicted, times the cost of the criminal sanction to the criminal. The *ex ante* expected value is the relevant figure in considering the individual's decision whether to commit a crime since a rational person would discount the costs of the criminal sanction by the probability he will actually suffer that sanction in deciding whether to commit the crime." Dau-Schmidt, *supra* note 143 at 10 n.48. See also Becker, *supra* note 167 at 191-92.

170 This has been demonstrated most emphatically in the context of tax evasion. See R. Kagan, "On the Visibility of Income Tax Law Violations," in *Taxpayer Compliance*, vol. 2, edited by J. Roth and J. Scholz (Philadelphia: University of Pennsylvania Press, 1989), 76.

171 See Becker, *supra* note 167 at 211; Posner, *supra* note 117 at 1207-8; S. Shavell, "Criminal Law and the Optimal Use of Nonmonetary Sanctions as a Deterrent" (1985), 85 Colum. L. Rev. 1232 at 1246; Cooter and Ulen, *supra* note 75 at 449.

172 See Pyle, *supra* note 164 at 40, citing I. Erlich, "Participation in Illegitimate Activities: A Theoretical and Empirical Investigation" (1973), 81 J. Pol. Econ. 521.

173 See R. Freeman, "Crime and the Employment of Disadvantaged Youths," Working Paper no. 3875 (Cambridge, MA: Harvard University, National Bureau of Economic Research, 1991); J. Lott, "Do We Punish High-Income Criminals Too Heavily" (1992), 20 Econ. Inq'y 583; D. Nagin and J. Waldfogel, "The Effects of Criminality and Conviction on the Labor Market Status of Young British Offenders" (1995), 15 Int'l. Rev. Law and Econ. 107.

174 See Nagin, *supra* note 164 at 20.

175 S. Klepper and D. Nagin, "Tax Compliance and Perceptions of the Risks of Detection and Criminal Prosecution" (1989), 23 Law and Society Rev. 209; S. Klepper and D. Nagin, "The Deterrent Effect of Perceived Certainty and Severity of Punishment Revisited" (1989), 27 Criminology 721.

176 See Nagin, *supra* note 164 at 34; M. Tonry, *Malign Neglect: Race, Crime, and Punishment in America* (New York: Oxford University Press, 1995); R. Adelstein, "The Moral Costs of Crime: Prices, Information, and Organization," in *The Costs of Crime*, edited by C. Gray (Beverly Hills: Sage, 1979) 233 at 247.

177 See G. Stigler, "The Optimum Enforcement of Laws" (1970), 78 J. Pol. Econ. 526 at 534.

178 See N. Katyal, "Deterrence's Difficulty" (1997), 95 Mich. L. Rev. 2411 at 2451-52.

179 See Nagin, *supra* note 164 at 36; J. Andreoni, "Reasonable Doubt and the Optimal Magnitude of Fines: Should the Penalty Fit the Crime?" (1991), 22 RAND J. Econ. 385.

180 See F. Beutel, *Some Potentialities of Experimental Jurisprudence as a New Branch of Social Science* (Lincoln: University of Nebraska Press, 1967) at 224-379; N. Walker, *Crime and Punishment in Britain*, 2nd rev'd ed. (Edinburgh: University Press, 1968), 241 n.3; M. Foucault, 1975, *Discipline and Punish: The Birth of the Prison*, 2nd ed. (Vintage Books 1995), 14; Adelstein, *supra* note 176 at 247.

181 As economists say, law is a "preference-shaper." See Dau-Schmidt, *supra* note 143; Katyal, *supra* note 44 at 2442-49.

182 See generally R. Ellickson, *Order Without Law: How Neighbors Settle Disputes* (Cambridge, MA: Harvard University Press, 1991); P. Robinson and J. Darley, *Justice, Liability, and Blame:*

Community Views and the Criminal Law (Boulder, CO: Westview, 1995), 201-2; Robinson and Darley, *supra* note 143 at 457-58, 477-88, 494-99.

183   See Robinson and Darley, *supra* note 143 at 468-71; D. Dana, "Rethinking the Puzzle of Escalating Penalties for Repeat Offenders" (2001), 110 Yale L.J. 733 at 776-77; D. Kahan, "Social Meaning and the Economic Analysis of Crime" (1998), 27 J. Legal Stud. 609.

184   See Robinson and Darley, *supra* note 143 at 468-71; Dana, *supra* note 183 at 772-73; J. Lott, Jr., "An Attempt at Measuring the Total Monetary Penalty from Drug Convictions: The Importance of an Individual's Reputation" (1992), 21 J. Legal Stud. 159; Seidman, *supra* note 143 at 337.

185   *Ibid.*, 474-75, 481-82.

186   See D. Kahan, "Between Economics and Sociology: The New Path of Deterrence" (1997), 95 Mich. L. Rev. 2477 at 2481.

187   Nagin, *supra* note 164 at 35.

188   See D. Kahan, "Social Influence, Social Meaning, and Deterrence" (1997), 83 Va. L. Rev. 349 at 356-57.

189   Marginal deterrence describes the capacity of graduated sanctions to induce offenders to commit a lesser rather than a greater offence. See Stigler, *supra* note 177 at 526-27; Posner, *supra* note 117 at 1207.

190   Stigler, *supra* note 177 at 527.

191   Katyal, *supra* note 44 at 2407.

192   *Ibid.*, 2445.

193   *Ibid.* See also Robinson and Darley, *supra* note 143 at 481-82.

194   There is some empirical support for this phenomenon, especially in African American communities with very high incarceration rates. See M. Mauer and T. Huling, *Young Black Americans and the Criminal Justice System: Five Years Later* (Washington, DC: Sentencing Project, 1995).

195   See discussion *supra* notes 35-41 and accompanying text. See also Bailey, *supra* note 86 at 519-21. Naive users may escape conviction by virtue of the *mens rea* requirement, but more sophisticated users would likely face liability. See discussion *supra* notes 37-8 and accompanying text.

196   See Lessig, *supra* note 45 at 125; Bailey, *supra* note 86 at 515-17. In some circumstances, however, digitization may increase visibility. Automated searching technology facilitates the detection of infringing material that is nonsecurely posted on bulletin boards and websites. This type of unsophisticated, low-level infringement is arguably more visible than its real-space analogues. See Ballon, *supra* note 139 at 735; Lessig, *supra* note 65 at 182.

197   See Bailey, *supra* note 86 at 514-18. For example, the MPAA has attempted to identify the Internet Protocol (IP) addresses of P2P users distributing movie files. See L. Gomes, "Recording Industry Targets Gnutella Amid Signs Napster Usage Is Falling," *Wall Street Journal*, 4 May 2001, B6; F. Ahrens, "'Ranger' vs. the Movie Pirates," *Washington Post*, 19 June 2002, H1. But as Liebowitz asserts, this practice may be thwarted by the use of dynamic IP addresses, which are already in common use. See Liebowitz, *supra* note 97 at 15. See also D. Chmielewski, "Swappers Sprint to Cloak Identities," *SiliconValley.com*, 14 July 2003, <http://www.siliconvalley.com/mld/siliconvalley/6300393.htm?> (8 January 2004).

198   Bailey, *ibid.*, 524-29.

199   See discussion *supra* notes 64-67 and accompanying text.

200   Robinson and Darley, *supra* note 143 at 458.

201   *Ibid.*, 458, 475-77.

202   *Ibid.*

203   See Johannes Andenaes, "The Scandinavian Experience," in *Social Control of the Drinking Driver*, edited by M. Laurence et al. (Chicago: University of Chicago Press, 1988) 43; R. Hingson, "Prevention of Drinking and Driving" (1996), 20 Alcohol Health & Research World 219; Robinson and Darley, *supra* note 143 at 476-77.

204   See Hingson, *supra* note 203.

205   In Canada the police may arbitrarily stop vehicles to check for signs of impairment in the course of either fixed or roving patrols. See *R. v. Hufsky*, [1988] 1 S.C.R. 621; *R. v. Ladouceur*, [1990] 1 S.C.R. 357. United States courts have been slightly less accommodating. The

Supreme Court has permitted fixed roadblocks screening every vehicle (*Michigan Department of State Police* v. *Sitz*, 496 U.S. 444 [1990]) but has forbidden random roving stops (*Delaware* v. *Prouse*, 440 U.S. 648 [1979]). Subsequent lower-court decisions under state and federal law have been mixed, with a majority permitting fixed roadblocks stopping cars pursuant to neutral criteria (such as stopping every *n*th car). See J. English, "Sobriety Checkpoints Under State Constitutions: What Has Happened to *Sitz*?" (1998), 59 U. Pitt. L. Rev. 453.

206 See Hingson, *supra* note 203.
207 Robinson and Darley, *supra* note 143 at 487.
208 For a discussion of these costs, see Hingson, *supra* note 203.
209 See Hingson, *supra* note 203.
210 The music industry is particularly unsympathetic. Many people believe that the major record companies engage in anticompetitive practices. See B. King, "Slagging Over Sagging CD Sales," *Wired News*, 17 April 2002, <http://www.wired.com/news/mp3/0,1285,51880,00.html> (8 January 2004). There is some evidence to support this view. See J. O'Donnell and D. Lieberman, "FTC Cuts Deal That Could Make CDs Cheaper, Time Warner to Drop Minimum Advertised Prices," *USA Today*, 10 April 2001, 1B; S. Castle and C. Arthur, "Brussels to Investigate Inflated CD Prices," *The Independent* (London), 27 January 2001, 10. Similar views are held about some of the largest players in the software industry, including most obviously Microsoft (which courts have found guilty of anticompetitive activity. See *United States* v. *Microsoft*, 253 F.3d 34 (2001 D.C. Cir.).
211 Research in cognitive psychology confirms that people respond to vivid and dramatic events more readily than to less dramatic events even where the risk posed by the latter is objectively greater. See P. Slovic, "Perception of Risk" (1987), 236 Science 280 at 283.
212 See Litman, *supra* note 102.
213 Liebowitz (*supra* note 97 at 15) describes the conundrum faced by content producers as follows:

> It is painful to imagine the authorities trying to monitor individual computer users and then prosecuting copyright infringers, often teenagers, for downloading music and other files. Yet that is exactly the specter that faces copyright owners, who do seem willing to undertake it. They might do well to consider, however, the public relations fiasco that the American Society of Composers, Authors, and Publishers created when it decided to enforce copyright against summer camps, including the Girl Scouts, who believed that they were no longer allowed to sing copyrighted songs around the campfire. The blizzard of negative publicity engendered by that action required ASCAP to backpedal at full speed. Teenagers trading copyrighted songs may not create the same degree of empathy as young girls singing around the campfire, but lots of parents have such teenagers and the record industry will have to be very careful not to alienate the public while punishing otherwise law-abiding infringers.

214 For support for this assertion, one need only look to the knighting of Rolling Stones singer Mick Jagger, who was arrested and imprisoned for possession of amphetamines in 1967. See L. McLaren, "A Knight in Black Armour?" *Globe and Mail*, 12 June 2002, R3.
215 17 U.S.C. § 1204.
216 See discussion *supra* note 65.
217 See, for example, H. Packer, *The Limits of the Criminal Sanction* (Stanford: Stanford University Press, 1968); Hart, *supra* note 106.
218 See, for example, K. Roach, *Due Process and Victims' Rights: The New Law and Politics of Criminal Justice* (Toronto: University of Toronto Press, 1999).
219 For example, the recording industry has recently initiated lawsuits against large numbers of file sharers. The effectiveness of this strategy in deterring infringement remains to be determined. See L. Holloway, "Recording Industry to Sue Internet Music Swappers," *New York Times*, 26 June 2003, C4; T. Bridis, "Subpoena Onslaught Aimed at Illegal File Sharing," *Washington Post*, 19 July 2003, E1; "File Swapping Dips After Threats," *BBC News*, 15 July 2003, <http://news.bbc.co.uk/2/hi/entertainment/3066981.stm> (8 January 2004);

M. Musgrove, "File Swappers to RIAA: Download This!" *Washington Post*, 6 July 2003, F7; L. Walker, "Music Pirates, on the Run? Or Just on Vacation?" *Washington Post*, 20 July 2003, F7; "Subpoenas Sent to File-Sharers Prompt Anger and Remorse," *New York Times*, 28 July 2003, C1; L. Rainie and M. Madden, *Pew Internet Project and Comscore Media Metrix Data Memo: The Impact of Recording Industry Suits against Music File Swappers* (Washington, DC: Pew Internet and American Life Project, 2004), <http://www.pewinternet.org/reports/index.asp> (accessed 8 January 2004); J. Schwartz, "In Survey, Fewer Are Sharing Files (Or Admitting It)," *New York Times*, 5 January 2004, C1.

4
Criminalization in Private: The Case of Insurance Fraud

Richard V. Ericson and Aaron Doyle

If crime is an offence against the state, what happens when private institutions displace the state or when the state itself is run like a business? Today, social life is increasingly regulated by private institutions rather than by government. For example, in Canada approximately two-thirds of security providers are now employed in the private sector (Law Commission of Canada 2002, 10). One very powerful, but often invisible, private institution that governs many aspects of our lives is the insurance industry. Private insurance is a central institution embodying the tendencies of contemporary society toward governance beyond the state (Rose 1999; Ericson, Barry, and Doyle 2000; Ericson, Doyle, and Barry 2003; Ericson and Doyle 2004). In a society increasingly oriented toward both risk and privatization, the insurance industry is the key market-based alternative to government for risk management. Yet, although private insurance is one of the most pervasive and powerful institutions in our society, it is given scant attention by social scientists.

This chapter is based on our empirical examination of the social processes by which insurers define and regulate fraud by claimants in property and casualty (home, auto) and workers' compensation lines of insurance. Fraud by those working in the insurance industry and by service providers, such as doctors, is also a significant issue, as we discuss elsewhere (Ericson, Doyle, and Barry 2003). Here we focus on claimant fraud. We examine a major expansion in the last twenty years of insurers' efforts to crack down on insurance fraud. We ask what it means for insurers to say that claimant fraud is a "crime" in this context given that fraud is still very largely defined and dealt with internally by insurance companies. Thus we ask "what is a crime?" as it is defined in practice in the expanding world of private justice.

The chapter builds on the extensive sociological and criminological literatures problematizing how certain behaviour and individuals are criminalized by focusing here on what happens when definitions of crime shift as the crime is policed by private institutions and mechanisms. In a society increasingly regulated or governed by private institutions rather than by governments, does the state still cast a long shadow by means of the law's role in governing the justice processes of these private bodies, or, alternatively, are the law and the criminal justice system increasingly estranged or pushed into the background by private institutions?

The data presented in this chapter are derived from a broader research program on the insurance industry and how it governs many aspects of contemporary social life (Ericson, Barry, and Doyle 2000; Ericson, Doyle, and Barry 2003; Ericson and Doyle 2004). We have conducted 224 open-focused interviews in Canada and the United States for this broader project. Interviewees included people with a wide range of responsibilities in the insurance industry,[1] professionals in expert systems that serve the industry, representatives of consumer associations, members of the general public who were consumers, industry regulators, senior civil servants, and politicians. Observational research included attending industry conferences and observing sales operations, loss-prevention operations, and claims-related examination practices.[2] For this chapter in particular, we draw on our many interviews with insurance-company executives, adjusters, and fraud investigators, on numerous industry documents, and on our firsthand observations – for example, at two insurance-claims centres and at an industry conference on fraud.

The Rise of the "Fraud Problem"

More than thirty years ago, H. Laurence Ross conducted a classic sociological study of adjusters at three US auto-insurance companies, reported in his book *Settled Out of Court*. Ross (1970, 45) found that:

> The adjuster typically believes that few people cut false claims from whole cloth, but that nearly everyone exaggerates his loss. This exaggeration is expected, and the adjuster sees his job as being to reduce the valid claim to an appropriate size. The claimant discovered in an exaggeration is the rule, rather than the exception, and nothing is gained by embarrassing him. Even more is this the case when exaggeration is expected but dishonesty cannot be proven, as in the case of subjective pain and whiplash injury.

In the thirty years since the study by Ross was published, some things have not changed in the insurance industry, but others have shifted dramatically. Just as Ross found then, today many in the industry still assume that a large proportion of claimants exaggerate. However, Ross barely discussed fraud in his book (*ibid.*, 95-6), noting simply that a "small minority" of claims warranted further investigation due to the possibility of fraud. Ross's book was a classic study of the "law in action" – not of criminal law, but instead of the law of torts related to the attribution of negligence in motor-vehicle accidents. Criminal law was little mentioned by Ross. However, since Ross wrote, there has been an explosion of insurance-industry antifraud efforts, not only targeting wholly fabricated claims, but perhaps more important, also cracking down on the mere "exaggeration" described by Ross as a somewhat routine part of the claims process.

In Canada industry associations and spokespersons now regularly proclaim that "insurance fraud is the second leading source of criminal profits next to drugs." A brochure on fraud distributed to policyholders of an auto insurer declares that "10 percent to 20 percent of all claims are fraudulent ... [T]hat means $160 to $320 million of your premiums are paid to people who don't deserve them." Another document from the same company was more precise, stating that in 1996 fraud cost $308 million, 15 percent of all claims costs. An antifraud investigator for this company used this same figure during an interview, followed by the opinion that it "is probably being conservative, because where I grew up everybody tries to screw us." The industry production of insurance-fraud "facts" is also exemplified in the following industry association document:

> The crime of insurance fraud is growing in Canada; its economic impact is exceeded only by that of tax evasion. Property and casualty insurers in Canada believe that at least 10 to 15 percent of household, automobile and commercial insurance claims are fraudulent – either completely fraudulent or inflated. That's about $1.3 billion a year in fraudulent claims that must be paid from the premiums of all policyholders ... [I]nsurance fraud has costly secondary consequences; staged "accidents" and deliberately set fires, medical examinations required because of false personal-injury claims and, of course, the wasting of costly and all-too-scarce police resources. Consumers are unaware that even the padding of a legitimate claim – often called "opportunistic" fraud or claims "build up" – is illegal.

According to Homesite Insurance in the United States, insurance fraud cost consumers $120 billion in 1999 and "continues to rise."

Alongside antifraud publicity campaigns, there has been a massive expansion of private-policing personnel and technologies in the insurance industry in the last two decades in Canada and the United States. The first Special Investigation Units (SIUs) of private police within American insurance companies were established in the 1970s (Ghezzi 1983) and have multiplied dramatically since the mid-1980s (see also Clarke 1989, 1990, confirming the increased policing of insurance fraud). In 1992 approximately 240 companies had SIUs. However, by 1997 approximately 1,200 companies had such units. This expansion in SIUs has been accompanied by the hiring of more investigators within each company's SIU. During the same five-year period, one major company's SIU grew from approximately 300 to 1,200 investigators. As Dornstein (1996, 332) observes:

> In the early 1980s, there were still hardly enough SIU investigators in the Northeast [US] to field a softball team, and meetings were held in the backs of diners; by the early 1990s, there were national and international associations of SIUs with memberships in the many thousands ... Often lost in the alphabet soup of industry trade groups are the tens of thousands of private investigators working on contract to insurers ... [such as in] Photo Surveillance which has more than 100 agents nationwide completely outfitted with custom vans, cameras, and in some cases, camouflage jumpsuits designed to look like shrubbery.
>
> In January 1992 the American property and casualty insurance industry's new message about fraud took on a new air of seriousness and urgency when a former U.S. Army general stepped forward to announce the formation of the National Insurance Crime Bureau (NICB), with himself as the first director. Arnold Schlossberg, Jr., had come to the NICB directly from the Pentagon, where he served as one of the higher-ups in the Bush administration's "war on drugs" ... [General Schlossberg] talked about insurance fraud as a criminal threat to the American way of life equal in many ways to drug trafficking in terms of its economic cost and its creeping erosion of moral values.

Although the NICB is wholly funded by insurers, its president described it as a "social welfare agency." Insurers and the government-affairs branch of the NICB have also been very effective in influencing the American criminal justice system to take a harder line with insurance fraud. In the US, civil and criminal penalties for insurance fraud have increased. Almost every American state now defines insurance fraud as a felony rather than a misdemeanour. Most states have enacted legislation creating state-government fraud bureaus, which are often partly funded by the insurance industry. Parallel crackdowns were evident in various Canadian jurisdictions. For example, one provincial auto insurer not only conducted extensive publicity campaigns, but also expanded its own Special Investigation Unit as well as the surveillance functions performed by its adjusters. Moreover, it is a major contractor with the private investigation firms in the province, which are primarily used to conduct photo surveillance on claimants to ascertain whether they are engaged in physical tasks that would belie their claimed disabilities. In 1995 there were approximately 4,400 such assignments. There is also an effort to mobilize neighbours, fellow employees, and others as informants – for example, through an informant tip line.

Measurement Difficulties and Slippery Definitions

Certainly, claims costs are extremely large and have grown very dramatically in some areas – for example, soft-tissue injury claims for auto insurers. However, despite industry statements, the scope of claimant fraud and the extent to which it is responsible for these escalating costs remain extremely difficult to discern. With soft-tissue injury claims, for example, the problems of capturing what might be fraud are immense: Medical science on the subject is extremely limited; medical, legal, and insurance systems are themselves iatrogenic and lead to increasing costs; and claimants themselves, rather than being deliberately fraudulent, may have extreme difficulty comprehending various signals as to the nature of their injuries (see Ericson and Doyle 2004, Ch. 3).

Indeed, measuring fraud would be extremely difficult even if one took the realist position that there is a precise amount of insurance fraud "out there." Most crime in general goes unrecorded. Insurance fraud in particular is secret, not self-disclosing; the victim is not a private individual but both the insurer's bottom line and, indirectly, insurance consumers. Even when fraud is discovered, it is most often not dealt with formally.

Beyond this, there is considerable fluidity in defining precisely what is meant by fraud. The scope of the fraud problem is of course linked to how the boundaries of fraud are drawn. In public contexts, stressing the need to crack down on fraud, insurers offer a broad definition of fraud as any intentional deception that exposes the recipient to unjustified losses. For example, in a popular-magazine article on insurance fraud, the executive director of the Canadian Coalition Against Insurance Fraud offered the following definition: "It's any act or omission resulting in illicit collection of property and casualty insurance benefit ... [from] fabricated claims, to inflation or padding of legitimate claims and false statements on applications."

In everyday working contexts, defining exactly what does and does not constitute fraud is more problematic, and the scope narrows. A definition from an insurance-company manual for claims adjusters says that fraud occurs when the claimant misrepresents facts with the intention of having the insurer act on them. As the manual states: "For fraud to exist there must be a false representation of fact, knowledge of the statement's falsity by the person making it, and intent by the insured that the insurer will act on it." While this definition is broad and encompassing, the manual immediately narrows the formulation by adding, "Slight exaggeration in the amount of the claim itself will not constitute fraud ... however falsifying documents to support an exaggerated claim would constitute fraud."

We found that this type of blurry distinction between mere "exaggeration" and fraud is typical in the industry. Although insurers describe insurance fraud as one of the most serious economic crimes, insurance-fraud investigators may also make a distinction between the "average offender" and the "criminal offender" (Baldock 1997). Indeed, adjusters and many others in the industry see that exaggeration of claims has long been a routine and typical part of the business of insurance, as Ross (1970) found thirty years ago.

The barrier between what those employed in the industry understand as "fraud" and what is mere "exaggeration" is highly permeable. In the extreme case, some industry executives simply conflate the cost of "fraud" with claims costs in general. For example, Ontario auto-insurance executives we interviewed indicated that revamped provincial auto-insurance legislation had cut down on "fraud." They indicated that they knew this simply because auto-claims costs in general had decreased.

One auto-claims adjuster we interviewed said that while "everyone exaggerates," fraud is clear-cut falsification of a document or material evidence. Her company offered a five-hour training session that tried to specify the fine line between exaggeration and fraud. Another interviewee, involved in organizing this training program, was asked how the line was drawn. He replied, "If *you* could give us the answer to this, you'd be a hero."

Others in the industry make parallel distinctions between "soft-core" abuse of the system and "hardcore" criminal fraud. We interviewed a consultant who developed data-analysis systems to detect insurance fraud. He said that an example of "soft-core" abuse in auto-insurance claims is when a claimant's minor neck injury is portrayed as a major injury, usually on the urgings of a lawyer. "Hardcore" fraud, by comparison, would cover the activities of an "injury ring" that stages a fake auto accident followed by multiple claims from several "injured" parties. Similarly, an investigator for a workers' compensation insurer distinguished between "20 percent abuse" and "5 percent criminal fraud" among all claims. He said "abuse" is largely accounted for by "malingering individuals ... off [for] a couple of extra weeks longer than necessary simply because they've gone back to the doctor and said, 'I need a couple of extra weeks' ... we're in an injury system, not an adversarial system. On balance of probabilities, we give the nod to the claimant."

Even though "soft-core abuse" or "exaggeration" is described by some insurance personnel as not distinctly criminal and, indeed, as something that many or most claimants do, it is also seen within the industry as the more expensive part of the "fraud" problem overall, as compared to "hardcore" fraud. A recently completed survey of 353 American property and casualty insurers (Insurance Research Council/Insurance Services Organization 2001) revealed that the "soft-core" problem was seen as more costly. Thus, while industry antifraud publicity campaigns dramatize individual examples of wholesale "hardcore fraud," such as staged auto accidents, they are also targeted at reducing what is perceived as a more expensive "soft-core" problem by deterring "average" claimants from exaggerating their losses.

None of the numerous interviewees we asked to define fraud referred to criminal codes or legal definitions. A number struggled to define fraud at all. In practice, insurance adjusters and investigators take a pragmatic approach to defining fraud. For example, when asked to define fraud, an insurance-claims investigator employed by a multinational management-consultant firm replied, "Well it's easy. You see we're not the cops, so it's easier. We pursue it when we're paid to pursue it, and that's it ... we're driven by our clients ... they're driven by fear and self-interest." A manager of special investigators for an auto insurer said that this pragmatic approach to fraud has three elements. First, it must be determined that the claimant intended to deceive for personal gain. Second, the magnitude of the loss must be great enough to make further investigation worthwhile. Third, further investigation and possible sanctions must be both viable and efficient. If investigative options appear foreclosed, or adequate sanctions are not available, the determination of fraud dissipates.

While definitions are slippery, the detection of what adjusters perceive as "fraud" in everyday claims adjusting is nevertheless routine. In a vehicle hit-and-run insurance-claims centre that we studied, out of an average of sixty-five claims each day, six were judged fraudulent based on material damage assessment. These claims were denied on the spot. However, an additional thirteen claims were believed to be fraudulent but not investigated further because the company decided it was more expedient to pay the claim. Cases involving personal injuries and disabilities are even more ambiguous and difficult to assess. Studies of bodily injury claims arising from vehicle claims in Massachusetts (Weisberg and Derrig 1991, 1992) judged 31 percent (n = 597) of one sample and 47 percent (n = 1,154) of another sample to have involved dishonesty in the claim.

Insurers do not routinely produce such data, however. Where fraud is suspected but not pursued for reasons of expediency, there may be no data collected at all. Even when fraud is detected, it may not be recorded on company records if a resolution is reached with the culprit. As we have seen, these data inadequacies and fluid definitions do not inhibit industry spokespersons from producing dramatic numbers to sustain a view that fraud is a very serious risk to the industry and consumers. However, other industry insiders admit that such figures have little statistical foundation. In an editorial entitled "The Mismeasure of Fraud," written by the editor of *Canadian Insurance* magazine, the following assessment is made:

> Although we have seen in countless media the estimate of fraud in Canadian property and casualty insurance – 10-15 percent of claims or roughly $1.3 billion – few actually know where this measurement came from or, for that matter, how accurate it is. My exhaustive research has turned up only one reference to this number. A judgment in a 1992 New Jersey Supreme

Court case stated that "insurance fraud is a problem of massive proportions that currently results in substantial and unnecessary costs to the general public in the form of increased rates. In fact, *approximately ten to fifteen percent of all insurance claims involve fraud.*" No one really knows how much these particular judges knew about fraud, but the estimate lives on. Since the Canadian Coalition Against Insurance Fraud clearly borrowed the name from its US counterpart (Coalition Against Insurance Fraud), it is quite likely that this number was also extrapolated to fit the Canadian environment. (Harris 1998, 5, emphasis in the original)

Indeed, it may be argued that the prevalence of insurance fraud is ultimately unknowable, except to the extent that insurers make it into a problem. As the social-reaction perspective indicates with crime in general (Ericson 1975, 1993; Ditton 1979), fraud is an artifact of how the insurance industry organizes to deal with it. As related to us by a senior official in an insurance private-policing operation:

The scary part is, as we continue to increase the fight, we continually uncover more and more fraud. So people say, "You are putting all these dollars in there, but the problem is increasing." You can't say something is fraudulent until you find it. There's been such a growth in "insurance fraud." It has probably always been there; it is just that more has been uncovered than ever before.

Reasons for the Crackdown
Insurance-claims costs are very large, whether legitimate or not. Even if quantification is impossible, the industry certainly has a broad range of evidence – both from various research and from their own claims experience – that exaggeration of claims has always been widespread and that a substantial portion of the public does not regard padding of claims as a serious crime. Furthermore, outright fabrication of claims – for example, through staged accidents – is a significantly costly problem.

Yet a number of sources suggest that an industry crackdown has been driven partly by reasons other than simply a perceived growth in the fraud problem. A US industry executive indicated to us that the massive boom since the 1980s in fraud policing has been driven in part by increased pressure on insurance companies to keep premiums down. In the past, increased claims costs could more easily be passed on to the consumer in higher premiums, and companies may have been reluctant to antagonize consumers with fraud policing. The executive indicated, however, that regulations in various states that restrict premium increases – for example, those resulting from Proposition 103, introduced in California in 1988 – forced the companies instead to take stronger "antifraud" measures in order to reduce claims costs and to bolster their competitive position and profits. The executive's comments have been supported by some recent analyses by legal and business scholars. As Jaffee and Russell (2002, 31) write, citing Rosenfield (1998), "Prior to Proposition 103 ... the costs of fraud ... were simply passed on to consumers ... [W]hen Proposition 103 placed a ceiling on premium levels, the firms had to control fraud and their expenses in order to maintain their profit levels." Insurers would have been reluctant to police fraud as heavily prior to Proposition 103 because of possible consumer backlash. As Jaffee and Russell (2002, 32) go on to suggest:

> It is essential for this argument, of course, to understand why insurance firms did not find it in their best interest to control fraud ... even before the passage of Proposition 103. A possible mechanism for this effect is based on the consumer ill-will that an insurance firm may create when it falsely accuses a customer of fraud. In this case, there may be a "bad equilibrium" in which all firms in the industry ignore insurance fraud, in order not to create a reputation as a firm that falsely accuses its customers. In this situation, it is possible that a major regulatory change such as Proposition 103 may push the system toward an alternative "good" equilibrium, in which all firms in the industry fight fraud.

A recent statement on insurance fraud in the United States from the Insurance Information Institute (2002) similarly acknowledges that insurance companies faced a cost crisis in the mid-1980s that was partly responsible for the industry introducing a crackdown on fraud at that time:

> In the mid-1980s, the rising price of insurance, particularly auto and health insurance, together with the growth in organized insurance fraud, prompted many insurers to reexamine the issue. They began to see the benefit of strengthening antifraud laws and more stringent enforcement as a means of controlling escalating costs.

A similar price crisis to that of the 1980s developed in the first years of the new millennium due to factors including rising injury costs, the poor performance of insurers' investments on the stock market, and the financial toll of terrorist attacks against the US on 11 September 2001. In Canada the spiralling price of auto insurance was central to provincial election campaigns in New Brunswick, Nova Scotia, and Ontario in 2003, leading to various steps toward freezing or reducing rates. In this context, Dan Danyluk, chief executive of the Insurance Brokers' Association of Canada, said that atop his list of tips for consumers upset with huge premiums was to report insurance fraud to the police: "It's your moral and ethical responsibility ... and it lowers your insurance" (*Globe and Mail, Report on Business,* 21 June 2003, C3).

An earlier crackdown on fraud in Ontario came after provincial government legislation led to reduced premiums. A provincial auto-insurance company we studied in another Canadian province was also operating under a government-mandated freeze in premium increases. As in other contexts, this prompted a heavy crackdown on fraud as one method to contain costs.

An interviewee who did fraudulent-claims data analyses for the insurer said that a massive increase in fraud surveillance was introduced because "they were squeezed for money, so they wanted it. And it looked like ... a cost-free way. You don't have to raise premiums, you don't have to lower your service, you just get cash. And no one is going to stand up and say, 'I'm the fraud lobby,' and lobby for keeping the money. So it looked good."

What Does It Mean to Say Fraud Is a Crime?

In asking what it means for insurance companies to say fraud is a "crime," it is important to understand exactly what such a crackdown involves. More cases are actually criminalized now, but these still constitute a tiny fraction of the incidents defined as "fraud" or "potential fraud" of which companies are aware. There are considerable efforts to publicize these cases. However, "fraud" is far and away most often dealt with by the summary justice of simply denying claims, even when cases are referred to SIUs. Central to the crackdown are publicity campaigns. The symbolism of the criminal justice system is invoked mainly as a deterrent not only to "hardcore fraud" but, perhaps more importantly, to the more costly problem of the everyday padding of claims that has long been seen as a normal part of the business. For example, the New York State Insurance Department (2003) recorded a steadily increasing number of "fraud reports" – from 19,196 in 1999 up to 20,247 in 2000 and 26,028 in 2001. As the department put it, "The rise in reporting is due in large measure to the Bureau's commitment to work closely with insurers to ensure that no *potential* fraud goes unreported" (our emphasis). The criteria for "potential fraud" are unspecified. However, only a very small percentage of these reports of "potential fraud" are criminalized. In 1999, out of 19,196 "fraud reports," there were 390 arrests and 194 convictions. Similar data showed that in the early 1990s, only 0.5 percent of reported insurance-fraud cases in California were prosecuted (McKenzie 1993, cited in Tennyson 1997).

Our data indicate that when enforcement is deemed necessary, in the vast majority of cases it is handled internally through the summary justice of denial of claims. We interviewed a former police officer who was now an insurance-fraud investigator with a private investigation company. He said that, despite the crackdown rhetoric, insurers mostly do not consider prosecution to be worth the time and money:

You'd never get that type of [punitive] sentence first of all for somebody who was a first-time offender on fraud cases, a $20,000 deal. You'd get a suspended sentence, conditional discharge ... There's more of a penalty [through internal means]. And why clog up the system with another case that will take years to solve, and by the end of it nobody is going to get a real penalty? He'll probably end up getting his money.

Similarly, Ghezzi's (1983, 526) study of three Massachusetts SIUs found:

The SIUs spend an average of three weeks investigating each case. Then they recommend that the claim be either paid or denied. If the claim is denied, the claimant may file suit against the company. Although exact figures were not available, respondents from the companies I studied reported that suits against them were rare. (Roughly 10 per cent of total dollars denied to claimants are ever paid following litigation.) Criminal court action taken by Massachusetts insurance companies against claimants is also rare. Due to the circumstantial nature of insurance fraud, respondents estimated that since the inception of the SIUs, fewer than five per cent of the cases they investigate are presented to the district attorney. A case must be airtight and involve a lot of money or a large number of defrauders before the district attorney is usually willing to prosecute.

Although even those cases given to SIUs are seldom criminalized, insurers still work in concert with the criminal justice system, especially the police. Insurance investigators often have access to police information, either because it is purchased or because they are former police officers who have ongoing relations with the police (Ericson and Haggerty 1997). Relationships with the police and the dramatization of insurance fraud as a crime are also employed for symbolic deterrence purposes. For example, a provincial-government auto insurer that we studied perceived that it had a very high level of fraudulent hit-and-run claims. A common situation involved claimants who may have damaged their own automobiles in single-vehicle accidents and were facing various penalties, such as increased premiums. Such a claimant has an incentive to lie and thus reports that another driver who fled the scene caused the damage instead.

To deter hit-and-run fraud, the insurance company entered into a partnership with the city police department. A claims centre was constructed as part of the same building that contained police headquarters and a police division, and all hit-and-run claims were directed to this centre, conveying to claimants that such claims would be intensively scrutinized by police. Police who specialized in hit-and-run accidents became highly visible members of the claims team. The insurer also added a special phone line to which all claimants had to report their hit-and-run claims. Upon dialing this line, claimants immediately heard a message indicating that police would be involved in the investigation and outlining the criminal penalties for fraud. As a member of the insurer's staff reported, "we got about 30 percent hang ups ... so that was a few million bucks we got [saved] right away."

Despite the symbolic deterrence provided by the presence of police, the identification of fraudulent claims was actually based on expert analysis of material damage to the vehicles by specialist insurance staff. When fraud was determined, most frequently the insurer's response was simply to deny the claim and record the incident in the claims-data system.

Why Is Fraud Endemic and Often Tolerated?
Historically, a good deal of padding of claims by insurance customers has been tolerated. As Garland (1997, 186; see also Lianos and Douglas 2000; Garland 2001) observes about criminogenic situations more generally:

> The everyday conduct of economic and social life supplies countless opportunities for illegitimate transactions. Viewed en masse, criminal events are regular, predictable, systematic, in the way that road accidents are.

In the insurance relationship, fraud is but a factor in risk calculus, something taken into account in assessing acceptable levels of loss. The regulation of fraud cannot be too intrusive. As Garland (1997, 187) also observes, the criminogenic situation "has functional ends of its own that are easily disturbed by heavy-handed regulation." Regulation of fraud cannot upset the insurance relationship and its commercial values. It is precisely because fraud is often a normal, expected component of the insurance relationship that any intervention must be conducted with sensitivity to "business as usual."

> The "criminogenic situation" poses difficulties for government because it generally has a commercial or social value of its own which sets limits on crime control. Precisely because crime occurs in the course of routine social and economic transactions, any crime-reducing intervention must seek to preserve "normal life" and "business as usual." (*Ibid.*)

Despite public rhetoric by insurers about the need for crackdowns on fraud, fraud continues to be tolerated – often due to four related factors. First, evidence that would justify treating a claim as fraudulent is usually difficult to establish. Evidence problems are especially pronounced in some fields of insurance, such as personal-injury claims. An automobile or workers' compensation insurance claimant who says he or she is suffering from a soft-tissue injury, such as whiplash following an automobile or work-related accident, is a case in point. Medical science is notoriously unable to diagnose and treat this problem, and insurers are at a loss to determine where suffering ends and exaggeration begins, or where malingering ends and fraud begins (Sullivan 2000).

Second, it is very often simply better business to make a "nuisance payment" that closes the claims file on a suspected fraudster. Although insurance workers will not admit it, such nuisance payments have long been routine, especially as adjusters are under considerable supervisory pressure to close files quickly (Ross 1970). The indemnity principle is sacrificed to expedience (Heimer 1985; Baker and McElrath 1997). Moreover, the claimant's insurance contract conditions can be legitimately altered after the claim to transfer more of the cost to him or her – for example, through higher deductibles, lower limits, and more exclusions – and premiums can be raised to recover the claims cost over time.

The field of automobile-insurance claims for material damage exemplifies how nuisance payments are institutionalized in the process. Body shops routinely report that what was designated as claimable damage is actually old damage, but the insurer decides the cost of sending out an estimator to investigate further is not worthwhile. Claimants who have their stolen vehicle returned frequently use the opportunity to repair preexisting damage. We interviewed a fraud investigator for an auto insurer who described this scenario and how claimants are dealt with when confronted with fraud:

> Whenever someone gets a car stolen, at that point it is an opportunity for that person to get a lot of little things fixed on the car that were damaged already. And if we can't prove it was not damaged before, we give them the benefit of the doubt. So we grind our teeth, bite our tongue, and say we'll fix it. It is like a house insurance policy. You get broken into, your TV gets stolen, your VCR gets stolen, might as well claim the golf clubs at the same time because it is costing you $500 [deductible] anyway – golf clubs you never had ... [When a claim is denied] we give them a way out, give them a softer approach ... If you tell us you were involved with this, that you made a mistake, we will just leave it at that. We won't process your claim, but you just won't have a claim. We won't charge you with anything ... When we are busy we are trying to get closures ... It is time management.

Claimants may know that if they persist to a reasonable degree, they may be offered nuisance payments because adjusters need to close their files efficiently. If claimants are reasonable in finessing their claims, they may be able to garner extra compensation for their reasonableness.

The insurance adjuster's starting position in a claims settlement varies considerably with the field of insurance, type of claim, and market segment of the claimant. However, governed by auditing, quotas, and penalties for exceeding specified claims levels, adjusters may try to draw the line for negotiation at minimal levels. The adjuster's position may also be based on the experience that deception by both parties is frequent in the insurance relationship. Assuming that "everyone exaggerates," adjusters may try to minimize claims (Ross 1970). A former adjuster for an automobile insurer we interviewed said that his company's routine practice in personal-injury claims was "to deny until they hire a lawyer. So there's no question they were entitled to benefits, it's just denied them and hope they go away."

Knowing that claims fraud is routine, insurance operatives suspect every claimant. The insurance-governance system constitutes the private-justice category of "situational man," who is "the economic subject of interest ... a moderately rational, self-interested individual ... a consumer who is alert to criminal opportunities and responsive to situational inducements" (Garland 1997, 190). Fraud is seen as opportunistic. The insurance consumer has paid very substantial premiums for a long period – which have swelled the investment coffers of the insurer and been distributed to others insured in the pool who have suffered losses – and therefore a payback of extra magnitude seems justified in the event of a claim. An executive of a property and casualty insurance industry association articulated this sensibility:

> If people have a sense of what their responsibility is, then we're going to have fewer disappointed customers ... [A responsible policyholder is] an individual who understands the contract started in June of one year and ended in June of another and provides a peace of mind for that duration. If you didn't use it you get exactly what you paid for. A person who doesn't have a sense of that, after 20 years of paying for something you can't hold and you can't see, and you can't show your neighbours, is a person who is going to come into being an opportunistic fraudster. He will inflate the claim, cover the deductible. He will turn the Timex into a Rolex; he will do something to get his money back because he sees it still as his money. Not a sentiment he has for anything else he purchases.

Claims adjusters and investigators we studied took the view that a policyholder is not satisfied with paying thousands of dollars in premiums every year for various insurances and expecting only peace of mind in return. When the opportunity arises, even the most respectable person will seek extra benefit. An investigator for an auto insurer told us: "People pay into this fund every year a lot of money, and they see it being abused by others, and so when it's their turn, it's like they've hit the lottery. And it's like my turn to get the money, and it won't hurt anybody, the insurer has got lots of money."

An investigator for a workers' compensation insurer said his company conducted focus groups to better understand why claimants commit fraud: "We were amazed, every respondent, they knew somebody that was defrauding us. So it has just become accepted. And the hue and cry doesn't go out because it is not coming out of your tax fund, it comes out of your employer."

Much other research conducted or funded by the industry confirms the pervasiveness of the public belief that fraud is routine (e.g., Tennyson 1997). Such company research merely confirms what adjusters have known for many years (Ross 1970). The presumption of fraud, therefore, sometimes seems to be institutionalized in the claims relationship. There is a "decline of innocence" (Ericson 1994), part of a more general societal shift toward a presumption of guilt, and the burden of proof is shifted in the direction of the claimant.

This shift gives rise to a strong blame-the-victim approach. The former chief actuary of a property and casualty insurance company said in an interview that all claimants are treated as "fraudsters," leading insurers to take "financially the most expedient view of the claim. I will squeeze, extract, cajole; I'll do anything I can to keep the costs of the claim down. And I'll squeeze the customer, *victim*, in the process." A colleague who worked in the same company as a claims analyst said that at the height of traumatic experience, the auto-accident victim is blamed for not having prevented the accident in the first place and then for exaggerating his or her suffering:

> The number-one complaint people have with the claims process is that they're being treated as criminal: that essentially they're not being given the benefit of the doubt and that they're presumed guilty, and it's up to them to prove their innocence ... Especially after they've had a crash, they need some support mechanism, not being interrogated ... [W]hat it revolves around is the perception that people don't trust us because they feel we don't trust them, and it's the trust issue that's absolutely central to all this insurance business ... They want to feel that we can deliver on the promise. Because people are not actually buying a product, they're buying security, and they want to make sure that if something happens to them ... in fact we'll be there for them. It's the gap between the expectations and the actual realities of what happens when you actually have a claim that sets off the negative reactions.

In turn, then, the claimant may start with an inflated claim, suspecting that the adjuster will try to minimize it. The insurer's distrust thus becomes a self-fulfilling prophecy. A tendency for claimants to exaggerate may be tied to a distrust of insurance companies. One does not have to look far for evidence of distrust of insurers in popular culture. For example, in the 1998 Warren Beatty film *Bulworth*, the implication is that powerful insurance companies eventually have the senator played by Beatty killed after he turns against their interests. In the 2002 film *John Q*, the protagonist played by Denzel Washington takes hostages after a health-insurance company denies his son a life-saving operation. In a January 2002 episode of the popular television series *Law and Order*, entitled "Undercovered," an insurance executive was similarly portrayed as unjustly denying coverage for a bone-marrow procedure for a young girl, leading to her death from leukemia. The John Grisham novel and 1997 Francis Ford Coppola film *The Rainmaker* portrays a fictional insurance company, Great Benefits, brought to justice after it is revealed to have a policy of denying all claims. Trailers for *The Rainmaker* portray the lawsuit against the company by an underdog legal team as a David and Goliath struggle, highlighting one of the film's heroes, legal assistant Deck Shifflet, talking about the chance to "stick it to" a big insurance company. Given such visions of insurance companies circulating in popular culture, it is perhaps unsurprising that consumers may take their own small opportunities to "stick it to" insurance companies in the claims process.

The Rainmaker may seem like far-fetched fiction. Research by Ross (1970) found that the adjusters he studied were considerably bound by ethical constraints that limited the extent to which they would deny claims. Furthermore, Ross found no evidence that adjusters were monitored by supervisors in efforts to cap the level of payments they awarded. However, a 2001 opinion by the Utah Supreme Court in the case of *Campbell* v. *State Farm* paints a very different picture of the ethics of the claims process. The insurance company is well known for promoting consumer trust in itself because, "Like a good neighbour, State Farm is there." Despite the trustworthy image of State Farm, the Utah Supreme Court in 2001 *(Campbell* v. *State Farm Mutual Automobile Insurance Company No. 981564)* affirmed a judgment of $145 million in punitive damages against the company. The court stated that

> State Farm repeatedly and deliberately deceived and cheated its customers ... for over two decades, State Farm set monthly payment caps and individually rewarded those insurance adjusters who paid less than the market value for claims ... Agents changed the contents of files, lied to customers, and committed other dishonest and fraudulent acts in order to meet financial goals ... For example, a State Farm official in the underlying lawsuit in Logan instructed the claim adjuster to change the report in State Farm's file by writing that Ospital was "speeding to visit his pregnant girlfriend." There was no evidence at all to support that assertion. Ospital was not speeding,

nor did he have a pregnant girlfriend ... The only purpose for the change was to distort the assessment of the value of Ospital's claims ... State Farm's fraudulent practices were consistently directed to persons – poor racial or ethnic minorities, women, and elderly individuals – who State Farm believed would be less likely to object or take legal action ...

Second, State Farm engaged in deliberate concealment and destruction of all documents related to this profit scheme ... State Farm's own witnesses testified that documents were routinely destroyed so as to avoid their potential disclosure through discovery requests ...

Third, State Farm has systematically harassed and intimidated opposing claimants, witnesses, and attorneys. For example, State Farm published an instruction manual for its attorneys mandating them to "ask personal questions" as part of the investigation and examination of claimants in order to deter litigation ... The record contains an eighty-eight page report prepared by State Farm regarding DeLong's personal life, including information obtained by paying a hotel maid to disclose whether DeLong had overnight guests in her room ... There was also evidence that State Farm actually instructs its attorneys and claim superintendents to employ "mad dog defense tactics" – using the company's large resources to "wear out" opposing attorneys by prolonging litigation, making meritless objections, claiming false privileges, destroying documents, and abusing the law and motion process.

Taken together, these three examples show that State Farm engaged in a pattern of "trickery and deceit," "false statements," and other "acts of affirmative misconduct" targeted at "financially vulnerable" persons.[3]

Similarly, the Supreme Court of Canada recently upheld $1 million in punitive damages against Pilot Insurance Company for bad faith (*Whiten* v. *Pilot Insurance Company* 2002 SCC 18). According to the facts as accepted by the Court, after the insured lost her home in a fire, Pilot Insurance repeatedly denied the claim on suspicion of arson, although fire and police officials and even experts hired by the insurance company itself stated that the fire was an accident. In the face of such evidence, the company instead tried to take advantage of the insured's difficult financial circumstances to extract a settlement.

Given such revelations about insurers, the insured may approach the claims process with an attitude of distrust, anticipating attempts to minimize claims. Claimants may be tempted to exaggerate preemptively, just as adjusters minimize preemptively. In the context of such mutual distrust, deliberate deception for financial gain by both parties becomes built into the claims process. For example, Gill et al. (1994) surveyed 383 people about their last home-insurance claims. Thirty-six admitted to falsifying claims. A number argued that this was justifiable given what they expected from insurers in the process. Explanations for fraud included:

- To cover cost and time of getting valuation. To cover cost of incidentals not claimed for. Because we will probably get knocked down anyway.
- The insurance companies are screwing as much money as possible from their customers; therefore I shall screw them for as much – if not more.
- Many people today are making false claims. As a result of this, insurance policies are increased. In order to offset these increases, it leaves me no choice but to join in the rat race. (*Ibid.,* 75-6)

The authors noted that "particularly striking was the strength of resentment against insurance companies on the part of both legitimate and fraudulent claimants" (ibid., 80).

Such resentment may also stem from rising premiums, resulting in a vicious circle, as Ghezzi (1983, 523) found concerning auto-insurance fraud in Massachusetts:

> The cost of insurance has created highly publicized tensions between the insurance industry and state consumer groups. Policyholders have responded to these steep rates by submitting large numbers of padded and fraudulent claims in an attempt to recapture part of their premium expenses. As a result, fraudulent claims have produced even higher rates.

While deception has long been institutionalized in the insurer-claimant relationship, this is exacerbated in the contemporary moral economy, which has become a "moral maze" (Karstedt and Farrall forthcoming) and which,

> by re-distributing responsibilities and risks for consumers, citizens and business, and by re-shaping the weights between governments and markets, has engendered a sweeping change of ... formal as well as informal rules and norms ... The relentless promotion of self-interest, autonomy and responsibilization has cut deep into the normative fabric of trust, fairness and legitimacy that regulates markets, and produces conformity as well as a consensus on such rules and regulations. The increasing anonymity and commodification of life in market societies (where citizens find themselves caught between "big business" and "big government") impact on wider normative patterns of trust and citizenship values, on legal attitudes and alienation among citizens as consumers and vice versa.

One story drawn from our interviews with insurance consumers illustrates how exaggerated claims can become morally neutralized in the commercial transaction between insurer and claimant. Certainly the claimant was not a stereotypical "criminal": She was middle-aged, married with children, a university graduate, operator of a small business from her home, a practising Christian, and block captain for her local chapter of Neighbourhood Watch. The insurance claim was made after a major winter storm in which most properties in her area suffered some damage as well as lack of electricity for an extended period. The claim was for rental of an electrical generator that she told the insurance company she had hired, when in fact she had borrowed it gratis from a neighbour. When asked to explain her fraudulent act, the claimant referred to her relationship to the insurance company, situational opportunity, and social justice. She had a longstanding relationship with the insurer, which had insured her farm property and been part of the community for generations. This brand loyalty was related to her economic relationship with the insurer. She had been paying premiums for a long period without any claims and, as block captain of Neighbourhood Watch, had been especially vigilant about security and loss prevention on the property. A situational opportunity arose to make the false claim because she knew from her neighbours that the insurer was not requiring receipts for this type of claim. All of these elements combined in what she regarded as a moral relationship of social justice. She originally made a claim for an item on the grounds of her property that was worth twice as much as the claim for the generator, but the original claim was denied because such a loss was not covered by the insurance contract. This denied claim created a discrepancy between the company's sales story of trust, a promise to be there when needed, and its claims story that the item was not covered by the contract. She felt that she deserved something regardless of the contract even though compensation for the generator was only half of what it would have been for the other item. She reasoned that while the insurer was facing substantial claims for the storm, it had a deep enough pocket to provide some compensation for what had been suffered more generally in the storm. Her moral neutralization of the fraud, and her own sense of moral economy, were strengthened further by the fact that she had also used the generator to help some of her neighbours, thereby saving the insurer from having to reimburse them for rentals. At the interview's conclusion, she related that in matters of insurance and risk, and in life and security more generally, God is her tutor: "If there is something that I've got to do, He'll give me a hint, and otherwise I'll muddle through as best I can. And I think He's given me fairly good directions."

Claims fraud is also tolerated because of broader considerations of social and economic relations. As we noted above with reference to Garland (1997), intensified policing of fraud may seriously disrupt the smooth flow of social and economic relations. For example, workers' compensation insurers face sensitive labour and management issues that make them reticent to police fraud too heavily. An executive of a workers' compensation insurer made this point in an interview. He said that while an auto insurer might successfully undertake initiatives, including publicity campaigns, to crack down on some aspects of disability insurance fraud, he was not able to do so. "Labour would consider it an affront to suggest that workers would be defrauding the system. They do not believe that [fraud] is a significant issue ... and [believe] that before you deal with that you should deal with [employers'] claims suppression, for instance."

Finally, relationship management is a component of how claims fraud is tolerated. In keeping with broader marketing trends toward relationship management (Slater 1997; Turow 1997), insurers foster special relationships with lucrative policyholders over time. The special relationship may include turning a blind eye to possible fraud. Policyholders who have falsified their claims will nevertheless contribute to ongoing profitability by providing additional premium revenue over time. They may also be customers in other lines of insurance that are especially valuable, leading the insurer to overlook a particular instance of an exaggerated claim.

A former senior vice president of a multinational insurance company said in an interview that he preferred to hire in-house adjusters, rather than rely on independents, because they are more sensitive to relationship management when making their judgments about claims. He said that in-house adjusters are socialized into "your culture, your philosophy," where "service is the name of the game." In-house adjusters know how to minimize or deny a claim more diplomatically, including those that entail fraud. They know when to pay claims to avoid conflict, always keeping an eye on the future premium revenue the claimant will contribute to that side of the ledger.

An additional aspect of fraud tolerance as part of relationship management with desirable customers is the possibility that an allegation might prove wrong. Given the equivocality of definitions of fraud, and associated evidence problems, allegations of fraud may be deemed false or unfair. It is usually easier not to bite the hand that feeds even if one's own hand is nibbled at.

The hit-and-run claims centre we discussed earlier featured considerable tension between insurance-claims staff and police. The nub of this tension was the police orientation toward criminal law enforcement, versus the insurance approach of customer service and tolerance of fraud. As one adjuster said of police:

> They don't have the competition, and they don't care about customer service. We had one officer here on site who would call a claimant a liar to his face, then he would take him into a booth and browbeat him ... That just rubbed the centre manager the wrong way ... We can't do that ...

We're in the customer-service business, but the police don't care ... [In one case the police told the claimant,] "if you try and put forth a hit-and-run claim, we'll charge you with criminal mischief." Well, we can't do that.

We just deny.

When Fraud is Policed More Heavily: Less Desirable Populations
Karstedt and Farrall (forthcoming) suggest that

an array of new forms of regulation and control is emerging, re-shaping the landscape of control, and slowly slipping from observation by citizens and criminologists ... Associations of insurers and banks establish task forces against fraud, the National Health Service and Health Insurers Associations [in Britain] establish specialist units to detect and prosecute fraud, the Department of Social Services (now Department of Work and Pensions) ran advertisement campaigns and a website against benefit fraud, borough councils run and build up fraud units to tackle fraudulent parking permits, and so on. These institutions establish their own definitions of "crime," their own procedures of tracking and prosecuting, and in particular of sanctioning – mainly by excluding citizens from their services.

Some less desirable populations of the insured are policed more intensely for fraud and may thus be more likely to be excluded. A substandard-market customer who might have padded a claim is less likely to be maintained as a policyholder than a superstandard customer. The provincial auto insurer we studied varied its approach to questioning claims considerably, depending on the locale of the particular claims centre and the socio-economic background of each centre's clientele. We also studied a company that operated exclusively in the superstandard property and casualty market. Part of its marketing strategy, made explicit in its advertisements, was to offer a superior claims service, which included in-house adjusters with a demeanour of professionalism and a "no-hassle" replacement of expensive losses. A claims manager for this company said that this approach was possible because of high premiums and the relationship management associated with these premiums. Taking claimants more at face value justifies not only the higher face value of insurance policies, but hopefully a view among claimants that

"Maybe I don't need to over-inflate that claim, or maybe insurance companies aren't as bad as I thought they were." And that's another way of combating fraud. I mean obviously we don't intend to pay anything more than we have to, but there are sometimes we do ... When people discover that you're not going to nickel-and-dime them to death, they tend not to do it to you. But ultimately it comes down to the relationship, or the conversation, between two individuals: How do you feel about the person you're talking to?

This contrasts with the approach of another insurance company that specialized in auto insurance for a high-risk clientele. This company, whose clientele is generally of lower socio-economic status, does not even bother employing regular insurance adjusters on staff or on contract – adjusters who would be skilled in dealing with claims relatively gently and diplomatically. Instead this company contracts with a firm of private investigators located in the same office building as the insurance company's headquarters in order to ensure a much tougher approach with this particular clientele. As ex-police officers, these private investigators are especially adept at detecting fraudulent claims and at having clients see the wisdom of withdrawing such claims. They are also skilled at the preparation of evidence and work closely with their former police-department colleagues in prosecuting the company's clients. This represents a very strong contrast with the more diplomatic approach to claims that we found is adopted by insurance firms targeting more upscale risk segments.

Adjusters and investigators make subjective and intuitive moral judgments of claimants to decide how much to blame them for their losses and what compensation is deserved.

A subcultural term within the industry for a claimant who represents a risk of fraud is "red." Although it is intended simply to denote a high risk, "red" can also be read as "communist," as signifying someone who is a source of what insurers call "social inflation": an increasing sense of entitlement to claims, which is therefore a threat to profitability. To ferret out reds, company manuals and training programs identify myriad "red flag" indicators. While a multifactorial analysis of red flags can be computer-assisted, it also requires the experienced and keen eye of the claims agent.

Baker and McElrath (1997, 147) found that property-claims adjusters "rely on their experience and intuition to assess whether the claims fit their expectations." One adjuster told them, "'I look at the car they drive, the other things in the house, the way they carry themselves.' Other social attributes mentioned were the character of the home or neighbourhood, employment status, business or professional background, immigrant status ... perceived wealth, and what another adjuster called 'a life-style that indicates a basic honesty'" (*ibid.*; see also Glenn 2000; Baker 2000).

Employment, income, and credit records are all read for suggestions of fraud potential. We interviewed an insurance-claims consultant who worked with insurers across North America to develop data-analysis systems that would help them to identify and reduce sources of excessive claims. He said that one technology he had devised was a "moral cost analysis" based on an assessment of the ratio of claims awards to the personal income of claimants. The technology measured the "claims award basis relative to need or desire and relative to opportunity ... $100 isn't anything to me ... Why would I lie for $100? I get more gain off the moral cost to me, in a sense it's just self-image ... [to] a street person down there, $100 is a bunch more." Those who have high moral-cost considerations in making a claim are naturally better risks. Those assumed to have no reputation to lose – in other words, the poor – are obviously not worth the risk.

We also found a number of examples of how ascribed race and ethnicity were used as red flags for potential fraud and of how particular ethnic groups were targeted for supposedly being prone to "scams." Of course these ascribed statuses cannot be used officially, but they are used unofficially. One claims-tracking specialist for an auto insurer told us that he routinely tracked race and ethnicity because certain groups have higher rates of claims and "hit probabilities" that may justify a potential fraud investigation. In fact, claims personnel we observed and interviewed regularly referred to race and ethnicity as key "red flags" for potential fraud. A claims manager for one multinational insurer told us that his staff starts with the name on the file as an indicator of ethnicity: "[We have] adjusters who will look at an insured and say 'that kind of person with that kind of name is likely to do this.'" One adjuster told us, "East Indian clientele are always looking to scam you." Another adjuster, working for a different company, said: "In the 1970s it was the Polish, in the 1980s it was the Chinese, and now it's Russians ... One of the people I used to work with, he said they actually have a claims adjuster who is East Indian ... He would tell all of the adjusters, 'Never believe a word that these East Indians say because it's our culture'... Is that stereotyping? Well, no, it's probably just smart."

Conclusion

In this chapter we have used the example of insurance fraud to illustrate how a "crime" is defined and dealt with largely through private-justice mechanisms. A seesaw battle of exaggeration and minimization has long been part of the insurance claims process. The boundaries of what constitutes "fraud" as opposed to mere "exaggeration" are fluid. Asked to define fraud, insurance investigators do not refer to criminal code or legal definitions, and face difficulty defining fraud at all.

If security of profits is not unduly threatened, or if it can be addressed through other means, such as increased prices and sales-contract conditions, padding of claims is tolerated. Economic pressures on insurers, and the inability to pass costs on to consumers, have been some of the key factors leading to an industry crackdown in which much more claimant behaviour has been defined as "fraud" in the last two decades than previously. However, such "fraud" is still dealt with outside the criminal justice system in all but a small minority of cases.

Instead, the crackdown mostly deploys the notion that fraud is a "crime" as a way to deny claims, particularly from less desirable customers, and to cut costs. The criminal justice system is invoked for symbolic purposes as a deterrent, and police play a supporting role by supplying information to insurance investigators on suspected claimants, often for a fee. Even during this era of crackdown, what might be defined as "fraud" by policyholders may be tolerated, especially if the client is otherwise respectable and of a desirable market. Preferred risks are doubly desirable as insurance clients: They are seen, on the one hand, to be affluent customers and perceived, on the other hand, as less risky in terms of claims. A private insurance company is in the business not of redistributing resources among the insured but of discriminating in favour of those who contribute to the goodness of the pool and the prosperity of the company (Gowri 1997; Ericson, Doyle, and Barry 2003). Thus a person who is not a fully desirable participant may be labelled a "fraud" risk and have his or her claim denied. Claimants who are denied have recourse to the civil courts but may be reluctant to persist with the perceived threat of criminal prosecution hanging over them. Those most likely to be denied – for example, the poor – may also be least able to seek legal recourse in fighting such denials. Meanwhile, those who do exaggerate claims – but are otherwise deemed worthy within the moral utilitarianism of the insurance institution – continue as valued participants.

Ross (1970) studied insurance adjusting as an example of the "law in action." In the insurance-claims contexts we have studied, the role of criminal law in action is largely a symbolic one. The police are mostly back-up players used for their symbolism and also to serve insurers' information needs. Despite insurers' public rhetoric concerning the immorality of the crime of fraud and the fact that the moral evaluation of particular claimants is often key in the decision to proceed with a fraud investigation, in industry practice the dominant morality by far is one of expedience. In an increasingly privatized society, the practical definition of insurance fraud becomes whatever is consistent with the smooth flow of business.

Notes

1   Our research focuses on private insurers as well as on a Canadian provincial-government auto insurer that is a Crown corporation: a government-business hybrid that displays a number of the characteristics of a private business.

2   The research was funded by the Social Sciences and Humanities Research Council of Canada, the Law Commission of Canada, the University of British Columbia, the Canada Council Killam Research Fellowship Program, and the Visiting Fellows Program of All Souls College, Oxford.

3   We thank Tom Baker for pointing out this example.

References

Ashworth, A. 2001. "The Decline of English Sentencing, and Other Stories." In *Sentencing and Sanctions in Western Countries,* edited by M. Tonry and R. Fraser, 62-91. New York: Oxford University Press.

Baker, T. 2000. "Insuring Morality." *Economy and Society* 29: 559-77.

–, and K. McElrath. 1997. "Insurance Claims Discrimination." In *Insurance Redlining: Disinvestment, Reinvestment, and the Evolving Role of Financial Institutions,* edited by G.D. Squires, 141-56. Washington, DC: Urban Institute Press.

Baldock, T. 1997. "Insurance Fraud." Paper #66. Canberra: Australian Institute of Criminology.

Clarke, Michael. 1989. "Insurance Fraud." *British Journal of Criminology* 29 (1): 1-20.

–. 1990. "The Control of Insurance Fraud: A Comparative View." *British Journal of Criminology* 30 (1): 1-23.

Ditton, J. 1979. *Controlology: Beyond the New Criminology.* London: Macmillan.

Dornstein, K. 1996. *Accidentally on Purpose: The Making of a Personal Injury Underworld in America.* New York: St. Martin's Press.

Ericson, R. 1975. *Criminal Reactions: The Labelling Perspective.* Westmead: Saxon House.

–. 1993. *Making Crime: A Study of Detective Work.* 2nd ed. Toronto: University of Toronto Press.

–. 1994. "The Decline of Innocence." *University of British Columbia Law Review* 28: 367-83.

–, and K. Haggerty. 1997. *Policing the Risk Society.* Toronto: University of Toronto Press; Oxford: Clarendon Press.

–, D. Barry, and A. Doyle. 2000. "The Moral Hazards of Neoliberalism: Lessons From the Private Insurance Industry." *Economy and Society* 29: 532-58.

–, and K. Haggerty. 2002. "The Policing of Risk." In *Embracing Risk: The Changing Culture of Insurance and Responsibility,* edited by T. Baker and J. Simon, 238-72. Chicago: University of Chicago Press.

–, A. Doyle, and D. Barry. 2003. *Insurance as Governance.* Toronto: University of Toronto Press.

–, and A. Doyle. 2004. *Uncertain Business: Risk, Insurance and the Limits of Knowledge.* Toronto: University of Toronto Press.

Garland, D. 1997. "'Governmentality' and the Problem of Crime: Foucault, Criminology, Sociology." *Theoretical Criminology* 1: 173-214.

–. 2001. *The Culture of Control: Crime and Social Order in Contemporary Society.* Chicago: University of Chicago Press.

Ghezzi, S. 1983. "A Private Network of Social Control: Insurance Investigation Units." *Social Problems* 30, 5: 521-31.

Gill, K., A. Woolley, and M. Gill. 1994. "Insurance Fraud: The Business as a Victim." In *Crime at Work: Studies in Security and Crime Prevention,* vol. 1, edited by M. Gill. Leicester: Perpetuity Press.

Glenn, B. 2000. "The Shifting Rhetoric of Insurance Denial." *Law and Society Review* 34: 779-808.

Gowri, A. 1997. "The Irony of Insurance: Community and Commodity." PhD dissertation. University of Southern California, Los Angeles.

Harris, C. 1998. "The Mismeasure of Fraud." *Canadian Insurance* (May): 5.

Hawkins, K. 1984. *Environment and Enforcement: Regulation and the Social Definition of Pollution.* Oxford: Clarendon Press.

Heimer, C. 1985. *Reactive Risk and Rational Action: Managing Moral Hazard in Insurance Contracts.* Berkeley: University of California Press.

Insurance Information Institute. 2002. *Hot Topics and Insurance Issues: Insurance Fraud.* <http://www.iii.org/media/hottopics/insurance/fraud> (accessed August 2002).

Insurance Research Council/Insurance Services Organization. 2001. *Fighting Insurance Fraud: Survey of Insurer Anti-Fraud Efforts.* IRC/ISO.

Jaffee, D., and T. Russell. 2002. "The Regulation of Automobile Insurance in California." In *Deregulating Property-Liability Insurance: Restoring Competition and Increasing Efficiency,* edited by J.D. Cummins. Washington, DC: American Enterprise Institute-Brookings Institution Joint Center for Regulatory Studies.

Karstedt, S., and S. Farrall. Forthcoming. "The Moral Maze of the Middle Class: The Predatory Society and its Emerging Regulatory Order." In *Images of Crime II,* edited by H.-J. Albrecht, T. Serassis, and H. Kania. Freiburg: Edition Iuscrim, Max Planck Institute.

Law Commission of Canada. 2002. *In Search of Security: The Roles of Public Police and Private Agencies.* Discussion paper. Ottawa: Law Commission of Canada.

Lianos, M., and M. Douglas. 2000. "Dangerization and the End of Deviance: The Institutional Environment." In *Criminology and Social Theory,* edited by D. Garland and R. Sparks, 103-25. Oxford: Oxford University Press.

McKenzie, S. 1993. *Insurance Fraud Literature Search/Summary of Key Findings.* Institute of Insurance and Pension Research Report, University of Waterloo.

New York State Insurance Department. 2003. "How Are We Doing? Some Current Statistics." <http://www.ins.state.ny.us/fd399_01.htm> (accessed September 2003).

Rose, N. 1999. *Powers of Freedom: Reframing Political Thought.* Cambridge: Cambridge University Press.

Rosenfield, H. 1998. "Auto Insurance: Crisis and Reform." *University of Memphis Law Review* 2, 1.

Ross, L. 1970. *Settled Out of Court.* Chicago: Aldine.

Slater, D. 1997. *Consumer Culture and Modernity.* Cambridge: Polity Press.

Sullivan, Terrence, ed. 2000. *Injury and the New World of Work.* Vancouver: University of British Columbia Press.

Tennyson, S. 1997. "Economic Institutions and Individual Ethics: A Study of Consumer Attitudes Toward Insurance Fraud." *Journal of Economic Behavior and Organization* 32: 247-65.

Turow, J. 1997. *Breaking Up America: Advertisers and the New Media World.* Chicago: University of Chicago Press.

Weisberg, H., and R. Derrig. 1991. "Fraud and Automobile Insurance: A Report on Bodily Injury Claims in Massachusetts." *Journal of Insurance Regulation* 9: 497-541.

–, and R. Derrig. 1992. "Massachusetts Bodily Injury Tort Reform." *Journal of Insurance Regulation* 10: 384-440.

5
From Practical Joker to Offender: Reflections on the Concept of "Crime"
Pierre Rainville

The Discipline of Law and the Indiscipline of Humour

This chapter focuses on making a distinction between merely inappropriate conduct and true criminal behaviour. The theme selected for this purpose is the punishment of practical jokes and humiliating humour. My analysis is thus concerned with the social disapproval of humour and laughter through Canadian criminal law.

The objective of this analysis is to determine the reasons for reprehensible or questionable behaviour being catapulted into the arena of criminal law. Thus my study is devoted to defining the respective boundaries between questionable or derogatory behaviour and truly criminal behaviour.

The study of the criminalization of jokes goes back to the very precepts of criminal law. The basic axiom is that only "serious misconduct" deserves criminal sanction.[1] The Supreme Court's judgment in *Zundel* strongly affirms this. In addition, in *Creighton* the Supreme Court stated that Canadian law does not lightly brand a person a criminal.[2] This principle lies at the heart of the question of penalizing humour.

Is it appropriate to label practical jokers "criminals?" There are numerous scenarios in which this question arises, some of the offenders in these cases being: a person who makes a phony bomb threat in an airport; someone who makes sexual contact as a form of inappropriate humour; an adolescent who points a gun at a friend and frightens him or her by giving the impression that he will shoot; the author of a threatening letter meant as a hoax; the pie-thrower; the exhibitionist who wrongly expects to make people laugh; individuals who hide other people's property as a joke; the joker who enjoys fooling a police officer by having the officer investigate an imaginary crime; the individual who suggests that another person commit a crime without suspecting that the person will take the advice seriously and will commit such a crime; the organizer of a military hazing or university initiation; the journalist or accused person who mocks a judge.

These few examples help in assessing the level of tolerance in criminal law and the reasons governing the characterization of behaviour as a crime.

As the preceding examples illustrate, the quest for pleasure or laughter may suddenly come up against criminal law. One might easily have thought the opposite. The very foundation of penal law is an interest in *serious* matters. At first glance, humour, joviality, and laughter seem to be too inoffensive to be among the concerns of criminal law.

Furthermore, the purpose of humour is to escape everyday constraints; it belongs to a domain far removed from the rigour of the law. Games, laughter, and humour act as a shield against the seriousness of this world. We thus tend to think that playful pleasure constitutes an area of "nonlaw" in the sense intended by Carbonnier,[3] the great legal scholar.

After all, is humour not the antidote of choice against anger, outrage, and irreversible acts – in short, against the irreparable? Does laughter not prevent us from taking even more harmful action against the victim? Are we not told that: "Humour prevents us from wallowing in pity or anger. It is the saving emotion, dominated by laughter."[4] As Freud points out, humour can counteract feelings of anger or fear by serving as a substitute emotion: "[T]he essence of humour resides in the fact that we spare ourselves from the affects that a situation should give rise to; by joking we place ourselves above such affective manifestations."[5] Besides, humour in all its forms is often a display against oppression; it is a form of self-help meant as an alternative to what might otherwise be a violent response. Criminal law should therefore be wary of prohibiting certain forms of annoying humour, for humour is often a substitute for violence or threats.

At the same time, humour often targets the very values that criminal law seeks to protect: Humour can attack morality,[6] safety,[7] property,[8] human dignity,[9] and the authority of the courts.[10]

Philosophers quickly understood the inherent challenge of humour: "What is funny relates ... to certain standards, to certain values."[11] Blondel states: "Laughter and games are allied with pleasure ... through *the transgression of standards and the substitution of new rules.*"[12]

Humour challenges existing standards. Getting undressed in the middle of the street as a joke is more or less an insult to morality.[13] Teasing a woman in public without permission by touching her breasts amounts to disparaging her sexual dignity. Throwing a pie in the face of a public figure in scorn belittles the victim's bodily dignity. In fact, humour is often expressed through acts of bravado.

Practical jokers intend to promote their own value system. The same goes for inappropriate sexual touching as for slanderous irony: "Laughter is a value judgment, and who should provide me with a set of values but myself."[14] A French philosopher appropriately comments:

In reality, the question of values underlies the question of what is serious. To approach an issue or an individual with seriousness is to give value to that issue or individual. Value can be defined through the seriousness with which we approach it. One is committed to what one values. When people are not serious, they are rejecting certain values. ... When I laugh at people, they have no value for me as long as I continue to laugh.[15]

Jurists must ask themselves whether the above-mentioned various transgressions are sufficient to justify criminal sanctions. This means that they must examine both the importance of the standard that has been mocked and the magnitude of the improper behaviour. Any such analysis requires a definition of the boundaries of criminal law: In this case, we have to draw the dividing line between disparaging behaviour and criminal behaviour.

Law in general – and criminal law in particular – has fallen far behind in studying the phenomena of laughter and humour. This deficiency is all the more unfortunate given that numerous related disciplines have made significant contributions to analyzing jokes and laughter. Sociology,[16] philosophy,[17] psychology,[18] psychiatry,[19] medicine,[20] psychoanalysis,[21] semiogenesis,[22] and literature[23] have devoted a number of studies to the theme. On the other hand, a genuine legal theory on laughter has yet to be expounded.

Criminal law experts who have taken an interest in the matter are few and far between, and the few lines written on the subject are most questionable.[24] There are many inaccuracies in Canadian academic commentary. Canadian jurists claim that a joke constitutes the perpetrator's motive for committing a crime. Therefore, a joker will not be acquitted. This is a widespread opinion, one that has gained much acceptance even in the Department of Justice Canada.[25]

To begin with, this vision of criminal law is contrary to case law. A careful review of the overall corpus of case law shows that criminal law on the subject is not as simple as legal commentators in Canada suggest. Contrary to what most writers feel, many offences have given rise to the prank defence – for example, fraud, mischief, public mischief, conspiracy, aiding and abetting, possession of a weapon for a dangerous purpose, and communicating with someone in a public place for the purpose of engaging in prostitution.[26]

The prevailing academic view conceals an even more serious problem. Erroneous generalizations by commentators demonstrate what little attention they pay to distinguishing between derogatory or improper behaviour, on the one hand, and criminal behaviour, on the other.

In doing so, current commentary is abdicating its function, which should be to draw the line between behaviour that is merely reprehensible and behaviour that is truly criminal. *Systematically thrusting practical jokes into the arena of criminal law amounts to detracting from and trivializing the very concept of crime.*

In fact, this error is not the prerogative of commentators. What should we say of the appeal courts that believe that practical jokes fall under the *Criminal Code* and, in the same breath, criticize prosecutors for filing criminal complaints for such ridiculous acts?[27]

Are we not trivializing the very concept of "crime"? Would it not be better to *define* crime in terms of thresholds of what is dangerous and what can be tolerated?

Thus my study takes a position opposed to contemporary Canadian commentary, returning its proper focus to the concept of crime. The next part of this chapter assesses the seriousness of the practical joker's behaviour. In what circumstances and according to what criteria does humour reach the level of seriousness at which it is considered a crime? To a lesser degree, I also examine the impact of the accused's intent to play a practical joke. Is the intent to utter or play a joke sufficiently blameworthy in itself to lead to criminal punishment? Does a practical joker possess the mental characteristics necessary for him to be properly described as a "criminal"?

Practical Jokes and Criminal Law: Deciding on Humour's Threshold of Danger

Considering whether practical jokes should constitute crimes requires an analysis of the danger of humour. It also requires some analysis of the required threshold of seriousness in criminal matters.

An assessment of this threshold of seriousness will be based on:

1 determining the danger of the act in question
2 determining society's threshold of tolerance.

Attention to the danger of the act in question unavoidably raises the following two questions:

• Can a practical joke mitigate the seriousness of the alleged conduct and consequently remove it from the definition of crime?
• Conversely, are there certain jokes that are intrinsically dangerous and reprehensible enough in a truly criminal sense?

Discussing legal responses to jokes also leads to an examination of society's tolerance level and, in turn, the tolerance level of criminal law. To what extent must criminal law be an arbiter of good taste? Does the punishment of impertinent behaviour fall within its purview? Is it correct to say that "misguided" humour should involve criminal law? Is this not, then, more or less punishing the joker's nonconformity and, thereby, departing from the ultimate purpose of criminal law?

All these questions essentially amount to defining the freedom each person has to be playful.[28]

The humour that criminal law views with suspicion falls into three categories:

1 humour as drift (humour that degenerates)
2 humour as pretense (humour that deceives)
3 humour as affront (humour that offends).

Humour As Drift (Humour That Degenerates)
Humour is ephemeral by nature.[29] Its life span may, however, be further shortened by an unforeseen event. The humour may get away from the joker and be offset by a sudden event, such as when bodily harm occurs to one of the players.

Practical jokes and games are sometimes the prelude to and even the unwitting impetus for a dangerous situation. A teenager amuses himself by pointing a firearm at a friend to scare him. He mistakenly thinks that it is not loaded, and then the irreparable happens. He pulls the trigger, a shot is fired, and his friend collapses and dies.[30]

Games are a form of escape, an escape from reality, but reality catches up with the players. Humour, which is supposed to be fleeting in nature, gives rise to situations with *long-lasting* consequences.[31] This is when the law comes into play.

When a joke does permanent damage, the magnitude of the consequences of humour becomes such that criminal law can no longer stand aside.

The more criminal law has to be concerned with the consequences of humour, the greater the importance of the joker's personal profile. The joker does not have the profile of a criminal. Accordingly, the traditional criteria of making an example and specific deterrence are blurred when dealing with a joker whose joke has gone awry. Protecting society is not the primary consideration even when the joke played by the accused has caused an unforeseen tragedy.[32] The immaturity of the act and of its perpetrator is undoubtedly of importance in sentencing.

Similar considerations prevail when studying a transfer application by a teenager charged with playing a joke that went wrong. Several factors may mitigate against transferring the teenager to an adult court. "The seriousness of the alleged offence *and* the circumstances in which it was allegedly committed" are among the Legislature's criteria for deciding on the transfer application.[33] Unforeseen consequences limit the seriousness of the alleged offence. There is no doubt that a joke will be part of the "circumstances" considered by the court. Whenever the joke does not counter the existence of one of the elements of the alleged offence, it may nonetheless remain a circumstance in favour of the accused: It shows an absence of malice and premeditation.

A joker's immaturity will also operate in his or her favour: The age and level of maturity of the teenager as well as his or her character and background are all factors that determine whether the proceeding should be heard in youth court.[34] *Prima facie*, the possibility of rehabilitation[35] should also work in the joker's favour, unlike in the case of a career offender. Besides, a less severe sentence will have to be rendered in the case of a joke with unforeseen consequences. The transfer of an adolescent to adult court loses some of its justification since the purpose of this measure is often to impose a heavier sentence.

This explains the *S. (R.S.)* ruling. A fifteen-year-old was convicted of homicide after an unfortunate joke ended in a man's death. The victim agreed, as part of a joke, to have his shoe sprayed with a flammable product. The fire spread quickly, and the victim died as a result of his burns. The judge denied the transfer application to adult court. He described the incident "[as] one of adolescent, even childish, inquisitiveness. The three boys were literally and figuratively playing with fire. They could not have known in their youthful ignorance, that the toluene would generate a fire that would spread so rapidly, with such intense heat and be so difficult to extinguish ... This accused is rather the type of immature adolescent to which the *Young Offenders Act* and the treatment resources provided thereunder are designed to respond."[36]

Humour As Pretense (Humour That Deceives)

Humour often creates illusions and false impressions.[37] There are many *Criminal Code* provisions designed to counter misleading appearances and deceptions: The *Code* prohibits forgery,[38] condemns perjury[39] and personation,[40] and prohibits counterfeiting banknotes.[41]

We have to analyze the distortions of truth and reality that criminal law regards as sufficiently dangerous and ask ourselves if it goes so far as to prohibit practical jokes and deceptions.

Humour enjoys disturbing reality. The practical joker passes him or herself off as someone else, pilfers something and pretends it disappeared, or shouts "fire" when there is none. Deception is one of the types of humour that the joker most values: His or her pleasure is derived from misleading the victim.[42] Deception consists of misleading someone by taking advantage of the person's gullibility in order to amuse oneself at the victim's expense.

Deception is precisely the type of humour that is most often targeted by criminal legislation. The *Code* condemns certain scenarios: Setting off a false alarm,[43] making a phony bomb threat,[44] interfering with boundary lines,[45] and counterfeiting money[46] are all examples of deception turned into crime. In labelling such conduct criminal, the Legislature rules that these forms of inappropriate humour have reached a degree of gravity that is serious enough for them to be prohibited.

In such cases, the joke is in itself an offence. It becomes a criminal offence because of the serious inconveniences it creates. The phony bomb threat is a perfect example. This offence, created by the *Aeronautics Act*, is a valid exercise of the federal jurisdiction over both criminal matters and aviation matters.[47] This offence involves two classic objectives of criminal law: safety and order.[48]

> 13. A person who is at an aerodrome or on board an aircraft must not falsely declare that:
>
> (a) the person is carrying a weapon, an explosive substance or an incendiary device.[49]

Section 13 of the *Canadian Aviation Security Regulations* is only concerned with *false* declarations. Criminalizing phony bomb threats amounts to punishing the practical joke. The real threat falls outside the scope of the section: A person carrying a bomb cannot be punished under this section. In other words, only unfounded words can be punished.

The section, therefore, focuses on the joke. The provision only takes the accused's state of mind into account to a limited extent. The accused must be aware of the false nature of his words, but the offence requires no intent to intimidate. Both the intent to intimidate *or* to make a joke constitute offences.[50] This is understandable. The boarding of the flight may be interrupted even if the accused immediately takes back his words. The flight crew is quite likely to take no chances and decide to conduct a search of the aircraft.

Penalizing jokes and tricks is still a rational process. The *Criminal Code* does not penalize every bad joke without exception. Criminalizing deception is usually subject to two criteria:

1 an immediate or future risk of harm
2 the convincing nature of the joke.

The harm that the Legislature wishes to prevent varies considerably from one offence to another. Public insecurity (particularly in transport), turmoil,[51] and financial insecurity are all evils to be suppressed by criminalizing deception.

That being so, the Legislature does not require that there be immediate and tangible harm. For example, section 437 of the *Criminal Code* prohibits wilfully making a false alarm. This tasteless joke is rightly penalized. Allowing false alarms turns all alarms into a trivial matter, causing the public not to take them seriously. The *future* protection of the public is just as important as the desire to prevent the needless turmoil that is suddenly caused by a false alarm.

A criminal penalty seems to have a second requirement: The "serious" nature of the joke must be obvious. Only jokes that are difficult to detect are prohibited. Four criminal offences support this: counterfeiting, personating a peace officer, personating a member of the Canadian Forces, and terrorist hoaxes.

Section 457 of the *Code* prohibits the counterfeiting of Canadian banknotes: It prohibits someone from printing anything in the "likeness of a current bank-note." However, the Legislature makes an exception if the likeness is greater than one and one-half times the length or width of the banknote and if the likeness is in black and white only, or if the likeness of the banknote appears on only one side. The Legislature wants to ensure that the joke can be detected.

In other words, the joke escapes punishment if no risk is involved. A deception that is easily detected goes unpunished, whereas one that has every appearance of reality is prohibited.

The seriousness of the joke forms the basis of its prohibition. Section 130(b) of the *Code* follows the same principle. It prohibits the wearing of any kind of badge that is "likely" to cause persons to believe that they are in the presence of a peace officer. A blatant joke is therefore not covered by the criminal law. Punishment depends on the joke's chances of success. Similarly, anyone who wears a uniform similar to that of the Canadian Forces is only penalized if the similarity is so striking "that it is likely to be mistaken therefor."[52]

Thus humour that can easily be discerned escapes all punishment. Conversely, the Legislature is extremely wary of hoaxers who intend to deceive their "victims." The quality of the deception increases the chances that it will be punished. In short, the danger involved in humour is often due to the fact that it is not easily discerned. The new criminal offence dealing with terrorist hoaxes illustrates this:

> 83.231 (1) Every one commits an offence who, without lawful excuse and with intent to cause any person to fear death, bodily harm, substantial damage to property or serious interference with the lawful use or operation of property, (a) conveys or causes or procures to be conveyed information that, *in all the circumstances*, is likely to cause a *reasonable* apprehension that terrorist activity is occurring or will occur, without believing the information to be true.[53]

Not all terrorist hoaxes are prohibited. The readily apparent joke escapes a penalty. Only deceptions that are convincing enough to be taken seriously by a sensible person are dealt with.

Nevertheless, the Legislature is aware that penalizing humour amounts to punishing acts that are less dangerous than many other crimes. Most of the offences that have already been mentioned are generally punishable by mere summary convictions.[54] The Legislature deals with a joke for what it is. One need only compare the maximum sentence handed down for reproducing the likeness of a banknote with the maximum sentence handed down for actually counterfeiting money. Reproducing the likeness of a banknote is punishable by six months in prison, whereas the possession of counterfeit money is punishable by fourteen years' imprisonment.[55]

That said, not all punishable jokes are seen by the Legislature in the same way. A person who moors a ship to a buoy receives a maximum of six months in prison; on the other hand, a person who decides to hide the buoy faces a maximum of ten years' imprisonment,[56] demonstrating that not all "criminal" jokes have the same degree of danger.

Humour As an Affront (Humour That Offends)

"We can laugh about anything, but not in any fashion."[57]

Humour mocks and ridicules many values protected by criminal law: morals, public safety, personal property, human dignity, judicial authority, and so on. The seriousness of these attacks on the values of criminal law must be analyzed as well as whether they should be punished under the *Criminal Code*.

Four types of affront are examined here:

1 affront to physical dignity
2 affront to discipline
3 affront to reputation
4 affront to security.

Affront to Physical Dignity
Ridiculing someone sometimes takes the form of an attack on that person's physical integrity. Inappropriate sexual touching, pie-throwing, military hazing, and university initiations are all examples of ridicule that is detrimental to the victim's body.

Assessing the injury that has been inflicted on the victim lies at the very heart of the debate: Is it or is it not appropriate to punish this questionable sense of humour? Does ridicule experienced on a physical level suffice to carry a criminal sanction? Is this a genuine *injury* worthy of a criminal sanction?

Inappropriate humour and criminal humour are not easy to differentiate. The practical joker and the joker's victim will, more often than not, have contradictory ideas about what is funny. The criminal law must arbitrate between, on the one hand, the joker's belief that he is engaging in mere antics and, on the other hand, the victim's opinion that his or her self-esteem has been wounded, not to mention his or her physical dignity.

In determining the threshold of what is impermissible, these two conflicting perceptions must be confronted and weighed – not an easy task to perform.

The fine line between what is considered an immature act and what is considered illegal can be illustrated by a recent Canadian ruling. A male nurse was charged with sexual assault for having fondled the sexual organs of three mentally handicapped patients in public. He was charged with having placed his hands on the patients' breasts or testicles to "tease" them. Both the Quebec Court of Appeal and the trial judge noted that the accused was known for being cheerful and for being a practical joker.

The trial judge acquitted. The "disrespectful" acts were the result of a "total lack of maturity and proper conduct" but did not constitute sexual assault under the *Criminal Code*: "The sexual touching was more likely the result of a bad joke rather than an act of violence."[58] These acts lacked the hostility characteristic of an assault, and the accused was not motivated by criminal intent.

The Quebec Court of Appeal dismissed these arguments.[59] Its decision was based on three principles. The first concerned the scope of the crime of assault as set out under the *Criminal Code*. According to the Court, the word "force" in section 265(1) of the *Code* is open to interpretation:

> Subparagraph 265(1)(a) provides that a person commits an assault when he applies force intentionally to another person, directly or indirectly. However, the word "force" is vague. What degree of force is required to constitute assault? (Translated)

The Quebec Court of Appeal concluded that no act of violence is required: A mere unsolicited touch suffices. In my opinion, this conclusion takes into account the special nature of a sexual act. The mere brushing of sexual organs can certainly constitute a sexual act. It would then be absurd to exclude such an act from the scope of the crime of sexual assault. It would be just as wrong to absolve a person who commits an unsolicited sexual act on the grounds that his act was a display of tenderness for the victim rather than hostility.

The other two conclusions stated by the Quebec Court of Appeal in *Bernier* raise a far more important issue. The defence of *de minimis non curat lex*[60] and the prank defence do not have any *autonomous* scope in criminal law when the accused's act is *fully* consistent with the definition of an offence:

> With evidence that the offence was committed before him, the judge does not have the discretion to acquit the appellant on the grounds that the acts were harmless or that they were only done playfully. The seriousness of the acts can only be taken into consideration during sentencing.[61] (Translated)

This case was then taken to the Supreme Court, which dismissed Bernier's appeal without specifically addressing the prank defence.[62]

This case clearly illustrates the conflicting perceptions of the joker and the victim:

> Humour softens aggression, so much so that the joker most often feels that he is "innocent," in the etymological sense of the word; he is surprised by the effects of his joke; he feels his jokes are insignificant, if not trivial: no one dies from ridicule. As for the person who is the brunt of the joke, laughter only adds to the malevolence of which he is victim: being laughed at hurts and being ridiculed kills.[63]

That being so, criminal law cannot simply take the joker's view. This is because the joker's critical faculties are often faulty.

The solution adopted by the Quebec Court of Appeal in *Bernier* could also be supported by Freud. He is quite clear about the collapse in judgment that afflicts the joker. The joker is like the alcoholic:

> The most precious thing that alcohol can offer mankind is an altered state of mind. This is why it is more difficult for some than for others to relinquish this "poison." *Light-hearted humour, endogenous or toxic*, decreases inhibitions, judgment in particular, and therefore makes sources of pleasure, which repression had closed off, accessible once again. *It is very instructive to note how much the elation of humour makes us less discerning about the appropriateness of the humour involved.*[64]

This is not unlike the evidence in *Bernier*: According to his colleagues, only Bernier found his behaviour funny.

The joker either is unaware of the harm done to the "victim"[65] or finds it inconsequential:

To the degree that it *is* aggression, laughter remains a privileged aggression, watched over by a consciousness of inconsequentiality. That the consequences may seem real to others is largely beside the humorous point.[66]

Therein lies the tragedy of humour, at least for a jurist. Jokers are unaware of or underestimate the consequences of their acts. They feel that their behaviour is of minor consequence, whereas the victims often disagree with this – as in cases of personal property that disappears temporarily, a pie thrown in the face, threats that are uttered in jest but taken seriously by the person they were aimed at, and so on.

The conviction handed down in *Bernier* was nevertheless correct. The impugned conduct was squarely within the provision's aim, which is to protect the victim's sexual dignity. The joker made fun of his victims' sexual dignity: *his act indicated that his victims' sexual dignity was of no account.*

In addition, civil law challenges the theory that the embarrassment experienced by the victim of inappropriate sexual touching, perpetrated in public and in jest, is of no consequence. On the contrary, the victim's humiliation represents harm that entitles the individual to compensation.[67] Put simply, attacking a person's sexual dignity is a serious matter.[68]

In my view, the solution put forth in *Bernier* is not limited to the crime of sexual assault: It also applies to common assault. Military hazings or university initiations sometimes serve as a setting for assaults under the pretense of fun. The hazings that accompany certain initiation rites can amount to an assault under section 265 of the *Criminal Code*. The attack on the individual's physical dignity and on his or her freedom of movement are serious enough to be prohibited.[69] This constitutes harm that is truly criminal.

This can be seen from the evolution of French penal law: "Hazing" is now a criminal offence as such under the part of the *Penal Code* pertaining to attacks on personal dignity.[70] Collective humour, designed to forge bonds, is not necessarily enjoyed by all: "Humour is a way of life and a social bond – for the joker. However, humour can also destroy; it disrupts and excludes. It is then that it becomes a permanent dialectic ... of social belonging and social alienation."[71]

Throwing a pie at someone to humiliate is another kind of humour punishable as an assault.[72] As the philosopher Henri Bergson so aptly puts it: "Laughter is, above all, a corrective. When intended to humiliate, it must make a painful impression on the person against whom it is directed."[73]

Jokes and ridicule often go together, with laughter thriving on the victim's ridicule. One cannot help being reminded of the conclusion reached by the writer Marcel Pagnol, for whom "Laughter is a song of triumph; it expresses the laugher's sudden discovery of his own momentary superiority over the person he laughs at."[74]

The seriousness of humour and of its humiliating nature is already indirectly recognized by criminal law. Depending on the circumstances, mockery or derision can be considered an "insult" under section 232 of the *Criminal Code* and may raise the defence of provocation.[75]

It should thus come as no surprise to see how criminal law deals with humour when the section's function is to preserve the victim's physical *dignity*.[76] Throwing a pie to intentionally ridicule the victim challenges the very values that section 265 of the *Code* is designed to protect.

Throwing a pie at public personalities to make fun of them involves the victim's physical dignity. The attack on dignity is more pronounced since the incident takes place in a public setting to achieve its desired amusing effect. It is essential, for the pie-thrower, that the scene unfolds where people are watching. The joke he wants to achieve consists specifically of having the public – either at the scene or watching the joke on television or reading about it in the newspapers – laugh at the victim.[77] Ridicule needs an audience.[78]

The desire to ridicule often stems from the pie-thrower's desire for publicity and consequently from his or her wish to achieve some kind of sensational act. The animosity that may exist between pie-thrower and victim can also undermine the theory of belief in the victim's tolerance level.[79]

Instances involving pie-throwers also help set the boundaries for the criminalization of humour in another way.

The law does not prohibit jesting. Mockery, in itself, does not fall under the *Criminal Code*. One necessarily goes back to the words of the philosopher Alain: "Laughter braves all. There is great vengeance in laughter against respect that has not been earned."[80]

No, laughter only makes one guilty if it also affects the victim's bodily integrity.

There is a second criterion. Throwing a pie does not always mean a criminal conviction. The circumstances may exclude all malicious or reprehensible intent on the part of the joker.

The dividing line between lawful and unlawful must fall between the mere intent to *tease* and the intent to *ridicule*.[81] Whereas the intent to tease supports the argument of the accused's belief in the victim's tolerance, the intent to ridicule does not.

Consider the person who gets thrown into the swimming pool on her birthday and becomes so angry that she charges the perpetrator with assault. Or think of the person who gets a pie thrown in his face during an evening with friends or who has beer spilled over his head, again during an evening with friends. The jokers in these cases are innocent if they believe that their victims will also find the pranks funny. They are innocent if they believe that, after the initial shock, their victims will then laugh about it. *Laughter aimed at producing laughter cannot be prohibited.*

This defence is essential in common assaults.[82] *It protects the accused from the victim's misplaced and unpredictable reactions.* As Favre so aptly puts it: "The enemies of laughter lack flexibility."[83]

The victim's consent must certainly be determined subjectively, as in the crime of sexual assault.[84] Consent to contact is determined based on the victim's state of mind or verbal reaction.

The *mens rea*, however, must be defined in such a way as to allow the accused to assert his or her belief that the victim would not be offended by the joke. As a matter of fact, the Canadian courts have not ruled out the possibility of using an innocent-joke defence for common assault. On the contrary, the Quebec Superior Court was careful to point out that the events leading to a conviction for pie-throwing in *Robert* were inconsistent with the existence of a genuine joke.[85]

Conclusion The preceding illustrates two of the challenges humour presents to criminal law: Criminal law cannot leave the victim at the mercy of a joker's poor judgment. Conversely, criminal law must not cause the joker to risk a conviction on account of the victim's unpredictable reactions and total lack of humour. The way to achieve this is through the defence of the belief in the victim's tolerance. The victim must not be at the mercy of the joker *and* vice versa.

Affront to Discipline

A joke sometimes stems from a lack of discipline. Pleasure, in this context, is derived from defying orders. Such bravado is sometimes systematically punished in the context of disciplinary law.

Consider the rebellious prisoner who hastily swallows a given substance during a prison search for contraband material. He later admits that he was only joking and that he simply ingested coffee beans. He is charged with committing an act *"calculated* to prejudice the discipline or good order of the institution."[86] The conviction that ensues[87] seems inevitable.

The joke erodes the officers' authority. The joke is suspicious *in itself*. It mocks the authorities. The misconduct is an affront to authority. The joke is punishable since it represents disobedience. A so-called joke defence ought almost to be dismissed automatically.

Mere bravado is of interest to disciplinary law or military law. However, this kind of affront is of no concern to criminal law. Rebellious humour does not have the necessary seriousness required in criminal law.

Affront to Reputation

Laughter is innocence: it liberates; laughter is a defence: it disarms; laughter is an offence: it kills.[88]

The derision accompanying physical aggression can lead to a conviction for assault.[89] The criminalization of derision is much trickier when there is no physical aggression. The question then is whether the victim's humiliation or ridicule are enough to involve criminal law.

The Canadian *Charter* itself requires that two criteria be considered before punishing derision: the seriousness and the malicious intent of the humour at issue. Mockery falls under freedom of expression. Suppression of the prank therefore centres around two factors: the public nature of the derision and the accused's slanderous intent.

The truth of these observations can be verified by examining two criminal offences: spreading false news and defamatory libel.

Satire is rarely kept within bounds by criminal law. This can be seen from the constitutional fate of section 181 of the *Criminal Code,* which prohibits the publication of a tale or news that the accused knows *is false* and that causes or is likely to cause injury or mischief to a public interest. This provision was struck down by the Supreme Court in *Zundel*.[90] The Court faulted the Legislature for penalizing jokes that are akin to satire or parody. It referred to the writings of famous English writers such as Swift and Addison, arguing that it is not appropriate to prohibit all false news likely to cause injury or mischief to a public interest: Their writings were not truly criminal in nature.

Section 181 of the *Criminal Code* is invalid because the provision prohibits certain valid political satires.[91] Two principles emerge from this ruling:

1 A *false* statement made in jest is protected under section 2(b) of the Canadian *Charter.*
2 Section 181 of the *Criminal Code* is unconstitutional because it penalizes insufficiently dangerous behaviour.[92]

Yet other provisions in the *Criminal Code* target irony. Defamatory libel also prohibits satire. The *Criminal Code* condemns slanderous irony in sections 298 to 300: Defamatory libel entails exposing a person to "ridicule" through "irony."[93]

We must not be deluded by the broad scope of the offence. The courts stand guard: Two conditions must be met before a joke will be penalized. First, the seriousness of the humour at issue must be determined; second, its malice.

In order to be criminally harmful, the false irony must be divulged to a third party. Defamation presupposes an act meant to tarnish a person's reputation. Therefore, the author of a piece of writing meant to ridicule the victim must divulge it to a third party. As the Supreme Court explained in *Lucas*, no offence is committed if the author simply shows the defamatory writing to the victim.[94] Causing vexation or indignation to the victim is therefore not punishable as such. The cruelty inflicted upon the victim does not suffice. Only a public affront warrants a penalty. Only an affront that exposes the victim to external ridicule is criminal.

There must be witnesses to the victim's ridicule. Punishment depends on their presence.[95] The ridicule that is caused is condemned only if the victim's reputation is tarnished.

The seriousness of the humour comes into question at another level. The author of the text ridiculing the victim is only guilty if he or she wanted to defame the victim.[96] Inappropriate humour is therefore not prohibited as such.[97]

In short, mockery is a product of freedom of expression. Consequently, punishment of humour is subject to stringent conditions. The ridiculing text must be disseminated, and its author must be prompted by defamatory intent. A ridiculing text devoid of malice is unpunishable.

Conclusion   There are a number of techniques a judge can use to exclude innocent jokes from the arena of criminal law. Three of these techniques are constitutional in nature:

1 The judge can conclude that freedom of expression has been violated if the humour being punished by law is in a verbal or written form.[98]
2 The rules for division of powers provide a second shield. A provision under the *Criminal Code* that punishes behaviour that does not have the required degree of severity is invalidated under the *Constitution Act, 1867*. This rule is of significance when it comes to innocent jokes or any inappropriate behaviour that does not meet the degree of severity required to incur a criminal penalty.
3 The theory of overbreadth also acts as a safeguard: It prevents criminal law from punishing behaviour that is merely objectionable. For example, a law that targets innocent jokes can be declared contrary to section 7 of the Canadian *Charter.*

An essential principle of statutory interpretation can be added to these three constitutional guarantees:

4 When an offence is broadly worded, the courts have the right to limit its scope in order to prevent convictions on objectionable behaviour that is not serious enough. In other words, statutory interpretation may take into account that the impugned conduct does not attract public condemnation. As the Supreme Court held:

> [W]hen the legislature employs language as broad as it has here, I think it is open to the Court to refine it in light of what it perceives to be the degree of public condemnation any impugned conduct would be likely to attract.[99]

The Court is therefore responsible for interpreting the section in such a way as to abstain from punishing conduct that is perhaps derogatory but not strictly criminal.

The provisions of the *Code* must be interpreted in such a way that the philosophy of criminal law is respected. The intervention of criminal law is specifically reserved for acts that are sufficiently odious or dangerous. The rules of statutory interpretation must recognize this and promote, to the extent possible,[100] the interpretation that is most in keeping with the relatively modest objectives of criminal law:

> [T]he general underlying purpose of the criminal law must inform the interpretation of any provision which creates a crime. The criminal law is essentially a means whereby society seeks to prevent, and failing that, punish blameworthy conduct which strikes at the fundamental values of the community. The criminal law is, however, a weapon of last resort intended for use only in cases where the conduct is so inconsistent with the shared morality of society as to warrant public condemnation and punishment.[101]

This rule of statutory interpretation, which is meant to limit the scope of the criminalizing provision, seems totally appropriate in the case of an innocent joke. In short, the Court can make use of constitutional principles and rules of statutory interpretation designed to remove from criminal law behaviour that is not sufficiently offensive.

Affront to Safety

Section 264.1 of the *Criminal Code* condemns everyone who "knowingly" utters a threat either to cause death or bodily harm to any person or to cause vandalism to property.

The connection between humour, fear, and intimidation can be studied in the context of this offence. Three conclusions will emerge from this analysis:

1 Trivial words cannot be punished.
2 Ill-considered words cannot be punished.
3 Only malicious words are prohibited.

Trivial words are exempt from all punishment because they are devoid of seriousness. Ill-considered words go unpunished because the accused lacks criminal intent. On the other hand, malicious words should be penalized because they are meant to instil fear in the victim.

This triple distinction is in keeping with the argument made thus far. Punishment centres on two criteria: the seriousness of the humour at issue and the seriousness of the intent.

Trivial Words   Words that are not objectively threatening are exempt from any penalty. A joke that is obvious escapes penalization from the very outset:

> The *actus reus* of the offence is the uttering of threats of death or serious bodily harm ... To determine if a reasonable person would consider that the words were uttered as a threat the court must regard them *objectively*, and review them in light of the circumstances in which they were uttered, the manner in which they were spoken, and the person to whom they were addressed. Obviously, *words spoken in jest or in such a manner that they could not be taken seriously could not lead a reasonable person to conclude that the words conveyed a threat.*[102]

This passage from *Clemente* focuses on the *actus reus:* Objectively speaking, was a threat uttered? An objective test is used, as the issue has to do with the material element of the crime.[103] Whether the accused's comments are threats or not is entirely for the jury to assess.[104]

No *actus reus* exists in the case of an *obvious* joke. Let us review the factors listed by the Supreme Court for determining the threatening nature of the words that were used.

The manner in which the words were uttered must first be examined. For example, an accused who laughed without malice when he uttered the alleged words escapes punishment.

The context surrounding the words objected to can also anodize a threat. The following example is particularly eloquent:

> [I]t is incumbent upon the Crown to prove that the threat, from an objective point of view, was "serious" ... It must have been an utterance which, when objectively considered, fell outside the category of jest. By requiring the Crown to prove that the remark satisfied the objective test, comments such as "kill the referee" made at a hockey game by an overly enthusiastic fan are not caught in the web of criminal law.[105]

The trivial nature of the accused's words can also result from the apparent impossibility of carrying out the threat. If it is evident that the threat cannot be carried out, one can infer that the accused is joking or does not actually think what he or she is saying.[106]

The words will then not be threatening under the objective test noted in *Clemente*. In other words, there is no *actus reus* since no threat exists as such. The obvious inability to carry out the threat must lead to acquittal.[107] This, in my view, explains why a paraplegic confined to a wheelchair was exonerated for crying out to his neighbour that he would "slap her and kick her in the butt." The words were not threatening given the context and the handicap of the person who uttered the words.[108] It was therefore equally appropriate to acquit an accused who was small in stature and who, as he was forcefully removed from the courtroom, promised physical retaliation to the much larger bailiff. Such words convey a sense of powerlessness rather than a threat.[109]

Appearances, therefore, vouch for the accused's innocence. No threat exists if the accused cannot give credence to his or her words.

The first conclusion must be that there is no *actus reus* if the words can patently not be taken seriously. Such words do not allow a reasonable person to deduce that they constitute a threat. The situation would be totally different if the words were apparently threatening given the context in which they were uttered and the person they targeted.

The debate then shifts toward the *mens rea*. The accused have a right to claim that, despite the objectively threatening nature of their words, they did not intend to intimidate anyone. This is the hypothesis of ill-considered words.

Ill-Considered Words   Trivial words are not serious enough to be prohibited. In short, they are not intimidating.

Ill-considered words also go unpunished. The reason for this is completely different. Criminal law abstains from punishing these since the author of the unfortunate words is not motivated by criminal intent.

In essence, the seriousness of the words uttered by those accused is not enough to convict them. In order to be found guilty, an accused must be aware of the threatening nature of his or her words: The accused must be aware of the meaning of the words used.

For the Court to impose a penalty, it cannot simply rely on the apparent meaning of the words uttered.[110] It must question whether the accused wanted the words to have an impact on the victim.[111] The accused is only guilty if he or she intended to intimidate someone. As important as it is to approach the existence of a threat objectively, it is equally important *then* to ascertain what the accused intended by his or her words. The intent to be taken seriously is required:[112] Section 264.1 of the *Criminal Code* does not target words spoken in jest.[113]

However, the specific content of the alleged joke must be examined. *The type of humour is a determining factor:* A malicious joke makes the joker guilty. Intent to carry out the threat is not required under section 264.1 of the *Code*.[114] Only the intent to intimidate counts. Making the victim fear the worst and enjoying doing so is enough to make the joker guilty.[115]

However, words that are uttered without knowing that they will be taken seriously will lead to an acquittal. Even if the joker was indifferent to the consequences of his or her words, this would not, in my opinion, suffice to convict. The crime of uttering threats requires specific intent – that is, intimidation. We can refer to two Supreme Court rulings. The following definition is set out in *McCraw*: "A threat is a tool of intimidation which is *designed* to instil a sense of fear in its recipient."[116] In *Clemente*, the Supreme Court enlarged on this: "A denunciation to a person of ill to befall him; esp. a declaration of hostile determination or of loss, pain, punishment or damage to be inflicted in retribution for or conditionally upon some course; a menace."[117]

The purpose of the accused's words is therefore a determining factor. The words must be meant to intimidate. Mere recklessness does not seem sufficient.

This is understandable. Section 264.1 of the *Code* penalizes the expression of a thought.[118] Unlike assault, no threatening act is required.[119] Mere words are enough to convict. It should therefore not be surprising that the courts have raised the level of *mens rea* above that of mere recklessness. The same applies to conspiracy: The accused's indifference to the impact of the agreement in which he or she takes part would not be enough to convict.[120]

Just as the *actus reus* is reduced to its most basic meaning – the outward expression of a thought – the *mens rea* must also be restrictively defined. This is a safeguard against extension of the field of punishable conduct. Criminal law is not designed to prohibit the excesses of language. Rather, it simply punishes one for words that are uttered in order to scare another. Humour, loss of control, and fatigue are all factors that cast doubt on the accused's intent to be taken seriously.[121]

Ill-considered words, by definition, do not fall within the ambit of section 264.1 of the *Code*.[122] Words spoken in jest or in fits of anger are therefore not the only words to benefit from impunity. Words uttered without thinking entail acquittal. Words that are seemingly threatening ("I'm going to kill you if you don't shut up") are sometimes more like insults rather than actual threats. This is how it is when the accused and the victim are used to using such strong language during their arguments and when neither takes the exchange of words literally.[123] Empty words are not intended to be caught up in criminal law.

Conclusion

This study shows that two tensions exist that the law must resolve:

1 the tension between the practical joker and the victim of the joke
2 the tension between undue criminalization and the judge's subjectivism.

The Tension between the Practical Joker and the Victim of the Joke

The tension between the practical joker and the victim of the joke is the first conflict that criminal law must resolve. The concept of "crime" must reconcile individual self-fulfilment through laughter and humour, on the one hand, and the victim's need for protection from bad jokes, on the other.

Humour is naturally experienced differently by jokers and their victims. Jokers contend that they were only jesting;[124] they are shocked – and offended – by their victims' outrage.

But the joker's critical faculties are not always reliable. Freud notes the collapse in judgment that is often characteristic of a joker.[125] This collapse is at times so pronounced that criminal law cannot simply *abandon* the victim to the joker's sense of humour. Laughter is "taking a break from reason."[126] Therefore, the defendant's belief that the act is harmless or farcical is not a defence *as such*. The reverse would constitute an unquestionable danger: It would allow the joker's value system to take precedence over that of society's.

This explains why the concept of *mens rea* does not refer to the accused's beliefs about the appropriateness of the act. The accused's value judgments are not considered during the inquiry into his or her state of mind. The perpetrator's belief that the acts are innocent is of no help;[127] persons charged with war crimes cannot express their beliefs about the humane or inhumane treatment of their victims;[128] persons in possession of obscene material will be charged regardless of their claims that they merely found the images erotic.[129] The same is true for the practical joker. Criminal law does not concern itself with the accused's value judgments.

On the other hand, it is equally important to protect the joker from being convicted based on the "victim's" sensitivity or overreaction to the joke. Safeguards must be put in place; legal concepts must sometimes be formulated from scratch to prevent a conviction based on the victim's oversensitivity.

The concept of "defamatory intent" is a good example. It allows the joke to go unpunished as long as the joker is not motivated by malice.[130] The courts wisely ensured that this requirement was *added* to the legal enactment in order to prevent a person who is easily offended from seeking a criminal conviction against the joker.

The defence of belief in the victim's tolerance depends on the same factors. It protects the joker, such as the friendly pie-thrower, from the victim's unpredictable oversensitivity.[131]

This reconciles the respectability of the victim with the respectability of criminal law: One cannot be achieved at the expense of the other. This concern transcends the question of penalizing humour. The victim's subjectivism cannot be the primary influence shaping the scope of criminalizing provisions. The victim's strong emotions must not broaden the reach of the offence.[132]

The Tension between Undue Criminalization and the Judge's Subjectivism

The law must also resolve the tension between undue extension of criminal law, on the one hand, and the judge's subjectivism, on the other.

Criminal law is unduly extended by interpreting the *Code* in a manner that results in punishing acts that, by the courts' own admission, are devoid of seriousness.[133] In this case, the judge interprets the offence in a manner leading to the punishment of innocent jokes.[134] This approach distorts the concept of a "crime." To trivialize criminal law in such a way weakens its authority all the more. Humour may be trivialized, but the law may not.

The reverse is not much better. Allowing an "independent"[135] prank defence with universal application would grant the judge considerable discretion and would make him or her the arbiter of good taste. Such judicial subjectivism fits uneasily with the rule of law. The reservations of criminal law expert Don Stuart on the matter are therefore understandable to a large extent:

> Professor Atrens suggests that the courts have not yet established what type of prank will suffice and advances the view that "the only practical test may be the social acceptability of the accused's conduct." This seems to be a particularly vague yardstick and subject to the criticism that judges are encouraged to substitute personal ethics.[136]

The final consideration is definitely the most important. The purpose of play, of laughter, of humour is to escape the seriousness of the world. It is important to respect, as far as possible, this healthy quest for freedom and to establish "unlegislated" zones for individuals. The criminal lawyer must, then, at all costs resist the temptation to interfere in all spheres of life. If criminal law unduly enters into the arena of humour, humanity loses one of its few sanctuaries.

Acknowledgment
I would like to thank my research assistant, Me Mario Naccarato, for his most valuable assistance.

Notes
1 *R. v. Zundel*, [1992] 2 S.C.R. 731, 774. In *R. v. Malmo-Levine; R. v. Caine*, 2003 SCC 74, par. 133, the Supreme Court indicated that the prohibited harm must not merely be "insignificant or trivial."
2 *R. v. Creighton*, [1993] 3 S.C.R. 3, 59.
3 J. Carbonnier, *Flexible droit*, 8th ed. (Paris: L.G.D.J., 1995).
4 Translated from L. Guirlinger, *De l'ironie à l'humour, un parcours philosophique* (Nantes: Éditions Pleins Feux, 1999), 46.
5 Translated from S. Freud, *Le mot d'esprit et ses rapports avec l'inconscient*, 15th ed. (Abbeville: Gallimard, 1953), Appendix at 278. Humour becomes a mental attitude that "renders affective discharge pointless" (idem, 278, translated). René Poirier seems to agree wholeheartedly: "[M]oderate laughter constitutes ... an appeasement, a refuge for people. It liberates and relaxes, thereby disarming the malice or the arrogance that are often its secret origin" (translated from "Recherches et réflexions sur le rire, le risible, le comique et l'humour," *Bulletin de la Société française de Philosophie* 78 (1984): 125). See also M. Gutwirth, *Laughing Matter: An Essay on the Comic* (Ithaca: Cornell University Press, 1993), 65-67.

6 One need only consider off-colour humour: *Rawlinson*, [1998] O.J. No. 3864; *Underdahl*, [1995] B.C.J. No. 2810; *Hecker*, (1980) 58 C.C.C. (2d) 66; *Springer*, (1975) 24 C.C.C. (2d) 66; and *Niman*, (1974) 31 C.R.N.S. 51. Relevant, too, is the jurisprudential controversy with regard to communicating with prostitutes in public via simple mockery or witticism: See the cases of *Collins (B.V.)*, (1996) 188 A.R. 161; *Pake*, (1995) 45 C.R. (4th) 117 (C.A. Alta.); and *Archer*, (1997) 34 W.C.B. (2d) 339.

7 There are numerous examples, ranging from pointing a loaded firearm as a joke (*Johns*, [1995] A.J. No. 1018) to a false bomb threat (*Clavelle*, (1972) 10 C.C.C. (2d) 127).

8 Theft, fraud, and mischief are some of the crimes for which a prank defence may be invoked.

9 The situations are quite diverse, ranging from gratuitous threats to pie-throwing and sexual touching due to inappropriate humour. For example, see *Robert*, JE 2000-1553; *Bernier*, [1998] 1 S.C.R. 975, [1997] R.J.Q. 2404 (C.A.); *Dickinson*, [1995] N.S.J. No. 386; *Clemente*, [1994] 2 S.C.R. 758.

10 Hence the need to verify under what circumstances mocking a court amounts to criminal contempt.

11 Translated from L. Guirlinger, *De l'ironie à l'humour, un parcours philosophique* (Nantes: Éditions Pleins Feux, 1999), 15.

12 Translated from É. Blondel, *Le risible et le dérisoire* (Paris: P.U.F., 1988), 81, my emphasis.

13 See the case law quoted *supra* note 6.

14 Translated from A. Nguyen, "Le rire et la dérision," in *L'évolution psychiatrique*, 67-118 (Paris: Privat, 1955), 111.

15 Translated from J. Château, "Le sérieux et ses contraires," *Revue philosophique* 140 (1950): 441-65, at 464.

16 See especially D. Grojnowski, *Aux commencements du rire moderne: L'esprit fumiste* (Paris: Librairie José Corti, 1997); R. Escarpit, *L'humour*, 10th ed. (Paris: P.U.F., 1994); Marcel Pagnol, *Notes sur le rire* (Paris: Éditions de Fallois, 1990); C. Powell and G. Paton, eds., *Humour in Society: Resistance and Control* (New York: St. Martin's Press, 1988); M. Mulkay, *On Humour: Its Nature and its Place in Modern Society* (Cambridge: Polity Press, 1988); C. Wilson, *Jokes: Form, Content, Use and Function* (London: Academy Press, 1979); Gutwirth, *supra* note 5; E. Dupréel, "Le problème sociologique du rire," in *Essais pluralistes*, ed. E. Dupréel, 27-69 (Paris: P.U.F., 1949).

17 See also L. Guirlinger, *De l'ironie à l'humour, un parcours philosophique* (Nantes: Éditions Pleins Feux, 1999); V. Jankélévitch, *L'ironie* (Manchecourt: Flammarion, 1997); H. Bergson, *Le rire*, 9th ed. (Paris: Quadrige, P.U.F., 1997); É. Smadja, *Le rire*, 2nd ed. (Paris: P.U.F., 1996); Gutwirth, *supra* note 5; J. Morreall, *Taking Laughter Seriously* (Albany: State University of New York Press, 1983); Château, *supra* note 15; Grojnowski, *supra* note 16.

18 The following are only a few examples: A. Chapman and H. Foot, *Humour and Laughter: Theory, Research and Applications* (New Brunswick: Transaction Publishers, 1996); J. Émelina, *Le comique. Essai d'interprétation générale* (Paris: Sedes, 1996); A. Ziv, *Personality and Sense of Humor* (New York: Springer Publishing, 1984); P. McGhee and J. Goldstein, *Handbook of Humor Research* (Berlin: Springer-Verlag, 1983); N. Holland, *Laughing: A Psychology of Humor* (Ithaca: Cornell University Press, 1982); A. Chapman and H. Foot, *It's a Funny Thing, Humour* (Oxford: Pergamon Press, 1976); J. Goldstein and P. McGhee, *The Psychology of Humor* (New York: Academic Press, 1972); Wilson, *supra* note 16; Gutwirth, *supra* note 5; É. Souriau, "Le risible et le comique," *Journal de psychologie* 41 (1948): 145-83; E. Aubouin, *Technique et psychologie du comique* (Marseille: OFEP, 1948).

19 Nguyen, *supra* note 14.

20 E. Smadja, "Approche pluridisciplinaire du rire normal et des rires pathologiques," PhD thesis, Université d'Amiens, 1990.

21 See especially the special July 1973 issue of *Revue française de psychanalyse*, which is devoted to humour; P.-L. Assoun, "L'inconscient humoriste," in *L'Humour: Un état d'esprit*, ed. Gérald Cahen, 51-68 (Paris: Éditions Autrement, 1995); S. Freud, *Le mot d'esprit et ses rapports avec l'inconscient*, 15th ed. (Abbeville: Gallimard, 1953).

22 S. Vogel, *Humor: A Semiogenetic Approach* (Bochum: Studienverlag, Dr. Norbert Brockmeyer, 1989).

23 P. Schoentjes, *Poétique de l'ironie* (Paris: Éditions du Seuil, 2001); R. Favre, *Le rire dans tous ses éclats* (Lyon: Presses universitaires de Lyon, 1995); L. Pirandello, *L'humour et autres essais* (Paris: Éditions Michel de Maule, 1988); A. Sauvy, *Aux sources de l'humour* (Paris: Éditions Odile Jacob, 1988); G. Elgozy, *De l'humour* (Paris: Denoël, 1979); Grojnowski, *supra* note 16; Bergson, *supra* note 17; Émelina, *supra* note 18. On the position given to humour in theatre, see A. Ubersfeld, "Le jeu de l'universelle vanité," in *L'Humour: Un état d'esprit*, ed. Gérald Cahen, 115-23 (Paris: Éditions Autrement, 1995).
24 W. Holland, *The Law of Theft and Related Offences* (Scarborough, Ont.: Carswell, 1998), 197; D. Stuart, *Canadian Criminal Law: A Treatise*, 4th ed. (Scarborough, Ont.: Carswell, 2001), 218, 554-55; Department of Justice Canada, *Towards a New General Part of the Criminal Code of Canada*, framework document submitted for review to the Standing Committee on Justice and Solicitor General, Ottawa, undated, 113.
25 Department of Justice Canada, *supra* note 24 at 113.
26 This unprecedented case-law study was carried out by G. Côté-Harper, P. Rainville, and J. Turgeon, *Traité de droit pénal canadien*, 4th expanded and revised edition (Cowansville: Éditions Yvon Blais, 1999), 1101-15.
27 See *Mitchell*, (1981) 58 C.C.C. (2d) 252 (B.C. C.A.). An engineering student was charged with two counts relating to possession of house-breaking instruments. As a member of the stunts committee of the Engineering Undergraduate Society, the accused was entrusted with custody of four master keys that had been in the possession of the society for several years. He used one of these keys to enter a Faculty of Arts building at night in order to obtain letterheads of the Arts Undergraduate Society with which to perform a stunt intended to embarrass and confound students of the Faculty of Arts. He was acquitted by the trial judge on the grounds that section 351 of the *Criminal Code* requires some unlawful purpose as opposed to an innocent or childish purpose. The majority judgment in the Court of Appeal disagreed with this interpretation of the *Code*. Yet the Court urged the attorney general not to proceed with a new trial. The dissenting judge in the Court of Appeal felt that section 351 of the *Code* had not been violated: "All of that was incurred in an attempt to brand a student prank a crime" (257). The majority's ruling on the scope of section 351 is subject to criticism (Côté-Harper, Rainville, and Turgeon, *supra* note 26 at 1110-11).
28 As has been aptly said: "[L]aughter emerges as the wild card in the pack of our faculties, the one to which we owe the capacity to negotiate our perilous freedom ... Standing unobtrusive guard over our right to be wrong, laughter ensures that [human beings] may go on floundering for as long as [they do] not too catastrophically overstep the boundaries of the safely laughable" (Gutwirth, *supra* note 5 at 190). As noted earlier, determining the playful sphere of liberty of every person (or the "boundaries of the safely laughable") entails examining society's tolerance level and, in turn, the tolerance level of criminal law itself. My study does not purport to address the full range of legal responses to offensive jokes. For instance, whether and how employment law has to respond to ethnically and sexually offensive jokes will not be analyzed. My text focuses on determining what behaviours can properly be described as criminal. On the broader issue of tolerance in society, one can refer to M. Walzer, *On Toleration* (New Haven: Yale University Press, 1997).
29 "Kant says of the comic in general that one of its main features is to deceive another for only a while" (translated from Freud, *supra* note 5 at 14).
30 Case law on the subject is plentiful. One need only cite the following as examples: *R. v. Morrisey*, [2000] 2 S.C.R. 90; *R. v. Bartlett*, (1998) 38 W.C.B. (2d) 177 (Ont. C.A.); *R. v. Vaillancourt*, (1996) 105 C.C.C. (3d) 552 (Que. C.A.); *R. v. Shawn B.*, (1990) 78 C.R. (3d) 93; and *R. v. Morehouse*, (1982) 65 C.C.C. (2d) 231 (N.B. C.A.).
31 Injury to others, destruction of an object, and so forth.
32 See *R. c. Cantin*, [1982] C.A. 151. The accused took part in St. Sylvester celebrations with over three hundred people in a community hall. After joking around and drawing attention to himself, he took out his lighter and set some decorative fir branches on fire. The flames happened to spread to the building, which was set ablaze; forty-six victims perished in the fire. The Court of Appeal held that this poor joker did not have the profile of a criminal; it concluded that the eight-year prison sentence imposed on him placed undue

importance on the criteria of making an example and of protecting society. See also *R.* v. *MacKay*, (1980) 40 N.S.R. (2d) 616 (N.S. C.A.), and *R.* v. *Joyce*, (1977) 41 C.C.C. (2d) 24 (Ont. Prov. Crt.).

33   *Young Offenders Act*, R.S.C. c. Y-1, s. 16 (2)*(a)*. This *Act* continued to have statutory effect until the coming into force of the *Youth Criminal Justice Act*, S.C. 2002, c. 1, on 1 April 2003.

34   *Young Offenders Act*, R.S.C. c. Y-1, s. 16 (2)*(b)*.

35   *Young Offenders Act*, R.S.C. c. Y-1, s. 16 (2)*(d)*.

36   The Court of Appeal agreed with the judge's ruling that the transfer should be denied: *R.* v. *S. (R.S.)* (1999), 132 C.C.C. (3d) 449 (C.A. Alb.).

37   For example, in the contexts of fake banknotes printed as a joke, a fake diploma designed to deceive someone, and so on.

38   See the following sections of the *Criminal Code:* 366 (forging a document), 369 (reproducing the seal of a public body or a court of law), and 376(2) (counterfeiting a mark).

39   Section 131 Cr.C.

40   See sections 130 (personating a peace officer) and 403 (personation) of the *Criminal Code*.

41   Section 457 Cr.C.

42   A trick is a particular type of deception of which the point is to keep the victim unaware, for a while, that he or she is the object of a practical joke. One need only think of the individual whose personal property has disappeared. "A practical joke is usually not amusing to its victim until near its end or after the joke is over. It may be funny during its unfolding to relatively uninvolved bystanders – but usually only if they have received the proper message that the episode is a joke ... Usually the victim goes through the experience to the very end without consciously knowing that he is the butt of a joke, and without laughing. The 'it's all a joke' message is then put over and the victim is able to find humour in the joke. Significantly, the joker and the bystanders who are all aware of the play frame may be laughing already. But not the victim. He perhaps may never laugh, may never find this joke which has been perpetrated against him humorous; but, after the joke is labeled as such, then humour is at least possible for him" (Fry, quoted in Vogel, *supra* note 22 at 139).

43   Section 437 Cr.C.

44   Sections 77*(g)* and 78.1(3) Cr.C.

45   Sections 442 and 443 Cr.C.

46   Section 457 Cr.C.

47   Numerous criminal offences at the federal level are derived from laws other than the *Criminal Code*. One need only mention offences regarding toxic substances, hazardous products, and cigarette advertisements (Côté-Harper, Rainville, and Turgeon, *supra* note 26 at 57-60).

48   The offence of making a phony bomb threat, punished under the *Aeronautics Act,* has the same constitutional basis as sections 77*(g)* and 437 of the *Criminal Code*. A recent bill confirms my conclusion that phony bomb threats fall under criminal law. Bill C-17, introduced for first reading on 31 October 2002 (51 Elizabeth II, 2002) and titled *Public Safety Act, 2002,* proposes the criminalization of jokes that are suggestive of terrorist activity.

49   Section 13 of the *Canadian Aviation Security Regulations*, SOR/2000-111, adopted under the *Aeronautics Act*, R.S.C., c. A-3.

50   *R.* v. *Rinkenbach*, (1991) 12 W.C.B. (2d) 549 (Ont. Ct. Prov. D.), concerning section 23*(b)* of the *Air Carrier Security Regulations*. The *mens rea* is the intent to make a declaration in *public knowing it to be false*. The *mens rea* does not require the intent to mislead others. The person who makes such a joke yet does not believe that the joke will be taken seriously is therefore guilty. Sentencing courts are nevertheless lenient if the practical joker was not aware of the consequences that could follow from his or her joke: *R.* v. *Rinkenbach*, (1991) 12 W.C.B. (2d) 549 (Ont. Ct. Prov. D.); *R.* v. *North*, (1989) 8 W.C.B. (2d) 542 (N.W.T.S.C.).

51   We need only think of the phony bomb threat or section 178 of the *Criminal Code,* which prohibits a person from throwing an offensive volatile substance that is "likely to alarm" any person in a public place. Punishment therefore depends upon the potential turmoil that can be caused by the accused's act.

52   Section 419*(a)* Cr.C.

53 My emphasis. See section 32 of Bill C-17, cited *supra* note 48, which deals with the addition of section 83.231 to the *Criminal Code*; the section is designed to suppress certain types of terrorist hoaxes.
54 See sections 130, 419, 442 and 457 Cr.C.
55 Compare sections 450 and 457 Cr.C.
56 Compare sections 439(1) and (2) Cr.C. Similarly, a false alarm is an indictable offence and is liable to imprisonment for a term not exceeding two years (section 437 Cr.C.).
57 Translated from A. Comte-Sponville, *Petit traité des grandes vertus*, 3rd ed. (Paris: P.U.F., 1998), 281-82.
58 Translated from the Court of Appeal's summary of the trial decision. *R. v. Bernier*, [1997] R.J.Q. 2404, 2408 (C.A.).
59 *R. v. Bernier*, [1997] R.J.Q. 2404 (C.A.).
60 The *de minimis non curat lex* defence for assault has prompted an intense legal debate. This issue goes beyond an analysis of penalizing jokes. I cite only a few of the many cases on the subject: *Canadian Foundation for Children, Youth and the Law* v. *Canada (Attorney General)* 2004 S.C.C. 4, paras. 200-209 (per Arbour); *R. c. Robert*, J.E. 2000-1553 (Mun. Ct.); *R. v. Perivolaris*, (1998) 41 W.C.B. (2d) 124 (Ont. Ct. Prov. D.); *R. v. Kormos*, (1998) 37 W.C.B. (2d) 299 (Ont. Ct. Prov. D.); *R. c. Nadeau*, [1997] A. N-B. no 535 (N.B. Prov. Ct.); *R. v. Chau*, (1996) 31 W.C.B. (2d) 173 (Alta. Prov. Ct.); *R. v. Stewart*, [1996] O.J. No. 2704 (Ont. Ct. Prov. D.): The maxim would not come into play during a domestic dispute; one must therefore convict the husband who pushes his spouse and causes her to momentarily lose her balance; and *R. v. Burden*, (1984) 66 C.C.C. (2d) 68 (B.C.C.A.).
61 This conclusion seems correct. The role that the prank defence plays is dependent on the elements of the offence: "Joking does not constitute an 'autonomous' defence. Joking simply constitutes a corollary to the rule that the prosecution must prove all elements of the offence. As a consequence, it is pointless to invoke section 8(3) Cr.C. as authority for this so-called defence" (translated from Côté-Harper, Rainville, and Turgeon, *supra* note 26 at 1114).
62 *R. v. Bernier*, [1998] 1 S.C.R. 975.
63 Translated from Nguyen, *supra* note 14 at 76. This is made clear by the outrage of victims of inappropriate humour in *Bernier*, [1997] R.J.Q. 2404 (C.A.), and *Dickinson*, [1995] N.S.J. No. 386 (N.S. Prov. Ct.).
64 Translated from Freud, *supra* note 5 at 146 (my emphasis).
65 Bernier's sense of humour is reminiscent of a quotation from the philosopher Château: "The immature man ... is not an accomplished man, he is still a child unable to make sense of the world and to apprehend it objectively; he does not have the ability to see ahead, to foresee the whole of a situation and all the consequences of an act" (translated from *supra* note 15 at 459).
66 Gutwirth, *supra* note 5 at 66 (emphasis in the original). See also page 109 of the same work.
67 *Vachon* v. *Perreault*, J.E. 84-39 (Prov. Ct.).
68 The following convictions illustrate this point. In *R. v. Dickinson*, [1995] N.S.J. No. 386 (N.S. Prov. Ct.), the accused was found guilty of fondling the victim's breasts and slipping his hand under her skirt; the assault was held to be sexual in nature despite the accused's claim that he was only joking. See also *R. v. Delia*, (1992) 15 W.C.B. (2d) 671, [1992] A.J. No. 288 (Alta. Prov. Ct.). The Court convicted a man in his sixties of touching a female employee's inner thigh and knee during an eye examination. The appellant's acts were preceded by lewd jokes. The Court convicted the accused of sexual assault primarily on the basis of the accused's offensive jokes. The Court also rejected the defence's argument that the accused's Latin background and temperament minimized the importance of the incident. See also *R. v. Nguyen*, (2000) 50 W.C.B. (2d) 362 (Alta. Q. B.). *Contra, semble, R. v. Nadeau*, [1997] N. B. J. No. 535 (N.B. Prov. Ct.). Lastly, it should be borne in mind that the scope of *Bernier* will vary depending on the facts of the case and the charge; see the acquittal in *Rawlinson*, [1998] O.J. No. 3864 (Ont. Ct. J. Gen. Div.), in relation to the crime of "gross indecency," which was abolished by Canadian legislation in 1988.
69 This assumes the use of force under section 265(1)*(a)* Cr.C.
70 Section 225-16-1 of the new *Penal Code*. See, on the issue of prohibiting hazings, René de Vos, *Le bizutage*, Collection Médecine et Société (Paris: P.U.F., 1999).

71 Translated from Smadja, *supra* note 17 at 70. In this passage, Smadja summarizes the theories of authors who have studied the concepts of laughter and gaiety.

72 *R. v. Robert*, Quebec Superior Court, District of Montreal, 500-36-002212-002, 19 October 2000 (Barrette-Joncas, J.).

73 Bergson, *supra* note 17 at 150.

74 Translated from Marcel Pagnol, *Notes sur le rire* (Paris: Éditions de Fallois, 1990), 25. Pagnol's theory is reminiscent of the position held by Hobbes, cited by Smadja, *supra* note 17 at 20-21.

75 *R. v. Thibert*, [1996] 1 S.C.R. 37.

76 Spitting in someone's face constitutes assault: *R. v. Stewart*, [1988] R.J.Q. 1123 (C.S.P.).

77 The joke is akin to assault. Compare the following quotation from Gruner, cited by Vogel, *supra* note 22 at 13: "The two words, 'sudden' and 'glory,' make up the two elements necessary for any evoking of laughter. Why does a pie in the face of a pompous stuffed shirt make us laugh? We perceive the difference between the victim and ourselves; he is deflated, defeated, and a sloppy mess – and we are not. This perception makes us feel 'glorified.' But this perception of 'glory' must be *sudden*; the pie must splash into his visage as a surprise to us. After the surprise wears off the 'glory' is no longer 'sudden.' Suppose he sits around for several minutes with pie all over himself. We might even begin to feel sorry for the poor slob" (emphasis in the original).

78 This is recognized in section 299 Cr.C.

79 As an example, the defence of belief in the victim's consent was raised unsuccessfully in *Robert* since the factual evidence was completely silent on the matter: *R. v. Robert*, Quebec Superior Court, District of Montreal, No. 500-36-002212-002, 19 October 2000 (Barrette-Joncas, J.). In this case, the Court of Quebec had itself noted both accuseds' desire for vengeance against the minister at whom they threw a pie and whom they criticized politically: *R. v. Robert*, [2000] J.Q. No. 2919 (C.Q.); *R. v. Foisy*, [2000] J.Q. No. 2990 (C.Q.).

80 Translated from the philosopher Alain *(Système des beaux-arts)*, cited by Favre, *supra* note 23 at 122.

81 This remark concerns common assaults. It does not relate to sexual assaults; see *infra*, note 82.

82 The issue of inappropriate sexual touching must be approached differently. The accused must ascertain *beforehand* that the victim was consenting: section 273.2(b) Cr.C.

83 Translated from Favre, *supra* note 23 at 96. The victim who decides to file a complaint does not always present him or herself in the best light: "It is difficult to combat ridicule with serious complaint. ... The optimal strategy for the butt would seem to be to acquiesce to the ridicule and feign amusement" (Wilson, *supra* note 16 at 204).

84 *R. v. Ewanchuk*, [1999] 1 S.C.R. 330.

85 *R. v. Robert*, Quebec Superior Court, District of Montreal, No. 500-36-002212-002, 19 October 2000 (Barrette-Joncas J.). The Superior Court very properly noted the categorical statement of one of the accused: "We did not throw a pie at Mr. Dion to be funny" (translated). Only the Court of Quebec concluded that pie-throwing in jest cannot serve as a defence: *R. v. Robert*, [2000] J.Q. No. 2919 (Q.C.); *R. v. Foisy*, [2000] J.Q. No. 2990 (Q.C.). The Court of Quebec relies on *Boger*, [1975] C.A. 837 (theft), and *Bernier* [1997] R.J.Q. 2404 (C.A.) (sexual assault). The serious questions about the dismissal of the prank defence to theft in *Boger* should be noted (Côté-Harper, Rainville, and Turgeon, *supra* note 26 at 1107-10).

86 Section 39*(k)* of the *Penitentiary Service Regulations* (now known as the *Corrections and Conditional Release Regulations)*, my emphasis.

87 *Bechard v. Canada*, (1989) 7 W.C.B. (2d) 159 (Fed. Ct.).

88 Translated from Nguyen, *supra* note 14 at 110.

89 The pie-throwing cases previously discussed attest to this.

90 *R. v. Zundel*, [1992] 2 S.C.R. 731.

91 *R. v. Zundel*, [1992] 2 S.C.R. 731, 755-56 and 775.

92 *R. v. Zundel*, [1992] 2 S.C.R. 731, 774 and 776.

93 Section 298(1) deals with ridicule; section 298(2), with irony.

94 *R. v. Lucas*, [1998] 1 S.C.R. 439, 476-78.

95 Section 299*(c)* of the *Criminal Code* is therefore partially invalid: *R. v. Lucas*, [1998] 1 S.C.R. 439.

96 Despite the wording of section 300 of the *Criminal Code,* knowing the allegations to be false does not constitute a sufficiently guilty state of mind.

97 Hence the questionable nature of the conviction handed down in *R. v. Georgia Straight Publishing Limited et al.,* (1969) 6 C.R.N.S. 150 (B.C.Co.Ct.). Criminal proceedings were brought against the accused for defaming a judge. In a satirical newspaper, the judge was awarded the "Pontius Pilate Certificate of Justice" after he handed down an unpopular decision. The article reads: "To Lawrence Eckardt, who, by closing his mind to justice, his eyes to fairness, and his ears to equality, has encouraged the belief that the law is not only blind, but also deaf, dumb and stupid. Let history judge your actions – then appeal" ((1969) 6 C.R.N.S. 150, 151). The defence centred around two arguments: The text constituted a joke on the judge; moreover, the newspaper meant to attract the readers' attention to the unfair nature of the law (as opposed to defaming the judge). The Court dismissed these arguments and stressed that the alleged offence did not require any intent to harm. This statement of principle seems outdated. That the judge was defamed is inconclusive: The accused's intent to defame the victim is mandatory under *R. v. Lucas,* [1998] 1 S.C.R. 439.

98 The next step is to determine whether the punishment of humour is justified under section 1 of the *Charter.* This was what the Supreme Court had to determine in *R. v. Lucas,* [1998] 1 S.C.R. 439.

99 *R. v. Skoke-Graham* [1985] 1 S.C.R. 106, 134 (Wilson J.'s reasons). The case dealt with the interpretation of section 176 of the *Criminal Code,* which prohibits "anything" that is wilfully done to disturb the order or solemnity of religious worship.

100 Statutory interpretation is justified only if the wording of the provision lends itself to that: *R. v. Hinchey,* [1996] 3 S.C.R. 1128.

101 *R. v. Greenwood,* (1991) 67 C.C.C. (3d) 435, 445 (Ont. C.A.).

102 *R. v. Clemente,* [1994] 2 S.C.R. 758, 763 (my emphasis).

103 "The *actus reus* of the offence is the uttering of *threats* of death or serious bodily harm": *R. v. Clemente,* [1994] 2 S.C.R. 758, 763 (my emphasis).

104 In other words, the *application* of the objective criteria set out in *Clemente* is purely a question of fact: *R. v. Kafé,* (1996) 106 C.C.C. (3d) 569, [1996] A.Q. No. 83 (Que. C.A.); *Brochu* c. *R.,* JE 97-1841 (C.A.).

105 *R. v. Graham,* (1996) 108 C.C.C. (3d) 438, 445 (Prov. Ct. Alta).

106 As an example, see *R. v. McCain,* [2001] O.J. No. 2973 (Ont. Ct. Just).

107 *R. v. McCain,* [2001] O.J. No. 2973 (Ont. Ct. Just.). On the other hand, the objective impossibility of carrying out the threat is inconclusive if the accused can subsequently remedy it. The context in which the words were spoken can prove the obvious impossibility of carrying out the threats in the near future. One need only think of a prisoner who phones a third party and threatens to rough him or her up. As shown in this example, the obvious impossibility of going from words to actions does not necessarily remove the objectively threatening nature of the words. The conviction handed down in *Bilodeau* by René de la Sablonnière J. is entirely correct. As the judge noted, citing Beetz J. in *Nabis,* [1975] 2 S.C.R. 485, 492: "Whether the threat raised the possibility of imminent or remote danger is equally of no consequence" (translated from *R. c. Bilodeau,* C.Q. Que., 22 March 2000, No. 200-01-048647-998). The issue of whether the obvious impossibility of quickly carrying out the threats casts off any threat inherent to the words that are uttered is a matter of fact.

108 *Abdelhay* v. *R.,* J.E. 96-1210 (C.A.).

109 *Mobarakizadeh* v. *R.,* J.E. 94-816 (C.A.)

110 *Dyckow* c. *La Reine,* R.J.P.Q. 96-111 (C.A.): An accused who had come to the police station to lodge a complaint was physically removed. In a fit of anger, he threatened a police officer with physical retaliation; he was arrested but did not resist. The trial judge convicted him because his words were objectively threatening even though they lacked intent since he was inebriated. The Court of Appeal acquitted him and criticized the judge for having considered only the accused's words objectively; *R. v. Mathurin* (1990) 11 W.C.B. (2d) 490 (Que. C.A.): The accused was acquitted of having told his former girlfriend that she would "die." The trial judge convicted him on the strength of the usual meaning of the word, regardless of the intent. The Court of Appeal criticized the judge's use of an objective standard.

111 *R. v. Range*, (1998) 37 W.C.B. (2d) 365, [1998] B.C.J. No. 361 (B.C.C.A.): "First, it is not merely what the words spoken to another would convey but what the appellant meant or intended by them"; *R. v. P. (T.)*, (2001) 50 W.C.B. (2d) 542 (C.A. Ont.), [2001] O.J. No. 1316 (C.A.); *R. v. Mathurin* (1990) 11 W.C.B. (2d) 490 (Que. C.A.). The jury must be informed of the nuance: *R. v. Range, supra*; *R. v. Danis (N.W.T.S.C.)*, [1993] N.W.T.J. No. 69 (S.C.). It is for the jury to establish the accused's state of mind: *R. v. Kafé*, (1996) 106 C.C.C. (3d) 569, [1996] A.Q. No. 83 (Que. C.A.). Therefore, whether or not the accused intended to joke is a question of fact.

112 This requirement seems to have been initially set out in *R. v. Underwood*, [1987] B.C.J. No. 2972, (1987) 4 W.C.B. (2d) 266 (B.C.Ct.C.).

113 *R. v. P. (T.)*, (2001) 50 W.C.B. (2d) 542 (Ont. C.A.), [2001] O.J. No. 1316 (C.A.); *R. v. Clemente*, [1994] 2 S.C.R. 758, paras. 7, 8, and 12. The new crime of terrorist hoax seems to depend on the same factors; see *infra*, note 115.

114 *Bonneville c. R.*, J.E. 96-1856 (C.A.); *Mercier-Rémy c. R.*, [1993] R.J.Q. 1383 (C.A.). The Supreme Court had similarly interpreted the predecessor of section 264.1 of the *Criminal Code: R. v. Nabis*, [1975] 2 S.C.R. 485.

115 This is the basis for criminalizing terrorist hoaxes. The perpetrator of such a hoax is only guilty if there was actual "intent to cause any person to fear death, bodily harm, [or] substantial damage." See text of the forthcoming section 83.231 of the *Criminal Code*, cited *supra* at page 132.

116 *R. v. McCraw*, [1991] 3 S.C.R. 72, 81-82 (my emphasis).

117 The Supreme Court adapts this definition taken from the *Shorter Oxford English Dictionary*: *R. v. Clemente* [1994] 2 S.C.R. 758, 761.

118 See Beetz J.'s comments in *R. v. Nabis*, [1975] 2 S.C.R. 485, regarding the provision that preceded section 264.1 of the *Criminal Code*.

119 Section 265(1)(b) Cr.C. defines aggression thus: "A person commits an assault when ... he attempts or threatens, by an act or a gesture, to apply force to another person." Mere threatening words do not suffice: *R. c. Starnino*, Municipal Court of Montreal, 9 June 2000, No. 199 088 741 (Discepola, J.); *R. v. Cadden*, (1989) 48 C.C.C. (3d) 122 (B.C.C.A.). This is the prevailing interpretation of section 265(1)(b) Cr.C. despite the reservations of certain authors: G. Williams, "Assault and Words" [1957] Crim. L.R. 219. The Supreme Court recognizes these two schools of thought yet has not resolved the issue: *R. v. Nabis*, [1975] 2 S.C.R. 485.

120 "Conspiracy cannot be committed by mere recklessness as to the object of the agreement": *R. c. Lamontagne*, J.E. 99-2308, (1999) 142 C.C.C. (3d) 561 (C.A.). See also *R. c. Sauvageau*, J.E. 97-24 (C.Q.); *Lessard c. La Reine*, Que. C.A., No. 200-10-000029-806, 12 July 1982; E. Colvin, *Principles of Criminal Law*, 2nd ed. (Scarborough, Ont.: Carswell, 1991), 347: "It is not enough that an agreement creates a risk that an offence may be committed."

121 "The word knowingly imparts a certain degree of consciousness and understanding of the words used as well as the effect that they normally would produce." The Court rightly added that "people may say what they do not really mean when very upset": *R. v. Taylor*, [1998] B.C.J. No. 2988 (BCPC). Accused who get carried away in fits of anger and get acquitted are common: *Sigouin c. R.*, J.E. 2002-916 (C.S.); *R. v. P. (T.)*, (2001) 50 W.C.B. (2d) 542 (Ont.C.A.), [2001] O.J. No. 1316 (C.A.); *R. v. O'Connor*, [1998] O.J. No. 6198 (Ont. C. Just., Prov. Div.); *R. v. Bernans*, [1996] O.J. No. 5237 (Ont. C. Just., Prov. Div.): Given his fatigue, the accused got carried away and did not mean what he said; the *mens rea* therefore did not exist; *Dyckow c. La Reine*, R.J.P.Q. 96-111 (C.A.); *R. v. Beyo*, [1996] O.J. No. 4942 (Ont. C. Just., Prov. Div.); *R. v. Payne-Binder*, (1991) 7 C.R. (4th) 308 (Y.T.C.A.); *R. v. Lee*, Ont. Dist. C. (Flinn, J.), 19 January 1988, unpublished, as summarized in *R. v. MacKinnon*, (1989) 75 Nfld. and P.E.I.R. 195, [1989] P.E.I.J. No. 26 (P.E.I.C.A.); *R. v. Teixeira*, (1988) 93 A.R. 361 (Alta. Prov. Ct.): The court noted the Latin temperament of the accused, who had a tendency to speak without thinking.

122 It is important to recall Beetz J.'s concerns regarding too broad a definition for threats, "for countless are those who do not weigh their words": *R. v. Nabis*, [1975] 2 S.C.R. 485. This concern is reflected in subsequent decisions made by the Supreme Court, which exculpates any individual who utters threats in jest.

123   See *R.* v. *Underwood*, [1987] B.C.J. No. 2972, (1987) 4 W.C.B. (2d) 266 (B.C.Ct.C.).

124   "The joker most often feels that he is 'innocent,' in the etymological sense of the word; he is surprised by the effects of his joke; he feels his jokes are insignificant, if not trivial: no one dies from ridicule. As for the person who is the brunt of the joke, laughter only adds to the malevolence of which he is a victim: being laughed at hurts and being ridiculed kills" (translated from Nguyen, *supra* note 14 at 76).

125   See, *supra* my study of *Bernier* and Freud's comments at pages 134-36 and 138.

126   Translated from É. Blondel, *supra* note 12 at 81.

127   *R.* v. *Théroux*, [1993] 2 S.C.R. 5.

128   *R.* v. *Finta*, [1994] 1 S.C.R. 701.

129   *R.* v. *Jorgensen*, [1995] 4 S.C.R. 55; *R.* v. *Hawkins*, (1993) 86 C.C.C. (3d) 246 (Ont. C.A.).

130   *Supra* pages 139-40.

131   *Supra* pages 137-38.

132   The Supreme Court cases are careful to avoid such a problem. See its decisions regarding offences where a person causes a disturbance (s. 175(1) Cr.C.; *R.* v. *Lohnes*, [1992] 1 S.C.R. 167, 180-81) and offences where a person disturbs the order or solemnity of religious worship (s. 176(3) Cr.C.; *R.* v. *Skoke-Graham*, [1985] 1 S.C.R. 106).

133   The *Mitchell* case, (1981) 58 C.C.C. (2d) 252 (BCCA), is symbolic of this problem. This case is analysed *supra* note 27.

134   *Boger*, [1975] C.A. 837, embodies this error. In fact, this decision is contrary to the wording in section 322(1) of the *Criminal Code* and it disregards section 7 of the Canadian *Charter*. See Coté-Harper, Rainville, and Turgeon, *supra* note 26 at 1107-10.

135   That is, *in addition to* the elements of the offence.

136   Stuart, *supra* note 24 at 555. On the other hand, Professor Stuart's opinion that the joke stems from the accused's motive and does not give right to acquittal is too absolute. As proven in this chapter, the prank can, at times, negate the material element or the psychological element of the offence. All is dependent on how the offence is defined. This issue is studied in depth by Côté-Harper, Rainville, and Turgeon, *supra* note 26 at 1101-15.

6

Poisoned Water, Environmental Regulation, and Crime: Constituting the Nonculpable Subject in Walkerton, Ontario

Laureen Snider

This chapter examines the question "what is a crime?" by looking at how particular acts and actors come to be seen as noncriminal. Specifically, it looks at the constitution of the nonculpable subject, examining how and why environmental crime – in this case, the failure of the Province of Ontario to provide safe drinking water – is conceptualized and defined as an "accident" rather than a "crime." At the empirical level, the argument rests on an analysis of testimony to the public inquiry in the town of Walkerton, Ontario. At the theoretical level, the chapter examines the forms of expertise and the discursive frameworks employed in defining behaviour in order to show how discourses of criminality and noncriminality are produced. It probes the intimate connection between expert knowledge, authorized knowers, and forms of discipline/power. Since knowledge claims always work to the advantage of some interests and groups and to the detriment of others, this chapter will also investigate why certain knowledge claims are heard and others marginalized, a question intimately linked to issues of political economy and the construction of the neoliberal state.

The deadly E. coli contamination of tap water that occurred in Walkerton, Ontario, in May 2000 left 7 people dead and 2,300 others suffering illnesses of varying severity. The long-term consequences of these illnesses are still unknown, but possible complications include kidney failure and other life-shortening (and very unpleasant) illnesses. A public inquiry headed by the Honourable Dennis O'Connor was established to look into the contamination of the water supply in Walkerton (Part 1) and into the safety of Ontario's drinking water (Part 2). From October 2000 to August 2001, 114 witnesses testified in public hearings.[1] The initial report was released on 14 January 2002 (Walkerton Inquiry 2002).[2]

The regulatory body responsible for the safety of water in Ontario is the Ministry of the Environment. Established in the first wave of environmental activism in 1971, the ministry grew in staff, ambition, and power throughout the 1970s and '80s, reaching its peak in 1992 under the left-leaning

New Democratic government of Premier Bob Rae. In 1995 the Progressive Conservative government under Premier Mike Harris swept into power with an avowedly neoliberal agenda. Its goal was to cut Ontario's deficit, slash the size and complexity of government, and make Ontario business-friendly. The Ministry of the Environment was a primary and immediate target: The number of employees was cut from 3,100 full- and part-time staff in 1994/95 to 1,394 in 2000/01, a drop exceeding 50 percent. Fines against polluters declined 67 percent in the two-year period from 1995 to 1997. The ministry's budget fell from $711 million in 1991/92 under the New Democratic government to $223 million in 2000/01, a decline of 69 percent. The proportion of water treatment plants inspected per year fell from 75 percent of 630 plants in 1993/94, to 24 percent in 1998/99. The specialist teams responsible for visiting water-treatment plants, for collecting and testing water samples, and for conducting follow-up visits, were disbanded and water testing, formerly done in public government-operated laboratories, was privatized (*Toronto Star*, 8 July 2000, K1, K3; Snider 1999; Krajnc 2000; Walkerton Inquiry 2002).

While the speed and depth of cuts and the extent of deregulation under the Common Sense Revolution of Mike Harris's Tories may have been extreme, the policies, and the philosophy that drove them, are anything but unique. Varying combinations of decriminalization, deregulation, and downsizing have transformed regulatory arenas in the field once defined as corporate crime. In areas as diverse as false advertising, monopoly law, and occupational health, on issues from medical implants to drug safety, the antisocial and harmful acts of the corporate sector have been rethought and literally "re-formed" (Snider 1999, 2000, 2001a; Tucker 1995; Tombs 1996, 1999, 1992; Condon 1998).[3] Behaviours once conceptualized as fraud motivated by an individual or collective desire to maximize private profit at public expense are now represented as accidental oversights by well-meaning, overworked executives or as technical failures caused by bureaucratic complexity. Education, counselling, and pollution permits and licences have replaced fines and prison terms as the "penalties" of choice. The responsibility of government to safeguard the health and wellbeing of citizens by controlling the antisocial acts of business has been redefined as "regulatory overload" or "red tape." Mandatory, legally binding sanctions for violators came to be seen as interference with stakeholders. Criminalization, zero-tolerance policies, and "three-strike" laws, increasingly employed to discipline and censure antisocial acts in every other sphere, became "excessive" and "inefficient" when applied to the private sector – that is, to business.

The first part of the chapter examines the events in Walkerton, focusing on what happened. The second part looks at the framing of the inquiry and the rationales employed to constitute discourses of blame and exoneration as they emerged through the voices of witnesses and the language of law.

The chapter concludes with an examination of the challenge to neoliberalism posed by the O'Connor report, expounding the implications and significance of this challenge. And it returns to issues of culpability: How was culpability conceptualized; what were the rationales, discourses, and strategies employed; and how was nonculpability defended? What are the implications of these discursive formations for policies of criminalization and for the politics of law and order?

The Events in Walkerton: What Happened?[4]
Walkerton, Ontario, is a town of 4,800 people, located about 280 kilometres northwest of Toronto. It is a small-c and capital-C conservative town in a largely rural county, where residents believe in self-reliance and hard work. Many can trace their roots in the area back several generations. Originally settled by an Irish immigrant named Joseph Walker, who established a sawmill on the banks of the Saugeen River in 1850, it survived the economic vicissitudes of the nineteenth and twentieth centuries, experiencing neither extreme depression (except during the 1930s) nor extreme prosperity. With no major industries or public-sector employer dominating the town, its business people and a sprinkling of professionals, such as teachers and doctors, make a generally modest living by servicing area residents and farms, a smallish number of tourists in season (primarily passing through en route to cottage country farther north and west), and a small but growing population of retirees or second-home owners from the prosperous Golden Horseshoe communities to the south. Walkerton is ethnically and religiously homogeneous: The residents are primarily white Anglo-Saxons from British stock who self-identify as Protestant or Roman Catholic; the diverse, multicultural population found in larger Ontario cities is strikingly absent here. In this sense, it is a world apart.

On Thursday 18 May 2000, the first indications of a mysterious outbreak of illness in Walkerton became evident, with reports that twenty children were absent from Mother Teresa, the local separate school, two having been hospitalized with bloody diarrhoea. On 19 May a wave of similar illnesses swept through Brucelea Haven, a nearby senior citizens' home, with widespread complaints of diarrhoea, stomach pain, and nausea. Reports of illness continued to come in on 20 and 21 May, and the Walkerton hospital and area doctors were swamped with complaints, inquiries, and emergency visits over the long holiday weekend (Victoria Day). The medical officer of health for the Bruce Grey Owen Sound Health Unit, Dr. Murray McQuigge, was becoming increasingly concerned about the safety of the water supply. However, when the health unit contacted Stan Koebel, the general manager of the Walkerton Public Utilities Commission (PUC), the body responsible for water safety in Walkerton, officials were assured by Mr. Koebel that the water was safe.

This, as it turned out, was not the case: The water supply was contaminated with *Escherichia coli* 0157:H7 (hereafter called E. coli), a nasty and potentially fatal organism. Because E. coli has been primarily associated with food contamination – found in the guts and intestines of cattle, it is sometimes called "the hamburger disease" because of its association with undercooked ground beef (Pennington Group 1997; Pennington 2000) – and because there had never been a major, water-generated outbreak in the province, the health unit did not, at first, focus its investigations exclusively on water. (And when it did, officials were assured by the PUC manager, once on 19 May and twice on 20 May, that the water was okay.)

On Sunday 21 May, stool samples analyzed at the Owen Sound hospital tested positive for E. coli, thereby confirming what was by then widely suspected. (Indeed, as early as 19 May, staff at Brucelea Haven, the retirement home, had switched to bottled or boiled water.) An hour later Dr. Murray McQuigge issued a "boil water advisory," an order that was to remain in effect for seven months. (It was finally rescinded on 5 December 2000.) On 22 May the first death occurred; there was another on 23 May and two more on 24 May. In the end seven deaths were directly attributed to E. coli contamination; the youngest victim was two, and the oldest was eighty-four. As is common with such outbreaks, the old and the young suffered most, their immune systems being least able to combat the pathogens. Subsequent epidemiological studies estimated that a total of 2,321 people became ill: Of these, 1,346 were seen by area health professionals, 65 of these were hospitalized, and 27 developed Hemolytic Uremic Syndrome (HUS), a serious but not infrequent complication of E. coli poisoning. At this point it is impossible to say how many have suffered lasting kidney damage, or to specify what the long-term health effects will be.

After intensive investigation, the cause of the outbreak was traced to manure spread on a farm owned by the local veterinarian on or about 12 May, which entered Well 5, located on the south-east quadrant of the farm. This was not a large agribusiness but a typical Ontario cow/calf operation with an average of forty cows at any given time.[5] The farmer was following "best management practices" set out in Department of Agriculture guidelines, but a combination of climate and geology had allowed E. coli in the manure to enter Well 5, a major source of water for Walkerton. From 8 to 12 May, 134 millimetres of rain inundated the area, 70 millimetres falling on 12 May. Such spring rains are not unprecedented, but in the Walkerton area a rainfall event of that magnitude would normally happen only once every thirty years (Hearings, 15 January 2001). Although Walkerton obtains its water from three wells, Well 5 was the primary source from 9 to 15 May because the other two were, for different reasons, shut off or operating only periodically. Justice O'Connor (Walkerton Inquiry 2002, 13-14) concluded that "the residents of Walkerton were first exposed on or shortly after May 12."

For geological reasons, Well 5 is highly susceptible to pollution by surface water because it is located on "highly fractured bedrock." This means that bacteria can penetrate groundwater through fissures, fence post holes, or springs, thereby contaminating the bedrock and water supply. This vulnerability was recognized when the well was constructed in 1978; however, the certificate of approval issued by the Ministry of the Environment (MOE) in January 1979 attached no conditions to the operation of this well. According to government guidelines in place today under the "Ontario Drinking Water Objectives" (ODWO), passed in 1994, such wells must be equipped with continuous monitors of chlorine residuals, which sound an alarm and automatically shut off the well when polluted water overwhelms the disinfectant capacity of the chlorine. Measuring chlorine residuals is important because well water must be disinfected with "sufficient chlorine to inactivate any contaminants" (Walkerton Inquiry 2002, 14), the chlorine residuals indicating whether or not this has occurred.[6] Well 5 should have been equipped with turbidity monitors as well.[7] However, when the MOE developed a set of conditions to be applied to all new certificates of approval in 1992, and when the ODWO was amended to require continuous chlorine residuals and turbidity monitors on all wells subject to ground water contamination in 1994, existing systems such as Walkerton's were retroactively approved, or "grandfathered." Because they had been "safely operated" for decades, it was assumed they were safe.

The absence of chlorine and turbidity monitors puts extra pressure on the human operators of the water system and on the regulatory systems charged with detecting and correcting system failures. Unfortunately, Stan Koebel and his brother Frank, the foreman at the PUC, were not up to the job. Without automatic monitors, the chlorine residuals measure must be taken daily, by hand. This is the duty of the water-system operators. However, for more than twenty years the operators in Walkerton had "engaged in a host of improper operating procedures" (Walkerton Inquiry 2002, 182-83), such as taking water samples from the nearest and easiest source, typically the tap at the PUC office, mislabelling samples, making fictitious entries on the daily operating sheets, not using enough chlorine, inventing false chlorine residuals numbers, and submitting false annual reports to the MOE. The Walkerton PUC was required by ODWO rules to submit thirteen water samples per month, but the regulations were for "guidance" only and thus not "legally binding" (Hearings, 17 October 2000, 106). As a result, on 13, 14, and 15 May the foreman performed the required daily checks on operating wells but did not measure the chlorine residuals. Following usual operating practice at the Walkerton PUC (contrary to MOE guidelines and directives), he made the number up. On 15 May three water samples were sent to A&L Canada Laboratories for testing, and on 17 May Stan Koebel was informed that all three samples showed the presence of E. coli.

According to the notification protocol set forth in the "Ontario Drinking Water Objectives," these results should have been forwarded to the MOE office in Owen Sound, which would have informed the Bruce Grey Owen Sound Health Unit. However, the Walkerton PUC, which had been using G.A.P. EnviroMicrobial Services Incorporated since the privatization and closure of the provincially owned public-health laboratories in 1996, had changed labs in April 2000. The new laboratory owners were unaware of this directive, which was also not a legally binding guideline (Walkerton Inquiry 2002, 33). Thus on 19 May, when reports of sickness surfaced and questions were asked about the safety of the water, only Stan Koebel and PUC staff knew of the adverse test results. Koebel was concerned and immediately began flushing and disinfecting the system in the mistaken belief that this would quickly make the water safe again. He did not disclose the negative lab results to the health unit or to anyone else, probably because he was afraid of revealing that Well 7 had been operating illegally – that is, without a chlorinator. The new chlorinator, which had been sitting in the PUC workshop for several weeks, was not installed until "around noon" on 19 May (Hearings, 18 December 2000, 140). Ironically, as it turned out, Well 5, rather than Well 7, was the source of the contamination.

Stan Koebel was, and is, a man with a Grade 11 education who joined the Walkerton PUC in 1972 at the age of nineteen. He became foreman in 1981 and general manager in 1988, when his former boss retired. He was "grandfathered" into his position and received his Class 3 Water Distribution Operator Licence with no further training or testing. The licence was routinely renewed from then on. He had never read the "Ontario Drinking Water Objectives" (though a copy sat on the shelves of the Walkerton PUC offices) or the "Chlorination Bulletin." He, his brother, and all PUC staff routinely drank untreated water at the well sites, finding it to have a better flavour than chlorinated water. Indeed, he was often pressured by area residents to "reduce the chlorine taste" (Walkerton Inquiry 2002, 183). Although section 17 of Ontario Regulation 435/93 requires every operator to receive "at least 40 hours of training per year" (*ibid.,* 185) and to report this annually to the MOE, Stan Koebel attended a few workshops and conferences and was allowed to count a ten-hour business workshop on leadership and the supervision of employees as fulfillment of this requirement. Small wonder he thought that superchlorinating the system (which he did from 19 May on) would quickly make the water safe again. Small wonder he got the impression that MOE guidelines and directives weren't very important and saw daily measurement of chlorine residuals as one more useless, and probably unnecessary, piece of government red tape. This attitude to government regulation, already strong in the Walkerton area, was reinforced by the Conservative government's high-profile Red Tape Commission, a Cabinet-level committee set up to recommend "the elimination or amendment of any inappropriate regulatory measure" (*ibid.*, 462).

The Ministry of the Environment is the body responsible for ensuring water safety in Ontario. It is supposed to "enforce laws, regulations and policies on the construction and operation of municipal water systems, set standards, approve construction, certify system operators and oversee treatment, distribution and monitoring practices (*ibid.*, 231). As part of its mandate, it is required to conduct regular inspections, ensure that water-system operators have adequate knowledge and training, and prosecute and/or sanction individuals and businesses for violations. The Walkerton PUC was inspected in 1991, 1995, and 1998. Following standard practice in the Owen Sound office, ministry officials gave advance warning of inspections to PUC officials, thereby providing the office enough time to "get ready" and ensure the records were "presentable" (*ibid.*, 198-99). The 1995 inspection took two hours, and the inspector, John Apfelbeck, found E. coli in several water samples; the measured chlorine residuals in treated water were less than the required 0.5 milligrams per litre, and the required number of water samples were not being submitted for microbiological testing. Stan Koebel said he would attend to these deficiencies, but he did not. There was no follow-up by the MOE. Three years later inspector Michelle Zillinger reported that the problems identified in 1995 (and, in many cases, in 1991) were still uncorrected in 1998. And there was new evidence of unsafe water and inadequate operator training. She therefore recommended that mandatory abatement measures be taken against the Walkerton PUC to compel its managers and staff to comply with MOE requirements.

However, province-wide the MOE was operating in crisis mode. When the Conservatives were elected in 1995, the Ministry of the Environment was immediately targeted because, according to the new minister, Brenda Elliot, "the focus of the Ministry had drifted ... It was clear upon meeting stakeholders ... that the Ministry needed to be refocused to become more responsive, effective" (Hearings, 26 June 2001, 11). To her, it was "an over-regulated sector" (*ibid.*, 12), an affront to the Common Sense Revolution, whose goal was to "eliminate all red tape and reduce the regulatory burden" (*ibid.*, 15). The *Final Report of the Red Tape Commission,* issued in January 1997, singled out the MOE with 131 recommendations, versus 18 for the Ministry of Labour and 12 for the Ministry of Health (Walkerton Inquiry 2002, 464-65). It was chastised for "customer service problems" and "onerous reporting requirements" (*ibid.*, 464-65). In response the MOE assigned fifteen employees to produce a document entitled "Responsible Environmental Protection," which committed the ministry to becoming more "results-oriented, cost-effective and customer driven." It would henceforth provide "flexibility and certainty to industry" and "simplify rules and eliminate red tape";

it would also encourage "voluntary action" and "incentives," rather than penalties (*ibid.,* 462). Its new business plan, signed by the minister on 28 February 1996, instituted a $200.8 million budget cut and eliminated more than 750 employees. From 1995/96 to 1999/2000, the overall staff complement dropped from 2,065 to 1,374. Spending estimates were reduced from $411.3 million in 1995/96 to $270.6 million in 1998/99; they jumped to $406.7 million in 1999/2000, then fell to $229.1 million in 2000/01, prior to the water contamination in Walkerton. And operating expenditures decreased from $282 million to $174 million between 1995/96 and 1999/2000 (*ibid.,* 272).

To accomplish these cuts, senior managers drew up a list of "non-core programs," water testing being one of them (Walkerton Inquiry 2002, 272). Training budgets were slashed, and senior personnel were downsized, transferred, or fired. When privatization closed down the public laboratories in 1996,[8] MOE officials decided not to "force" legally binding regulations on private labs, opting instead for voluntary compliance. "There was a reluctance to enact a new regulation in conjunction with the privatization of laboratory testing" or to pursue mandatory accreditation because this would have delayed privatization (*ibid.,* 315). And given that all existing regulations were under scrutiny with an eye to abolition, suggesting new ones was definitely *not* a wise career move. "The regulatory culture created by the government through the Red Tape Commission review process" (*ibid.,* 33) made the passage of a notification requirement a nonstarter. The new philosophy saw water-system operators as the "real" owners of the resource; MOE officials were mere "overseers" (*ibid.,* 272).

The MOE office in Owen Sound was, of course, aware of the ongoing philosophical revolution. And it was coping with high turnover in personnel, crises in morale, increases in workload, and the loss of experienced staff (though it apparently suffered no significant overall staff reduction). Continuity and stability were nonexistent. Walkerton's PUC, for example, was overseen in 1995/96 by Larry Struthers; in 1996/97 by John Clark; by Struthers; and from October 1997 to April 1999 by Donald Hamilton, who was replaced by John Earl until Earl was moved to waste management, at which point Struthers took over yet again! Earl was back in charge in May 2000. This round of musical chairs was dictated by the fact that five environmental officers resigned or retired, while the territory and program responsibilities of the Owen Sound office increased (due to municipal amalgamation, another downsizing policy). And although the district supervisor of the Owen Sound office, Phillip Bye, repeatedly argued that these personnel losses were not a problem, when pressed by skeptical counsel, he finally allowed that "it was a challenge" (Hearings, 1 November 2000, 140). Earl and other environmental officers were less reticent, describing morale problems, overload, and stress (*ibid.,* 30 October 2000, 16-33). Phillip Bye also knew that his bosses in Toronto were totally opposed to mandatory controls and that communal water systems had become even "less of a priority" following the budget cuts of 1996 (Walkerton Inquiry 2002, 272; Hearings, 13 November 2000, 48). The number of annual planned inspections in the Owen Sound office fell from twenty-five in 1994/95 to ten in 1999/2000; the actual number of inspections fell from sixteen to ten; and the time spent on water safety issues fell by about half (Walkerton Inquiry 2002, 407-8). Bye therefore rejected Zillinger's advice and opted for a conciliatory, "voluntary" approach. Thus letters identifying the problems with Walkerton's water system were duly written, and the responsibility for acting on them shifted back to the Walkerton PUC and its commissioners.[9]

As O'Connor (Walkerton Inquiry 2002, 27) points out, this decision was "consistent with the culture in the MOE at the time." Follow-up was once again nonexistent: Several months later Stan Koebel received a letter from the MOE thanking him for "attending to the deficiencies raised" in the 1998 report – when, in fact, he had addressed none of them (*ibid.*, 203). The MOE's failure to act "sent the unintended message that these requirements ... were not important" (*ibid.*, 204).

Explaining Walkerton

Framing the Inquiry

Thus far I have examined what happened in Walkerton as reconstructed by the main players in the inquiry. I will now look at how the events in Walkerton were presented, conceptualized, represented, and understood. The focus here shifts from the "what" to the "how," though the two are entwined and overlapping. (To assume that there is a "what" independent of a "how" is to assume that one "real truth" can be extracted from an examination of the Walkerton case, which is problematic.)[10] Because there are many lenses through which this case can be viewed and because the lenses themselves vary historically and culturally (300 years ago the water contamination in Walkerton would have been explained in religious rather than scientific terms), it is important to understand the thought patterns, language, and concepts that constituted the inquiry's findings in the Walkerton case as represented in the questions of lawyers and the testimony of witnesses. What role did the discursive frameworks produced by the hearings play in defining the events in Walkerton as essentially non-criminal?[11] How do "we" as a society decide where blame is warranted and where it is not?

The initial framing of the inquiry took place through law, through the terms and wording of the *Public Inquiries Act,* then through the Order in Council that set out the scope and terms of this particular inquiry, then through the Ontario government's appointment of Dennis O'Connor as commissioner. Once that framework was in place, the selection of *what information was relevant* became vital. This judgment, made in the first instance by Justice O'Connor and counsel for the inquiry, determined which witnesses would be required to appear, which documents would be sought (and, if need be, seized), which testimony would be required or requested and in what order, and which parties would be recognized as having a legitimate stake in the case – that is, designated "parties with standing." Beyond this, what kind of expertise, knowledge, or information was deemed vital to explaining the events in Walkerton, what credentials were necessary for one to sit on the Advisory Panel or to secure commissions to write issue papers? Once these decisions had been made – a process accomplished without input from "the public" or from those living with the consequences of Walkerton's water contamination – the testimony presented at the hearings became decisive. Which versions of what caused the illnesses and deaths in Walkerton were presented, and even more significant, which versions were recorded in the O'Connor report? It is these versions that will shape (but not determine) the "truths" of the events in Walkerton, that will appear in history and social-science texts, that will be taught to the next generation of voters, policy analysts, and scientists, that will be labelled "real" or "accurate." Competing versions of these events, if they cannot be ignored, will be represented, at one end of the continuum, as "the ravings of loonies" or as "the pleas of special-interest groups" and, at the other end, as "alternate accounts" and "overlooked truths." While a number of factors shape where opposing accounts will end up in this hierarchy of credibility, the power that the advocates of a particular position can wield – their control of political, economic, and ideological resources – is always significant.

The Public Commission of Inquiry into Walkerton's water contamination was set up by the Ontario government on 12 June 2000. The commission's mandate was broad: to inquire into the circumstances "which caused hundreds of people ... to become ill, and several ... to die in May and June 2000, at or around the same time as *Escherichia coli* was found ... in the town's water supply"; to consider "the effect, if any, of government policies, procedures and practices" and "any other relevant matters ... to ensure the safety of Ontario's drinking water" (Order in Council, 13 June 2000, cited in Walkerton Inquiry 2002, Appendix A). The commissioner, Justice Dennis O'Connor, a man with impeccable legal credentials and experience, was called to the Court of Appeal in 1993. He chose two men as head counsel for the inquiry: Paul Cavalluzzo, with a background in administrative, constitutional, and labour law, called to the Bar in 1973; and David Stockwood, Q.C., called to the Bar in 1968. Both are senior partners in well-established, well-respected legal practices. Backing them up were three slightly more junior counsel: Ron Foerster, Ron Gover, and Freya Kristjanson. Those most involved in the hearings were Cavalluzzo, Gover, and Kristjanson.

Law equips public inquiries with broad and sweeping powers to subpoena witnesses to testify, search premises, and compel the release of documents deemed relevant. To fulfill this part of the mandate, an RCMP inspector and a constable were hired to assemble documents, interview witnesses, and prepare evidence.

The inquiry was an intensely legal affair. Not only were its terms dictated by law, but virtually all witnesses, victims, and every party with full or partial standing at the hearings hired counsel (many with partial or total subsidy from special legal-aid funds).[12] Their questions and interjections – particularly those of the commissioner and commission counsel – determined which information was presented and how. On any given day the hearing room contained several dozen lawyers in addition to the commissioner, (usually) Cavalluzzo and either Gover or Kristjanson, and the witnesses appearing that day. (On 25 June 2001, for example, seventy-five lawyers were listed in the day's roster of counsel.)[13] The regular routine went like this: The witness of the day was sworn in, his or her credentials, education, work experience and/or biography were elicited, and the examination commenced. Commission counsel, usually Cavalluzzo, took the lead and conducted the most intensive, far-reaching examination. This was followed by cross-examinations. Depending on the centrality of the witness, each was cross-examined by a dozen or more counsel for other parties with standing. Throughout the examination and cross, counsel would refer to backup or background documents. These were filed as exhibits – by 18 January 2001 there were 1,300 of them; by 8 March 9,600 new ones had been produced (Hearings, 18 January 2001, 93; and 8 March 2001, 198-99). Documents were taken from six ministries, the Cabinet Board Office, the Premier's Office, and the Management Board Secretariat. More than 50,000 were requested from the MOE alone (Hearings, 8 March 2001, 198-99).[14]

To carry out the commission's mandate, hearings were conducted in Walkerton from 16 October 2000 to 30 July 2001. Counsel made their final submissions to the commissioner from 15 to 27 August 2001. In all, 114 witnesses testified. From (roughly) 16 October 2000 to 28 February 2001 (Part 1A), the hearings focused on the primary actors, those directly involved in the events of May 2000: staff and first-line supervisors from the Walkerton PUC, the local health unit, and the MOE's area office in Owen Sound. The focus from 6 March to 30 July 2001 (Part 1B) was on explaining the events in Walkerton and preventing future water contamination. This goal was sought through science by means of expert panels on water purification and through government. The decision to seek answers in these two areas, made by the commissioner and commission counsel early in the framing process, was crucial.

Science[15] was consulted through expert testimony backed by issue papers. Twenty-four issue papers were commissioned by the Research Advisory Panel

on subjects from water supply to risk communication. Charged with providing scientific and practical advice to the inquiry, the panel consisted of
seven people with senior academic positions in the natural, applied, or social sciences and was chaired by a former federal deputy minister. Twenty-
six environmental groups, eight agricultural or farming organizations, the
chiefs of Ontario First Nations, health units, conservation authorities, and
private companies in the water business were given full or partial standing
in the second stage of the hearings (Part 1B).[16]

Government policy and practice were interrogated through expert panels
on the workings of government and regulation and through the testimony
of senior policy advisors, civil servants, and politicians. Deputy ministers of
the Ministry of the Environment under the former NDP government and
the present Conservative government testified, along with past and present
managers of the MOE's offices in Owen Sound and Kingston and its head
office in Toronto. The inquiry heard from staff in charge of investigations
and enforcement, from the director of laboratory services, and from the
project manager of approvals reform – the latter, Robert Shaw, tied with
Phillip Bye, the district supervisor of the MOE's Owen Sound office, for
most appearances before the inquiry (five times each). Finally, the inquiry
heard from the politicians themselves: Brenda Elliot and Norm Sterling,
who were the Cabinet ministers responsible for the Ministry of the Environment during the tenure of the Conservative government, and the premier himself.

In addition to public hearings and the issue papers commissioned by the
Research Advisory Panel, a series of Town Hall meetings to hear concerns
about drinking water safety were held in nine Ontario towns and cities:
Waterloo, Peterborough, Kingston, North Bay, Thunder Bay, Walkerton,
Windsor, Ottawa, and Toronto. All of these initiatives were intended to fulfill the stated aim of the commissioner, who announced early in the process
that the inquiry would seek "broad involvement" and be "open and accessible to the public." He made the decision to hold hearings in Walkerton
rather than Toronto, where most of the professional parties lived, and to
seek "the views, expertise, knowledge, perspective ... of as many different
sources as possible" (Hearings, 18 January 2001; Walkerton Inquiry 2002, 104-
5). This interpretation of his mandate made space for oppositional voices and
views, some of which were validated in the all-important inquiry report.

Conclusions of the Walkerton Inquiry
The O'Connor report, as it turns out, is an intensely critical report. It does
not contain platitudes to the powerful; rather it attacks the presumptions
that drove the Common Sense Revolution, the massive budget cutting exercises, the reluctance to enforce regulations, and the voluntary approach
to compliance. Regulation, O'Connor notes (Walkerton Inquiry 2002, 465),

was a "last resort" for this government. Under the Regulatory Impact and Competitiveness Test (an offshoot of the Red Tape Commission), regulation was to be reactive, rather than proactive, and would only be considered after all possible alternatives were eliminated, the costs to business justified, and the impact on competitiveness assessed in "early and continuous consultation with affected businesses" (*ibid.*, 464). Government targeting of the MOE was deemed to have been ill-considered: "[A]ssociated risks to public health were not properly analyzed or managed, repeated warnings ... were not acted upon" (*ibid.*, 406).

Most damning of all, O'Connor's conclusions and recommendations (Walkerton Inquiry 2002, 4-5) blame government cutbacks and neoliberal policies for the Walkerton disaster: "The provincial government's budget reductions led to the discontinuation of government laboratory testing services ... in 1996 ... The government should have enacted a regulation mandating that testing laboratories ... notify both the MOE and the Medical Officer of Health"; moreover, "the provincial government's budget reductions made it less likely that the MOE would have identified ... the need for continuous monitors ... and the improper operating procedures of the Walkerton PUC." No words are minced: Failure to pass a notification requirement resulted in "an additional 300 to 400 illnesses" – though it probably "would not have prevented [any] deaths" (*ibid.*, 406).

While the report holds the PUC operators, especially Stan Koebel, responsible for their "improper operating practices," which were, and are, "unacceptable and contrary to MOE guidelines and directives" (*ibid.*, 4), the bulk of the blame is *not* directed there. Stan Koebel "did not intentionally set out to put his fellow residents at risk" (*ibid.*, 183), and he was "sincerely sorry" (*ibid.*, 182). Walkerton's water contamination is primarily explained as a failure of government: The MOE "took no steps to ... inform [Koebel] of the requirements or to require training." "It would be unreasonable" for the MOE to expect operators of small water systems to understand "the science behind chlorination" (*ibid.*, 24). MOE inspectors should have detected and corrected these deficiencies (*ibid.*, 182). It "did not invoke any mandatory abatement measures or issue a Director's Order" (*ibid.*, 202). And "it is simply wrong to say," as counsel for the Government of Ontario did, "that Stan Koebel or the Walkerton PUC were solely responsible" (*ibid.*, 24).[17]

This understanding of the events in Walkerton was constituted through the public-inquiry process. It emerged from the testimony of 114 witnesses, thousands of pages of verbatim transcript notes – approximately 300 to 400 pages per day were transcribed and posted – and hundreds of documents and exhibits. From this excess of material, the following analysis focuses on the testimony of three key players, men whose fact claims and truth representations were at the heart of the blame/exoneration process. These are Stan Koebel, general manager of the Walkerton PUC; Phillip Bye, district supervisor of the MOE's Owen Sound office; and John Earl, the environmental officer responsible for the Walkerton PUC in May 2000. Bye appeared before the inquiry five times, on 25 October 2000, 13 and 14 November 2000, 20 June 2001, and 3 July 2001; Earl appeared twice, on 30 and 31 October 2000; and Koebel appeared three times, on 18, 19, and 20 December 2000.

However, all these witnesses were heard, only and always, through counsel. Lawyers acting for players, government, the commission, and all parties with standing elicited and reconstructed the actors' rationales and interpretations. Counsel asked the questions and accepted or challenged the answers. Indeed, nonlegal actors disappeared at the crucial final stage of the inquiry. Counsel alone was permitted to summarize arguments, reconstruct and reinterpret the truths of witnesses, infer motives, and impute causality. The language, assumptions, methodologies, and prejudices of counsel, then, provided the ultimate filter.

Within this privileging of law, additional credibility-structuring hierarchies can be found. The commissioner and commission counsel were primary. They did the initial and most comprehensive questioning of each witness, took as much time as they wished, and set the timetable, stage, and agenda for the cross-examinations that followed. Their comments – O'Connor himself was an active participant throughout – represent the perspective most evident in the report. (And, as discussed above, this version of events is the one usually represented as the "lessons of Walkerton.") However, cross-examinations are equally significant for our purposes because they shed light on competing versions of culpability, blame, and truth. The role played by counsel for the Province of Ontario was particularly significant: These men found themselves defending not just their clients (the officials in the Ministry of the Environment), but also the rationales and factual claims of neoliberal government itself.

Thus, while much of the interrogation and summation, particularly by noncommission counsel, was of the tedious, pro forma, "my client is blameless" variety, it does reveal the rationales of blame and exoneration, the terms and modes of thought, that these lawyers believe set the boundary between accident and wilful misconduct, between the venal criminal (the other guy's client) and the accident-prone employee or innocent bystander (their client). The final summations, lawyers' last chance to sway the audiences they need to impress, are particularly noteworthy. Here we see in starkest form those reconstructions that counsel think make a difference to how their client(s) are judged.

A broad assumption, or underlying belief system, can be identified that united all counsel. This was their basic belief in truth-finding through law and science. Law – or, more accurately, legal procedure – was the means through which the "truth" of the events in Walkerton would be attained. Science was the source of this truth. Thus, as we shall see, counsel, particularly outside counsel, put much emphasis on procedural correctness, on whether particular actors did what the law required of them in the proper – that is, the legal – way. Blame was properly, and deservedly, attached to the illegal act and actor; exoneration belonged to those whose conduct could be seen to have been procedurally correct. As Morrison (1995, 464) points out, the legitimacy of modern law, due to the elevation of form over content, resides in procedural correctness. Because it creates its own legitimacy through procedure, no meta-narrative is necessary to sustain its "truths." Thus the laws, statutes, and regulations governing water protection were set out in the first part of the hearings as noncontroversial, as pure information, as "simply informative" (Hearings, 17 October 2000, 85-115). Information presented at the hearings in accord with procedural rules of law was validated as "the evidence." This is why the initial decisions made by the commissioner and counsel about which witnesses would be called and which issues were relevant were so important. Once validated as "evidence," information could be denigrated, dismissed as "speculation," or derided as "conjecture,"[18] but it had to be dealt with. Information not presented was literally and conceptually not in the frame.

While law was the means, science was the answer, the purveyor and source of "truth," the pathway to "wisdom." This unquestioning faith in progress through science marks the inquiry as a thoroughly modernist exercise (Crosby 1997; Haggerty 2001; Morrison 1995). Science was accessed through the work of experts ("the scientists"), whose studies provided "fact." It was science as presented by experts that established all the central truths of the inquiry: the source of contamination (Well 5, not 6 or 7); the cause of the outbreak (E. coli from manure, not contaminants related to construction of a new water main on Highway 9); and the levels of chlorination that are sufficient and "safe." On all of these issues, the correct science was sought. This made it difficult to deal with the limits and ambiguities of scientific knowledge – to accommodate, for example, evidence that properly conducted tests of water safety sometimes yield false negatives and false positives (Hearings, 23 October 2000, 22, 40; 26 February 2001, 219-20) or that "too much" rain in too short a period may overwhelm the best-operated, best-chlorinated water system (Hearings, 28 February 2001, 239-40). In the academic world, science is contingent and challengeable, a matter of probabilities; certainty lasts until the next study is published. Scientific knowledge is the result of human decisions to hold some factors relevant and treat others as background assumptions: If the criteria of relevance change, so do the probabilities, so does "truth." As Haggerty (2001, 10) puts it, "truth is a social accomplishment." In the inquiry, on the other hand, science was the Holy Grail. In the end O'Connor's report challenged the prevailing assumptions of neoliberal government but not those of science. It *interrogated* government but *consulted* science.[19]

The preeminent role accorded science and the men of science[20] was apparent from the beginning. The first two witnesses on 16 October 2000 were scientists, and Mr. Cavalluzzo spent fifteen minutes laying out the credentials of each. Professor Howard was introduced as the author of more than 150 articles and a distinguished professor with the Groundwater Research Group at the University of Toronto. His curriculum vitae was given to counsel, and Cavalluzzo told the inquiry that he was "eminently qualified to testify" (Hearings, 16 October 2000). The second witness, Professor Huck, was presented as the Natural Sciences and Engineering Research Council (NSERC) chair in water treatment at the University of Waterloo, an expert on water supply, treatment, monitoring procedures, and distribution systems. Scientists appeared early and often in this inquiry – only government officials appeared more frequently – this being the first of Professor Huck's three visits. And scientists were treated as expert witnesses; others, by comparison, were "fact witnesses" (Hearings, 16 October 2000, Cavalluzzo at 172). All counsel – both commission and outside counsel – treated scientists with respect. Questions primarily asked them to expand upon and/or to clarify their central arguments. No subpoenaed evidence was presented on the data not discussed or the methodologies not explored, and no requests that they justify their explanations versus alternative accounts were made. The testimony of Professors Howard and Huck was described by the commissioner as necessary to ensure that "we are operating on a common frame" (*ibid.*, 171). Thirty-one of the 114 witnesses before the inquiry were invited as scientific experts: Of these, 21 had PhDs in the natural sciences, and 10 had MDs.[21]

"Fact witnesses," the players in the drama of Walkerton, *and* those whose expertise was not the science of water purification but the "science" of government, faced more skeptical audiences.[22] Their reconstructions of the "truth" did not go unchallenged, and blame, at both the individual and collective levels, was regularly attributed to them through a variety of rationales.[23] As always, commission counsel set the tone at the witness's first appearance.

Institutional failure was consistently probed in the hearings through questions requiring government officials to justify operating procedures or to explain why they had not used powers conferred on them by law. Thus when Phillip Bye made his first appearance at the inquiry on 25 October 2000, nine days after the hearings began, he was quizzed on the MOE's "Strategy Document" (its 1998 response to criticisms from the Red Tape Commission):

Cavalluzzo [counsel for the commission, reading from the "Strategy Document"]: "[I]t is the responsibility of the treatment plant and distribution system owners to supply safe drinking water to consumers. The MOE establishes drinking water and operating standards." (Hearings, 25 October 2000, 52-3)

Cavalluzzo: [This means that] "[t]he Ministry views itself as playing an advisory role." (*Ibid.*, 54)

Bye prevaricated in reply, and Cavalluzzo paraphrased Bye's reply as:

"Basically you're saying that ... [it is] for the municipalities to treat and distribute water ... and for the municipal Officer of Health to ensure it is safe." (*Ibid.*, 54)

Similar questions followed, as Cavalluzzo sought to establish institutional culpability by presenting evidence showing that the MOE responded to cutbacks by attempting to "responsibilize" the bodies it was legislatively obligated to police.

At Bye's next appearance Cavalluzzo (Hearings, 13 November 2000, 40) quoted from Bye's subpoenaed notes, prepared for an internal inquiry at the MOE. In these notes Bye explained the situation in the Owen Sound office: "Since the 1998 Report, 4-5 officers have handled Walkerton due to F80." (F80 was the early retirement scheme instituted by the Conservative government with the aim of cutting the size, cost, and power of the civil service.) Cavalluzzo suggested that this amounted to an "admission" of institutional failure. However, Bye repeatedly denied that cutbacks or downsizing had impaired the operation of the Owen Sound office. In a protracted series of questions, a clearly skeptical Cavalluzzo reminded Bye that his office had lost five officers between 1997 and 2000. Bye's only (reluctant) concession was to say that the situation had represented "a challenge" (*ibid.*).

Other counsel focused blame at higher levels of decision making, interrogating the policies and priorities of the Conservative government as a whole. Mr. Finch, for the Walkerton Community Foundation, says: "They decided to do business differently. But they had an obligation to do it properly" (Hearings, 15 August 2001, 141). Mr. Muldoon, for Concerned Walkerton Citizens, identified policy changes and resource and regulatory changes as being responsible for the "climate created by the province" that led to the events in Walkerton (Hearings, 16 August 2001, 8). He cited a subpoenaed letter from an MOE lawyer that advised against putting restrictions on the private sector. He then tied the perceived "impracticality" of such a regulation to the antiregulatory agenda of the Red Tape Commission (*ibid.*, 12). In the same vein, Muldoon referred to a "regulatory gap created as a result of the privatization of labs" (*ibid.*, 14), linking it to the "regulatory chill ... created" (*ibid.*, 15) and to the "*infamous* business plan of 1996" (*ibid.*, 27, my emphasis).[24] Similarly, Mr. Lindgren (Hearings, 15 August 2001, 178) argued that "[t]he cold stark denials of the province ... must be reviewed." These were attacks by counsel on neoliberalism itself, on the philosophy that drove the Common Sense Revolution in Ontario. Blame and culpability were thus attached to institutional decisions made at the highest levels of government. These attributions were only possible because O'Connor and counsel decided to put government philosophies and cutbacks in the frame, thus allowing witnesses to be called and evidence to be introduced that would make these links clear.

This perspective, and evidence, put counsel for the Province of Ontario (Hainey and Marrocco) on the defensive. Thus, instead of focusing their efforts on criminalizing Stan Koebel and the Walkerton PUC, they were repeatedly forced to describe and defend the Conservative concept of regulation. Regulation, they argued, must be seen as a "partnership," a consensual relationship between "adults," a contract between equals. Welfare-state ideologies, which see the state as protector of the citizen, were denigrated as immature if not ridiculous: "[S]ome people want government to save them from themselves" (Hearings, 16 August 2001, 75). Small towns and small-town officials, it was argued, are not "helpless, childlike, unsophisticated" (*ibid.*, 75-76). What Muldoon called "the regulatory chill" became, in the language of counsel for Ontario, the "culture of trust" between the MOE and municipal PUCs (*ibid.*, 138).

In addition to institutional failure, rationales of procedural failure were widely employed as mechanisms of blame and culpability. In his summation for the Walkerton Community Foundation, Mr. Trafford referred to the collective failure to heed warnings. There were "many, many red flags," "bells should have gone off at the MOE" (Hearings, 15 August 2001, 40-41). He also argued that "[t]he Ministry had an obligation to go back [to ascertain the safety of wells approved under the ODWO]" (*ibid.*, 13). Muldoon, representing Concerned Walkerton Citizens, questioned environmental officer (EO) John Earl: "Is it fair to say there is no protocol ... dealing with transition [transfer] of files [between EOs]?" Ignoring Earl's response Muldoon continued: "There is no procedure ... for notification?" (Hearings, 31 October 2000, 28-9).

The MOE was repeatedly faulted for not setting standards for PUC employees and for "dumbing down" the credentials required to become a water-testing technician. A former MOE employee testified that the simplified water-testing kits introduced with privatization allowed mere "chemical technologists" (as opposed to fully qualified microbiologists) to conduct tests they might have been unable to interpret (Hearings, 23 October 2000,

22, 40). Here we see the valorization of the scientist/expert used to critique one of the effects of privatization.[25]

The logic underlying failures of procedure gains its power from the concept of unheeded warnings. "You were warned" or "you knew" is a powerful strategy of blame because ignorance is seen – in "common sense," if not in law – as legitimating inaction and excusing mistakes. This accusation, applied with damning effect in O'Connor's report, originated in questions posed and answers accepted, or challenged, during the inquiry's examination of key government officials. It is here that subpoenaed documents were presented showing that the minister of the environment, Norm Sterling by this time, had received a letter from the minister of health telling him that he should require the newly privatized water-testing laboratories to report adverse results to the local officer of health. Government failure to hear and to act was repeatedly represented as incontrovertible evidence of institutional culpability (Hearings, 16 August 2001, 13). The inference was that the Ontario government *knowingly,* rather than accidentally, put human health at risk.

Thus counsel pointed out: "It was stated in the confidential business plan [subpoenaed] that risk to human health and the environment may increase" (Hearings, 15 August 2001, 142). And "[o]n many occasions ... ministry staff warned senior management, the MOE and Cabinet that the budget reductions presented risks to the environment and public health" (Walkerton Inquiry 2002, 409; Hearings, 12 April and 8 March 2001). The government's failure to conduct a "proper," or formal, risk assessment was similarly critiqued: "No analysis appears to have been made of the specific nature, scope or extent [of the risks], or of how they could be managed" (Walkerton Inquiry 2002, 41; Hearings, 4 July 2001). Counsel for Concerned Walkerton Citizens also noted that "[n]either the Deputy Ministers nor Cabinet requested a risk management plan" (Hearings, 16 August 2001, 28). Government, then, "was fully aware" (Hearings, 15 August 2001, 142) but did "no realistic analysis"; there was "no structural approach" (*ibid.,* 143).

The inadequacy of training and knowledge was also used to establish culpability. Counsel for the PUC commissioners and other local actors, and for the province, interpreted inadequate training as a failure of the individual. Stan Koebel was repeatedly depicted as too lazy or complacent or uninterested to avail himself of "easily accessible" training (Hearings, 19 and 20 December 2000, 244-45). On the other hand, counsel for the commission and for groups such as Concerned Walkerton Citizens interpreted this as a failure of government. Government failed to oversee its employees or to provide adequate resources, which produced inadequate staff who lacked the training, time, resources, or knowledge to do their jobs properly. Thus the cross-examination of John Earl by the counsel for Concerned Walkerton

Citizens asked: "[S]ubsequent to University [previous questions established that he had graduated with a BSc in 1974] how much formal training ... with communal water systems [did you have]?" Earl was then asked: "[S]o is it fair to say there wasn't any formal training [on] communal water systems?" The question was repeated four times in the context of his promotion from a level-three to level-four environmental officer and in connection with the introduction of new chlorination techniques, new strains of bacteria, and new laws and regulations (Hearings, 30 October 2000, 19, 20, 23, 26). Counsel also asked Earl to guess how much time he had spent on communal water systems since 1996 and, when he guessed 10 percent, presented data from subpoenaed MOE records showing that it was only 1.4 percent (*ibid.*, 23-24). Counsel zeroed in on the fact that Earl had "no awareness" of the 1996 or 1998 inspections reports on the Walkerton PUC (*ibid.*, 28) and that he didn't know the ODWO regulations (ibid., 81-83). Earl's supervisor, Phillip Bye, was repeatedly drilled on the content and the adequacy of the training received by environmental officers (Hearings, 13 November 2000, 42, 65-127; 15 August 2001, 35-40). And it was underlined in the final submissions that the cost of courses for EOs shot up from $60 to $600 per course when the training subsidy was removed by the Conservative government in 1996 (Hearings, 16 August 2001, 410).

Lenience and/or a failure to act was a rationale presented more often in these hearings as an institutional, rather than an individual, fault. Thus Cavalluzzo drilled Bye on the fact that he refused to issue a director's order to the Walkerton PUC in 1998 despite Zillinger's recommendation (Hearings, 13 November 2000, 60-110; 14 November 2000, Prehogan and Muldoon at 156-57). In the final summations, the MOE was castigated again for its "serious failure ... to enact ... appropriate legislation" (Hearings, 15 August 2001, 152), for its "serious oversight" in not requiring laboratories to report adverse results to the Ministry of Health (*ibid.*), and for its "soft approach to follow-up" (*ibid.*, 166). Counsel for the Province of Ontario, back on the defensive, countered that attacks on the government's policy of voluntary compliance were unwise and speculative, being based on nothing more substantive than "hindsight" (*ibid.*, 106).[26]

Most of the rationales of culpability discussed thus far focused on organizational rather than individual culpability. This was a product of the way the commission was framed. However, a bad-faith intent to deceive was the rationale, allegation, and judgment used most consistently at the individual level. An intent to deceive is the type of culpability most closely linked to traditional criminality and attributions thereof. In the Walkerton hearings, there were only a few exceptions to this pattern, which are noteworthy because they were exceptions. A lawyer representing Pollution Probe (Hearings, 23 August 2001, 187) accused the Conservative government of bad faith for providing "misinformation" through its business plan. The intent to deceive was seen in the fact that "the most critical decisions under the Common Sense Revolution were not posted [on the government's website]." They were not publicly disclosed. Similarly, Muldoon, for Concerned Walkerton Citizens, suggested that the ministers and Cabinet "rolled the dice ... thinking they'd get away with it [the cuts]." They made "a decision ... that was conscious ... deliberate" (Hearings, 15 August 2001, 30).

For the most part, however, a bad-faith intent to deceive was the rationale used to construct, censure, and shame the guilty individual rather than the organization. It was levelled most intensely and personally at the general manager of the Walkerton PUC, Stan Koebel (and, to a lesser extent, at the foreman, Frank Koebel, Stan's brother). Cherniak, counsel for Murray McQuigge, Walkerton's medical officer of health, said in his cross-examination of Stan Koebel: "[Y]ou and your staff have been falsifying the records ... for 20 years ... to mislead the MOE Inspectors" (Hearings, 20 December 2000, 177-78). A number of similar accusations were directed at Stan Koebel: "You were prepared to lie" (*ibid.*, Trafford at 214-16); "you were actively, purposefully lying or deceiving, correct?" (*ibid.*, Trafford at 216); you "created false entries" to "make a good impression" (*ibid.*, Hainey at 232-33). In his final submission, Hainey, for the Province of Ontario, accused the Koebel brothers of "lack of responsibility" and "lack of integrity." Stan Koebel, he also stated, "knew which information to falsify" and successfully deceived "the people he set out to deceive" (Hearings, 16 August 2001, 90, 98, 99, 101-2). Moreover, he noted, Stan Koebel was "dishonest and intolerant of regulatory direction" (*ibid.*, 153-54). Censures that constructed the individual as a damaged character, a bad sort of person, dishonest, and a liar and falsifier were liberally employed.

The assumption is that the culpable criminal person, the bad character, is not merely careless and that his or her mistakes are not caused by honest ignorance.[27]

Hainey cross-examining Stan Koebel: "You had educational material in your office, available to you." "There was money for training?" (Hearings, 20 December 2000, 227)

"You knew what you had to do, it was easy, you could have done it." (*Ibid.*, 246)

"It wasn't difficult." (*Ibid.*, 245)

"Just turn up the chlorinator." (*Ibid.*, 246)

"You knew perfectly well." (*Ibid.*)

Later, Marrocco, for Ontario, summed up the Koebels as being culpable individual subjects:

"People [like this] ... get lazier and lazier over time." (Hearings, 16 August 2001, 104)

There is no rationale of exoneration for the bad character/criminal. At the level of the organization, as we have seen, exoneration is justified on the grounds of "we did everything we could," or, in legal terms, we (the party in question) conformed to a "statutory [that is, legal] standard of care" (Hearings, 24 August 2001, 20). Institutions are complex, and "every water system is different"; therefore, officials cannot be expected to "micromanage" every aspect of their operations (*ibid.*, 32). Organizations, then, can be conceptualized and explained through organizational culture, a notion that shields all who act for and through an organization. No single person can be blamed for a culture since its creation is seen as a collective set of acts. The criminal, on the other hand, is a blameworthy, immoral individual who is wholly responsible for his or her character. During the hearings, all counsel acted on this set of assumptions.

Those resisting the primary rationales of exoneration tried to rescue the culpable individual through the rationales of honest belief, good faith, contrition/remorse, and ignorance. Counsel for Stan Koebel made much of the fact that he admitted his guilt and had apologized to the people of Walkerton. He was "genuinely tearful and distraught" (Hearings, 21 August 2001, 75). Koebel was described as "honest and forthcoming" and "a completely guileless individual" (*ibid.*, 19). "I reject the suggestion that he did not care ... that he is a rogue" (*ibid.*, 49). There was "no intent to deceive" (*ibid.*, 55); he is a "decent human being" (*ibid.*, 74-75). Counsel for Koebel presented him as an inadequate but well-meaning man who was ignorant of the need for chlorination and of the dangers of E. coli. As his lawyer pointed out, and O'Connor's report validated, Koebel believed that Walkerton had good water: He and his staff often drank untreated water at well sites; indeed, his family continued to drink Walkerton water as late as 23 May 2000 (Hearings, 15 August 2001, 133). Attributions of bad character were countered by the language of family values: Stan was a "hard worker," and so was his wife "of 20 years." They were serious and dedicated: Both went to work "at 6 a.m. on May 15," Stan to test the water, his wife to clean the PUC offices (Hearings, 20 December 2000, 267-68).

Counsel for the Province of Ontario used similar rationales to defend individual officials at the Ministry of the Environment. The senior bureaucrats who developed the MOE's budget-cutting document were described as "dedicated public servants," as people with "thirty-year career[s]" who had spent "many, many hours" discussing governance, risk, and public-health tradeoffs "many, many times" (Hearings, 24 August 2001, 54-57). Phillip Bye was characterized as a "competent and conscientious employee" with twenty-five years of unblemished service. As evidence of character and nonculpability, his five "willing" appearances before the inquiry were cited as well as his credentials as a father; he has four daughters and a son (Hearings, 22 August 2001, 127-64). However, Phillip Bye and John Earl were generally not seen as acting in bad faith or as bad characters; their failures were situated in and understood through the organizational lens as part and parcel of organizational errors and omissions.

Conclusion

This chapter has asked how the events leading to Walkerton's water contamination were conceptualized and explained as well as what narratives were employed by contending groups to construct truth and to legitimate government action (or inaction). One of its aims has been to understand how new combinations of regulatory discourses are fashioned. Analyzing discourse – defined here as "the meanings and assumptions embedded in different forms of language use, ways of making sense of the world, and their corresponding practices" (Comack 1999, 62) – lets us ask how certain ways of representing and subjectifying individuals and populations are linked to strategies of control (Garland 1999; Hunt 1996). But control is not an equal-opportunity game. Some populations – typically the young, the poor, minority groups, women in certain contexts – are controlled more, and more coercively, than others. Organizations are controlled less than individuals, corporations and governments least of all. However, the hegemonic power epitomized by corporations and government, and the truth claims that support it, inevitably produces resistance, counterdiscourses, and alternative ways of seeing, knowing, and doing (Foucault 1977, 1980, 1990). *"Although members of a power block can realize their will better than most of us can, and often at our expense, the goal of social fabrication according to some detailed blueprint is ... a modernist fantasy"* (Tombs and Whyte 2004, 9, my emphasis).

The O'Connor report, to the surprise of many, gave voice to opposing groups and alternate ways of seeing, rather than reinforcing the economically and politically dominant power block. It exposed to public scrutiny the machinations of power, the rationales of neoliberalism, the downloading of government responsibility. Then, through narrative, it showed the consequences of this process, with the deaths and illnesses suffered by the citizens of Walkerton playing a central role. This morality tale had considerable public appeal and attracted much media attention.[28] The Walkerton inquiry made visible the relations of power that gain strength from remaining invisible. "One of the key features and effects of power is the ability to operate beyond public scrutiny and thus accountability" (*ibid.*, 1). Through the framing of the inquiry, the selection of areas to be interrogated (that is, those seen as relevant), the documents seized, and the groups and interests authorized to appear, the inquiry and then the report validated certain voices of opposition and resistance. The voices of public-interest and environmental groups – groups written off as "special interests" by Ontario's government – were among them. These voices constituted the events in Walkerton as a failure of government, a culpable dereliction of public duty.

However, the O'Connor report, while strengthening some voices of resistance, is an essentially liberal document rather than a radical script. It challenges some of the knowledge claims emanating from Chicago School economics – the creed that drove the Common Sense Revolution and legitimated privatization, deregulation, and downsizing – but not others. Privatization, the belief that "the market [is] inevitably superior to politics as an allocative mechanism" (Fudge and Cossman 2002, 1), is not depicted as "the evisceration of democratic authority" (Bakan 1997). Rather, the problems with privatization are regarded as operational: Privatized water testing was not done "properly" because mandatory notification requirements were not enacted. Reregulation, rather than public ownership of collective resources, becomes the validated solution of choice. The report also demonstrates the modern state's overwhelming faith in reason, in technology and science, in experts and expertise (Bauman 1993, 1991; Morrison 1995). Science, as we have seen, had privileged status; it was seen as "objective, apolitical truth," thereby reinforcing "a powerful ideology in our culture about ... truth and knowledge" (Philipps 1996, 145-46). Corporate agriculture is not challenged, nor is the capitalist ethic that gives rise to it. Thus the message of the report is an optimistic one: We don't need to ban intensive farming or adopt less wasteful lifestyles; we can have safe, plentiful, clean water if we repair regulatory agencies and heed the wisdom of science.

On the other hand, the technical discourse of science is used here to challenge, rather than to legitimate, power – in this case, the neoliberal government of Ontario. And the report embraces the unfashionable welfare-state notion that government has an obligation to protect the health, environment, and life chances of citizens – rather than, as neoliberalism would have it, to merely increase the shopping options of consumers. Market forces, it suggests, cannot replace government; deregulation and downsizing can be taken too far. It endorses the idea that there is such a thing as *public* interest and suggests that governments forget this at their peril. The style of the inquiry is as notable as the content. The commissioner championed the ideal of openness and demonstrated it through the inquiry's procedures. Holding the hearings in Walkerton, releasing the report there, and putting the stories of its residents front and centre all illustrated a tangible commitment to telling the stories and validating the truths of those who lived the disaster. The truths of the events in Walkerton were not seen as the exclusive property of science and government. In this sense, too, O'Connor's inquiry speaks to an older tradition, one in which the public inquiry serves as a genuine examination of government rather than as an exercise in public relations and "spin" control.[29]

What does all of this say about the constitution of criminality? As noted at the outset, the truths of the events in Walkerton were not heard in the context of criminal responsibility because this kind of legal and legalistic consideration is explicitly ruled out, defined as irrelevant, by the public-inquiry process. And it is also true that the decision to hold an inquiry established a noncriminal frame. (How often do we hold public inquiries into street crimes?)[30] Nevertheless, the hearings were very much about culpability – where it resides, why and how it is determined. The individuals actually involved in protecting the local water supply were repeatedly constructed as culpable actors. While the O'Connor report puts the onus on government, rather than on the Koebel brothers, criminal charges were nevertheless laid against them (see note 11). Criminal prosecution was clearly not excluded by the inquiry process.

O'Connor and commission counsel struggled repeatedly with the notion of cause. In the final summations, the commissioner challenged every lawyer who appeared to present and defend his[31] notion of causality against that put forth by the commissioner. A lengthy debate was conducted with counsel for the Province of Ontario in which chief counsel Hainey defined cause as "that which produces an effect or consequence" so that "but for a certain act or omission, [the event] would not have occurred" (Hearings, 16 August 2001, 60-61). This, he argued, is "the well-known legal approach to causation." In response and rebuttal, O'Connor presented the analogy of the speeding car on an unsafe road, wherein the driver, car manufacturer, and municipality are all causes of the ensuing accident. The role of prevention in the attribution of causality was also debated: O'Connor told Trafford that "there are many acts that would have prevented it [water contamination], but did not necessarily cause it" (Hearings, 15 August 2001, 24). Legal concepts of diligence and due diligence were also linked to cause (*ibid.*, 38-41; Hearings, 16 August 2001, Hainey and Marrocco at 55-70, McLeod and Martin at 147-49).

Throughout these discussions, organizational culpability and blame were most often conceptualized as acts not taken, warnings not heard, and technologies not purchased (Hearings, 15 August 2001, 40, 173-78). As noted above, Muldoon, for Concerned Walkerton Citizens, was one of the few who argued that not doing something can make an organization criminally negligent whether bad intent is present or not. To him, the culpability of the Ontario government arises from the fact that what happened in Walkerton could or should have been foreseen; it was "a predictable, preventable tragedy" (*ibid.*, 9). For most of the other players, however, criminal responsibility cannot reside in an organization, because responsibility for an organization's acts are collective (and institutional hierarchy usually ensures that no individual actor can be singled out anyway). Criminality resides at the individual level. It is about the blameworthy legal subject, about character flaws in individuals, about willed and wilful misconduct. This emphasis is reinforced by Canada's *Criminal Code* and common law. Canada and the United Kingdom (unlike the US), have historically employed something called "identification theory," which holds that criminal conviction in the case of institutional negligence is only possible where culpability can be traced to the "directing mind" of an organization (Puri 2001, 615).[32]

For those who wish to hold organizations accountable for the harm they do, this is one of the central challenges of the Walkerton case. If neither the law nor the public can "see" crime except through the body of the individual bad actor, the possibilities of disciplining the most powerful entities in the modern social order – the organizations dominating our economic and political systems – appear slim. While public opinion is always contested and in flux, it is in no sense democratically derived, given the disproportionate influence exerted by those with economic and political power and their structural ability to sponsor, publicize, and promote particular definitions and reconstructions of events. Such views of crime sustain a biased criminal justice system and reinforce a most unequal status quo. Public opinion plays a significant role in democratic states because censure is negotiated and laws must be argued into existence. If criminality, the ultimate censure and stigma, cannot be seen in anything but individualistic and moralistic terms, as the bad act committed by the bad actor, it is hard to see how the harmful antisocial acts of powerful organizations will be disciplined or challenged.

Notes

1 Throughout the hearings and beyond, verbatim testimony of all witnesses during examinations and cross-examinations was available at <http://www.walkertoninquiry.com> (accessed January to November 2002). Transcripts were accessed from the Walkerton Inquiry site, through <http://www.tscripts.com>, then Walkerton transcripts, organized by date and date of witness testimony.

2 The second report, released 23 May 2002, came too late to be discussed in this chapter. However, it is as hard-hitting as the first report, calling on the Ontario government to spend $800 million to ensure pure drinking water in Ontario. This is almost four times the annual budget of the entire Ministry of the Environment! Among the ninety-three recommendations are calls for the province to pass a *Safe Drinking Water Act* making the provision of safe water a legal requirement and to rebuild the "gutted" and "depleted" Ministry of the Environment (*Globe and Mail*, 24 May 2002, A1, A7; *Toronto Star*, 24 May 2002, A1, A18-19).

3 I recognize that some prefer the term "reregulation" to "deregulation" (or "decriminalization"). However, "reregulation," I would argue, is inaccurate – many state laws have simply disappeared (Snider 2000, 2001a, 2001b). Second and equally important, it understates the symbolic and ideological impact of removing regulatory and criminal law. Declaring an act a crime is a claim that a particular behaviour represents a social (public) harm. It justifies

state action against perpetrators "in the interests of all." Deregulation, or decriminalization, makes the opposite claim, symbolically telling various publics that these particular
behaviours are not harmful, not serious, not matters for public concern.

4   The primary source for this section is the *Report of the Walkerton Inquiry* (Walkerton Inquiry
2002, 1-38), supplemented by newspaper reports and witness testimony at the public inquiry. See <www.walkertoninquiry.com> (January to November 2002).

5   On 8 November 2000 the inquiry heard from Percy Pletsch, a retired Walkerton chiroprac-
tor who was born on this farm and lived there until July 1986. Mr. Pletsch testified that he
and his father before him had always kept "about 20" cows and some sheep. He remembers
when Well 5 was drilled because it caused the water in his own well to "lose its taste." A
member of the Walkerton Town Council himself from 1959 to 1963, Mr. Pletsch said that
the town never made any attempt to buy the land around the well to preserve the quality
of water in Well 5 (Hearings, 8 November 2000, 70-113).

6   The "Chlorination Bulletin" (March 1987) stipulates that the chlorine residuals must measure 0.5 milligrams per litre after fifteen minutes of contact. If this level had been maintained in Well 5 from 12 to 19 May, experts say (and the O'Connor report agrees) that the
outbreak would never have occurred (Walkerton Inquiry 2002, 14, 105-57).

7   Still water deteriorates more rapidly than water in motion; turbidity monitors keep water
circulating through the pipes, water towers, and reservoirs that make up the typical water-
distribution system.

8   Private water-testing laboratories and water-testing fees were first allowed in 1993, but few
municipalities switched from the public labs until they were closed down.

9   All inspection reports went to the Walkerton PUC commissioners as well as to Stan Koebel.
Unfortunately, these men, like many elected officials in small towns, saw their jobs in
strictly financial terms. Their primary concerns were to avoid spending and to keep municipal taxes down. Indeed, the PUC account was in surplus. Moreover, they were preoccu-
pied with another Conservative initiative, the privatization of electricity, enacted in
November 1998, and with municipal amalgamation, passed two months later. (The latter
gave Stan Koebel's office two new wells to oversee.) Testimony revealed that they spent
well under 5 percent of their time worrying about water (Walkerton Inquiry 2002, 218-52).

10 This does not mean that there are no real facts – 7 people died and 2,300 suffered real pain
and real illness. E. coli contamination of the water supply was the proximate, physical
cause; we know this from the science of water purification. However, there are many perspectives, not just one, from which to interpret these events.

11 While the primary focus of the O'Connor report was on organizational rather than individual culpability, the Ontario government always insisted that Walkerton's water contamination was a criminal matter. Thus, on 23 April 2003, the Ontario Provincial Police
laid criminal charges against Stan and Frank Koebel. On 23 April 2003, the Ontario Provincial Police laid seven charges against Stan Koebel for public endangerment, forgery, and
breach of trust. Five similar charges were laid against Frank Koebel as well.

12 Rates were set at $56 to $104 per hour for "junior" lawyers, rising to $192 per hour for the
most senior counsel, with a maximum of ten billable hours per day. "Reasonable" travel
expenses to and from Walkerton and accommodation expenses were covered with receipts.
The inquiry recommended funding for eight of the nineteen parties with standing in Part
1A of the hearings and for eleven of twenty-one such parties in Part 1B. Funding was
recommended for individuals, such as Stan and Frank Koebel and the Walkerton PUC
commissioners, but also for public action groups, such as Concerned Walkerton Citizens
and the Walkerton Community Foundation.

13 The transcripts list counsel relevant to each day's hearings at the beginning of the record.
It is impossible to know how many of them were actually physically present in the hearing
room at any given time.

14 Thousands and thousands of pages of exhibits were filed, some submitted by the witness or
by counsel on his or her behalf and some obtained by counsel for the inquiry through
search warrants – the inquiry seized a large number of private government documents, memos,
and e-mails. Despite the massive amounts of paper and the vast array of characters, Justice

O'Connor and commission counsel did an excellent job of organizing and orchestrating the process – at least insofar as this is reflected in the transcripts.

15 The assumptions, arguments, and data that underlie the "truth" claims embodied in the word "science" are not interrogated here. Thus "facts," in this context, refer to conclusions on which scientists, today, have reached consensus: for example, the science of water purification.

16 Parts 1A and 1B of the hearings overlapped. Key witnesses such as Phillip Bye appeared during both.

17 The Ontario government, in response to the events in Walkerton, revised the ODWO and the "Chlorination Bulletin," instituted new reporting requirements, made corrective action mandatory, and posted four new requirements for owners of waterworks. There is no indication, however, that government has abandoned its antiregulatory stance or the neoliberal perspective that drove it.

18 See the heated debate on this distinction waged between the commissioner and Marrocco, the lawyer for Ontario, during the final submissions (Hearings, 16 August 2001, 109).

19 I am not suggesting that scientific knowledge has no substantive basis or that scientific facts are merely a social construction. I am suggesting that the inquiry needed an infallible God, science providing the closest facsimile modernity allows. The truths on which science has reached consensus are unchallengeable in the same way that the truth of God's existence was unchallengeable in fifteenth-century Europe.

20 Nearly all of the natural scientists were men.

21 This excludes those with scientific credentials and degrees who appeared as fact witnesses, such as government officials in the Ministry of the Environment.

22 This is not to suggest that they were treated rudely. The commissioner and his counsel set the tone, and it was polite, often tough, but fair. Justice O'Connor was particularly gentle with "laypeople," those not accustomed to the legal process.

23 I have used "rationales" rather than "discourses" because, if discourse is defined as "the meanings and assumptions embedded in different forms of language use, ways of making sense of the world, and their corresponding practices" (Comack 1999, 62), then the logics used here were more narrow and focused.

24 The online transcripts allow no emphasis at all. The testimonies and questions are presented verbatim, right down to discussions about how long to allow for lunch.

25 However, it is the procedural defect, rather than the fact of privatization, that is questioned.

26 The government's argument was undermined by the fact that the legislation introduced after May 2000 reversed this stand. And claims of its efficacy were undermined by blitz inspections ordered in response to Walkerton's water contamination. Of the 659 water-treatment plants inspected, 367 had "significant deficiencies," inadequate sampling was found at 267, and the MOE issued 343 legally binding orders for mandatory compliance (Hearings, 23 August 2001, Mallson for Energy Probe at 113-14).

27 Ignorance, after all, can be remedied, even forgiven; laziness and incompetence cannot.

28 That the victims of Walkerton were always presented as *innocent* is important. It gave the story more public appeal and probably accounts for the intensity of public response, an intensity that forced the Conservative government to call a public inquiry in the first place. (My thanks to Steve Bittle of the Law Commission of Canada for pointing this out.)

29 While it may be stretching truth to call this a Canadian tradition, the O'Connor report follows the example set by Thomas Berger's inquiry in 1973. Here the judge and his staff took the inquiry to the people of the North, hearing testimony in the tents and churches and school basements of the Inuit nation. Based on their stories, Berger recommended against the construction of a pipeline. His recommendation was upheld by the Government of Canada and stood for twenty-five years.

30 Steve Bittle of the Law Commission of Canada drew my attention to this distinction.

31 All of those presenting at the final summations were men.

32 This may change: On 12 July 2003, Bill C-418 was introduced to broaden criminal liability and thus make it easier to hold organizations responsible for wilful antisocial acts.

References

Bakan, J. 1997. *Just Words: Constitutional Rights and Social Wrongs.* Toronto: University of Toronto Press.

Bauman, Z. 1991. *Modernity and Ambivalence.* Cambridge: Polity Press.

–. 1993. *Postmodern Ethics.* Oxford: Blackwell.

Comack, E. 1999. *Locating Law: Class, Race & Gender.* Halifax: Fernwood Publishing.

Condon, M. 1998. *Making Disclosure: Ideas and Interests in Ontario Securities Regulation.* Toronto: University of Toronto Press.

Crosby, A. 1997. *The Measure of Reality: Quantification and Western Society, 1250-1600.* Cambridge: Cambridge University Press.

Foucault, M. 1977. *Discipline and Punish: The Birth of the Prison.* New York: Pantheon Books.

–. 1980. *Power/Knowledge: Selected Interviews and Other Writings.* Edited by Colin Gordon. New York: Pantheon Books.

–. 1990. *History of Sexuality.* New York: Vintage Books.

Fudge, J., and B. Cossman. 2002. "Introduction: Privatization, Law and the Challenge to Feminism." In *Privatization, Law and the Challenge to Feminism,* 3-40. Toronto: University of Toronto Press.

Garland, D. 1999. "Governmentality and the Problem of Crime." In *Governable Places,* edited by R. Smandych, 15-44. Aldershot, UK: Ashgate/Dartmouth.

Haggerty, K. 2001. *Making Crime Count.* Toronto: University of Toronto Press.

Hunt, A. 1996. "The Governance of Consumption: Sumptuary Laws and Shifting Forms of Regulation." *Economy and Society* 25: 410-27.

Krajnc, A. 2000. "Wither Ontario's Environment? Neo-Conservatism and the Decline of the Environment Ministry." *Canadian Public Policy,* March.

Morrison, W. 1995. *Theoretical Criminology: From Modernity to Post-Modernism.* London: Cavendish.

Pennington, H. 2000. "Recent Experiences in Food Poisoning." In *Food, Science, Policy and Regulation in the Twentieth Century,* edited by D. Smith and J. Phillips, 223-38. London: Routledge.

Pennington Group. 2000. *Report on the circumstances leading to the 1996 Outbreak of Infection with E. coli 0157 in Central Scotland.* Edinburgh, Stationery Office.

Philipps, L. 1996. "Discursive Deficits: A Feminist Perspective on the Power of Technical Knowledge in Fiscal Law and Policy." *Canadian Journal of Law and Society* 11, 1: 141-76.

Puri, P. 2001. "Sentencing the Criminal Corporation." *Osgoode Hall Law Journal* 39, 2/3 (Summer/Fall): 612-53.

Snider, L. 1999. "Relocating Law: Making Corporate Crime Disappear." In *Locating Law: Race/Class/Gender Connections,* edited by E. Comack, 183-206. Halifax: Fernwood Publishing.

–. 2000. "The Sociology of Corporate Crime: An Obituary." *Theoretical Criminology* 4, 2: 169-205.

–. 2001a. "Abusing Corporate Power: Death of a Concept." In *(Ab)Using Power: The Canadian Experience,* edited by S. Boyd, D. Chunn, and R. Menzies, 112-30. Halifax: Fernwood Publishing.

–. 2001b. "Feminist Political Economy and Law." Paper presented at the conference *Feminist Political Economy and the Law: Revitalizing the Debate.* Institute for Feminist Legal Studies, Osgoode Hall Law School, 24 March.

Tombs, S. 1992. "Stemming the Flow of Blood? The Illusion of Self-Regulation." *Journal of Human Justice: Special Issue on Corporate Crime* 3, 2: 1-18.

–. 1996. "Injury, Death and the Deregulation Fetish: The Politics of Occupational Safety Regulation in United Kingdom Manufacturing Industries." *International Journal of Health Services* 26, 2: 309-29.

–. 1999. "Death and Work in Britain," *The Sociological Review* 47, 2: 345-67.

–, and D. Whyte. 2004. "Scrutinizing the Powerful? Crime, Contemporary Political Economy and Critical Social Research." In *Researching the Powerful,* edited by S. Tombs and D. Whyte. London: Peter Lang.

Tucker, E. 1995. "And Defeat Goes On: An Assessment of 'Third-Wave' Health and Safety Regulation." In *Corporate Crime: Contemporary Debates,* edited by F. Pearce and L. Snider, 245-67. Toronto: University of Toronto Press.

Walkerton Inquiry. 2002. *Report of the Walkerton Inquiry.* Part 1. *The Events of May 2000 and Related Issues.* Dennis R. O'Connor [commissioner]. Toronto: Ontario Ministry of the Attorney-General.

Contributors

Steven Bittle is a senior research officer at the Law Commission of Canada, and a graduate student in the Department of Sociology, Queen's University.

Jean-Paul Brodeur is a professor at the Université de Montréal, Centre international de crimonolgie comparée.

Wendy Chan is an associate professor in the School of Criminology, Simon Fraser University.

Nathalie Des Rosiers is president of the Law Commission of Canada and a professor in the Faculty of Law, University of Ottawa.

Aaron Doyle is an assistant professor of sociology, Carleton University.

Richard V. Ericson is a professor of criminology and director of the Centre for Criminological Research, University of Oxford, and a Fellow of All Souls College, Oxford.

Geneviève Ouellet is a graduate student at the École de Crimonologie, Université de Montréal, and a researcher in the Research Group on Terrorism and Intelligence.

Steven Penney is a professor in the Faculty of Law, University of New Brunswick.

Pierre Rainville is vice dean of Graduate Studies and Research, Université Laval.

Laureen Snider is a professor in the Department of Sociology, Queen's University.

Index

Printed and bound in Canada by Friesens
Set in Stone by Artegraphica Design Ltd.
Copy editor: Robert Lewis
Proofreader: Jonathan Dore
Indexer: Patricia Buchanan